Travel Trends

A report on the 2000 International Passenger Survey

London: The Stationery Office

ISBN 0 11 621477 5
ISSN 1360–5895

A National Statistics publication
Official statistics bearing the National Statistics logo are produced to high professional standards set out in the National Statistics Code of Practice. They undergo regular quality assurance reviews to ensure that they meet customer needs. They are produced free from any political interference.

Contact points
For enquiries about this publication, contact
Josh Lovegrove
Tel: 020 7533 5765
E-mail: josh.lovegrove@ons.gov.uk

To order this publication, call The Stationery Office on **0870 600 5522.** See also back cover.

For general enquiries, contact the National Statistics Public Enquiry Service on **0845 601 3034**
(minicom: 01633 812399)
E-mail: info@statistics.gov.uk
Fax: 01633 652747
Letters: Room 1.001, Government Buildings, Cardiff Road, Newport NP10 8XG

You can also find National Statistics on the internet - go to **www.statistics.gov.uk**

About the Office for National Statistics
The Office for National Statistics (ONS) is the government agency responsible for compiling, analysing and disseminating many of the United Kingdom's economic, social and demographic statistics, including the retail prices index, trade figures and labour market data, as well as the periodic census of the population and health statistics. The Director of ONS is also the National Statistician and the Registrar General for England and Wales, and the agency administers the statutory registration of births, marriages and deaths there.

Contents

Page

Introduction

Chapter 1

Chapter 2

Chapter 3

Chapter 4

Chapter 5

Appendices

Travel Trends 2000

ACKNOWLEDGMENTS

Editor :	Nikki Bennett
Production Manager:	Josh Lovegrove
Authors:	Habiba Ahmed Alyson Whitmarsh
Maps:	Alistair Dent Nick Richardson
Production Team:	Nathan Kaneshanathan Angie Osborn Peter Samani David Savage

Introduction

The International Passenger Survey (IPS)

The main aims of the survey

How the data are analysed

Changes in sampling methodology

Introduction

Travel Trends presents the main results from the International Passenger Survey (IPS) which collects information on travel to and from the United Kingdom.

Although concentrating on the findings of the 2000 survey, this edition contains information on long and shorter-term trends.

What is the International Passenger Survey?

The IPS is a sample survey carried out by the Office for National Statistics (ONS) for itself and a number of other Government Departments. The results are based on face to face interviews with a sample of passengers as they enter or leave the UK by the principal air, sea and tunnel routes.

Travellers passing through passport control are randomly selected for interview. Over a quarter of a million interviews were conducted in 2000 representing about 0.2 per cent of travellers. The interviews were conducted on a voluntary and anonymous basis with a response rate of 81 per cent. The survey covers both adults and children.

The main aims of the IPS are to:

a) collect data on both credits and debits for the travel account of the UK balance of payments;
b) provide detailed information about overseas visitors to the UK for tourism policy;
c) provide data on international migration;
d) collect travel information on passenger routes as an aid to aviation and shipping authorities.

Since the IPS was started in 1961, its coverage has been extended to include all the main air, sea and tunnel ports or routes into and out of the UK. The only routes excluded from the survey are sea routes to and from the Channel Islands, the land border with the Irish Republic, and cruise ships travelling to and from the UK. Estimates of spending are supplemented with figures from the Economic Advisor's Office in Jersey, which provides information with respect to the Channel Islands.

About 90 per cent of passengers entering and leaving the UK are covered by the survey. The remainder are either passengers travelling at night, when interviewing is suspended, or on those routes too small in volume or too expensive to be covered. These non-sampled routes and time periods are, however, taken into account when calculating weights for the IPS contacts.

ONS produces results from the IPS on a monthly, quarterly and annual basis. (Please see appendix F for details). A fuller description of the IPS methodology can be found in appendix B of this report.

The IPS is a large continuous survey and ONS wishes to acknowledge the large part played by the interviewers throughout the year, and to thank the respondents for the information they have provided.

How is the IPS analysed?

The records in the IPS database are mainly identified by their 'flow'. Flow is described as the direction of travel of the visitor combined with whether they are a UK resident or an overseas resident. There are, therefore, four main flows on the IPS:

a) overseas residents departing from the UK;
b) UK residents departing from the UK;
c) overseas residents arriving in the UK;
d) UK residents arriving in the UK.

For the purposes of this publication, only data relating to overseas residents departing from the UK and UK residents arriving in the UK have been used. This is because the IPS interviews for these groups of travellers take place at the end of the visit when factual information about visit duration and spending is available. This is felt to be more complete and reliable than the information gathered at the beginning of a trip when intentions regarding duration and spending may not prove to be accurate.

Mode of transport

Being a group of islands, only two main modes of transport to and from the UK, namely air and sea, were available until 1994. The Channel Tunnel between the UK and France began operating towards the end of 1994 and information regarding this mode of transport is available from quarter four 1994.

Journeys by sea and tunnel can be further analysed to show whether a vehicle was taken on the trip and, if so, the type of vehicle that was used.

Country of residence or visit

For overseas residents visiting the UK, this is the main country of residence of the visitor. For UK residents travelling abroad, it is the main country of visit.

For areas of the world outside the European Union, many countries are shown within groups rather than having been listed separately. Although the IPS can identify all countries individually, it would be impractical to show all these. Also for many countries sample sizes are too small to give accurate estimates. For some tables, countries are shown grouped into major areas of the world. A description of the countries included in groups is given in appendix C.

A larger number of countries than appear in this publication, can be identified in the Travel*pac* CD-ROM.

In addition to the country groupings, some analyses are shown by major areas of the world. The areas used are:

a) North America;
b) EU Europe;
c) Non EU Europe;
d) Other Countries.

EU Europe is defined (for all years in this publication) as consisting of the **current** member countries. For Germany, for the years before reunification in 1991, the states of the then East Germany do not appear within the Germany total and therefore are not included within the EU Europe totals.

Purpose of visit

Many reasons for visits are recorded on the IPS. These purposes have been amalgamated into four main categories:

a) Holiday;
b) Business;
c) Visiting friends or relatives (VFR);
d) Miscellaneous.

The categories describe the main purpose of the visit and where it is not possible to determine this, the visit is shown within the miscellaneous category. Note that people migrating or travelling as crew of aircraft, ships or trains, for example, are excluded from analyses in this publication.

Conference and trade fair visits, which can be separately identified and analysed from the IPS, are included in the business category. Visits made for study, medical treatment and shopping appear under the miscellaneous category.

Independence

The IPS collects information on whether tourists travel independently or on some form of package trip. The holiday purpose category is split into two sectors in this publication to show package holidays as well as total holiday visits. Other main purposes have not been disaggregated although it is possible to do this if required from the Travel*pac* CD-ROM or from analyses commissioned from marketing agents.

Age and gender

Respondents are classified into seven age groups. Questions on exact age are not asked on the survey as it is felt that people may be disinclined to give accurate answers, and age groups are normally sufficient for users' needs. Information on the gender of respondents is also collected.

UK region of visit

For overseas residents, information is collected regarding the place of stay during their visit to the UK. Information is collected and recorded by the towns where the person has stayed for at least one night. Within this publication, however, this is shown by county. People who do not stay in any particular place or who do not stay overnight are shown separately.

UK region of residence

For UK residents, the IPS records the area of residence and for the first time this information appears in a table in Chapter 5.

Making analyses over a specific time period

Although the IPS data are collected throughout the year, national estimates are produced by quarter in a process known as 'weighting'. A single quarter therefore becomes the minimum period over which most detailed analyses of the IPS data can be made. Quarters are then summed to form years.

IPS interviewing on routes to and from the Irish Republic

There is a major discontinuity in the time series shown in this publication between years up to and including 1998, with 1999 and 2000. From quarter two 1999, the IPS commenced interviewing on air and sea routes between the UK and the Irish Republic. These detailed results have been used within this publication. To enable 1999 data to be analysed, records for quarter one 1999 were constructed, based upon interviews conducted in quarter one 2000, but weighted to the traffic volumes of quarter one 1999. For the years up to and including 1998, estimates of visitor numbers, their spending and nights stayed on routes between the UK and the Irish Republic and their characteristics were based on data provided by other sources.

Analysis of the new data has shown that a large number of Irish visitors are transiting through the UK on their overseas visits, and are thus not tourists to the UK according to IPS definitions. Also, the 1999 and 2000 interviews showed that a number of European and commonwealth visitors made combined visits to the UK and the Irish Republic; these visits were previously recorded as visits from residents of the Irish Republic. These factors combine to reduce the number of overseas visitors to the UK, particularly the estimates of visitors from the Irish Republic, but they do increase the number of visitors from certain countries. Those countries particularly affected are: Australia, New Zealand, Canada, Germany, and the Netherlands.

The data from the IPS Irish interviews also affect estimates of spending and nights. These showed that the previous spending per visit estimates of Irish visitors to the UK were overstated, whilst UK residents' spending per visit in the Irish Republic was previously understated.

The details of visitors from the Irish Republic enable more complete duration of stay and regional breakdowns to be produced for 1999 and 2000. This leads to discontinuities between the duration of stay and regional profile from the IPS between 1998 and 1999.

In summary, the major effect resulting from IPS interviewing on routes to and from the Irish Republic is to improve the quality and detail of the 1999 and 2000 estimates (chapter 4 and 5 of this publication). The discontinuities from this change affect time series estimates of visitors to and from the Irish Republic, with some smaller effects for other countries (chapters 2 and 3).

For more information on the discontinuity, please contact the IPS team by phone on 020 7533 5765 or by e-mail to ips@ons.gov.uk.

Please note:

a) Spending data exclude fares to and from the UK;

b) Visits and spending information regarding travel to or from the Irish Republic for years up to and including 1998 are included in the totals figures in this publication, but may not always appear in the rows and columns. Consequently, rows and columns in tables may not always sum to the totals. Full data for travel to and from the Irish Republic is shown from 1999;

c) Expenditure data relating to the Channel Islands are included within the European Union totals but are not shown separately. This means that spending for European Union countries will not always sum to the European Union totals shown;

d) Expenditure data of overseas visitors transiting the UK, but not staying overnight, are included within the all purposes totals, but are not shown separately. This means that spending for overseas residents' visits by purpose will not always sum to the all purposes totals shown.

Interviewing for the IPS at Gatwick Airport

Chapter *1*

Travel and Tourism 1980 to 2000

Overseas residents

- *In 2000, 25.2 million visits made to the UK - double the number in 1980 - with a record £12.8 billion spent in 2000*

- *Decline in visits to the UK for the second year in a row - fall of half a million since 1998*

UK residents

- *Record 56.8 million visits abroad in 2000 - more than three times the number in 1980 - with record levels of spending*

Balance

- *More than two visits made by UK residents abroad for every overseas residents' visit to the UK*

- *Widening gap in UK residents' visits abroad and overseas residents' visits to the UK due largely to differences in holiday visits*

- *Record deficit of £11.4 billion - nearly £2 billion more than in 1999*

Chapter 1

Travel and Tourism 1980 to 2000

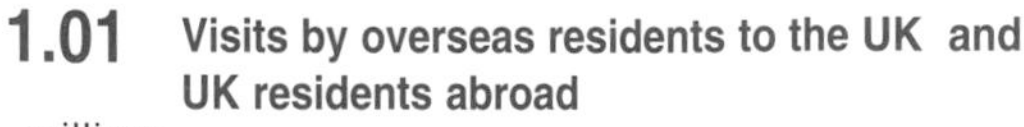

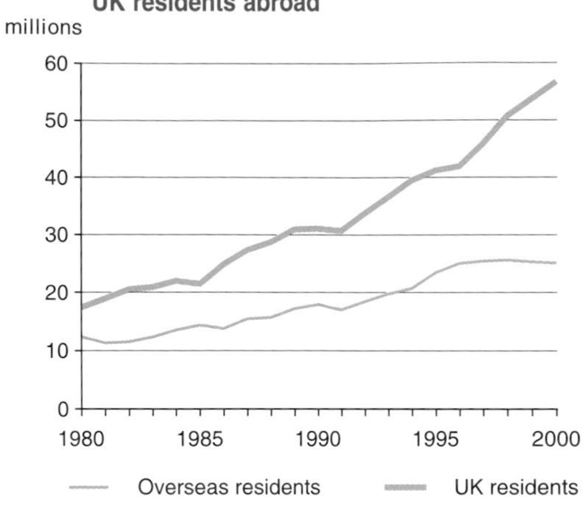

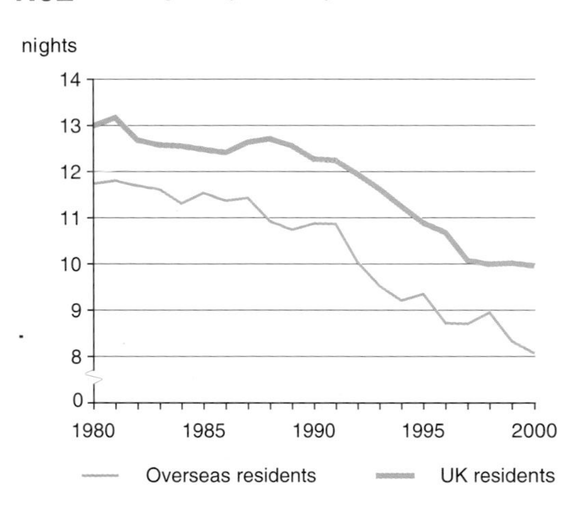

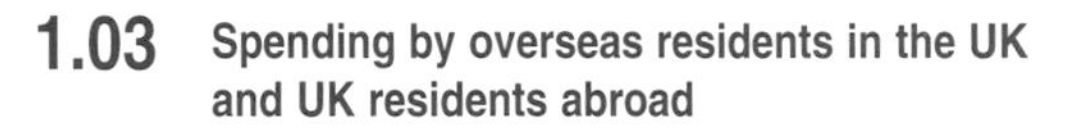

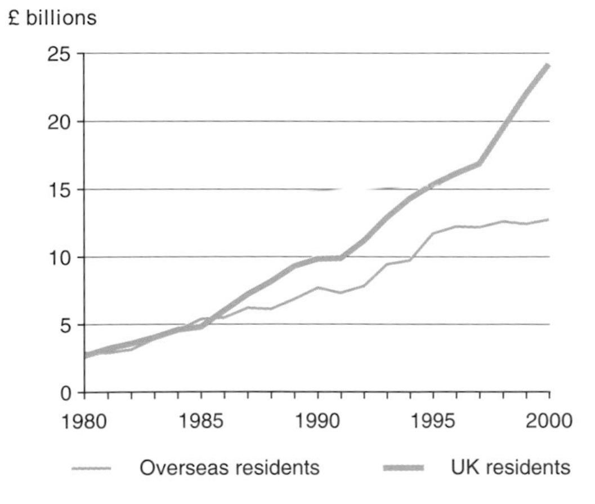

This chapter examines the long-term trends in tourism to and from the UK over the last 20 years.

Tables 1.01 and **1.02** show the total number of visits made by overseas residents to the UK and by UK residents abroad, together with the number of nights, and amount of money, both in current and constant 1995 prices, spent on these visits.

Number of visits, nights and length of stay

Figure 1.01 shows that the upward trend in tourism abroad by UK residents continued into 2000, with almost three million more visits in 2000 than in 1999. There was a decline in the number of overseas residents visiting the UK for the second year in a row, falling by half a million since the peak in 1998.

Between 1980 and 2000, the number of overseas residents' visits to the UK doubled from 12.4 million to 25.2 million, growing at an average annual rate of 3.6 per cent. Over the same period, UK residents' visits abroad grew at an average annual rate of 6.1 per cent, rising to 56.8 million in 2000, over three times the number in 1980. The gap in the number of visits to the UK and visits abroad has widened since 1997 due to continued growth in UK residents' visits abroad but a levelling off in visits by overseas residents to the UK. In 2000, for each overseas resident visit to the UK there were more than two visits made by UK residents abroad.

In 2000, overseas residents stayed 204 million nights in the UK compared with 146 million in 1980, a rise of two-fifths. UK residents spent 567 million nights abroad in 2000, two and a half times the 228 million in 1980. **Figure 1.02** shows that overseas residents stayed an average of 12 nights per visit in 1980, falling by a third to eight nights in 2000. In comparison, UK residents stayed an average of 13 nights abroad in 1980, falling by a quarter to 10 nights in 1997, since when average length of stay has remained broadly the same.

Spending

Figure 1.03 shows that in 2000, UK residents spent £24.3 billion abroad, nine times higher than the £2.7 billion spent in 1980, equivalent to an average annual growth rate of 11.5 per cent. In comparison, spending by overseas residents visiting the UK in 2000 was four times higher than in 1980, rising from £3.0 billion to a record £12.8 billion, an average annual growth rate of 7.6 per cent.

Figure 1.04 shows that since 1986 the deficit in the travel account of the balance of payments has continued to increase to a record of £11.4 billion in 2000 because of the different growth rates in spending for UK and overseas residents' visits. Similar trends have been observed in spending based on 1995 constant prices (i.e. with the effects of inflation removed).

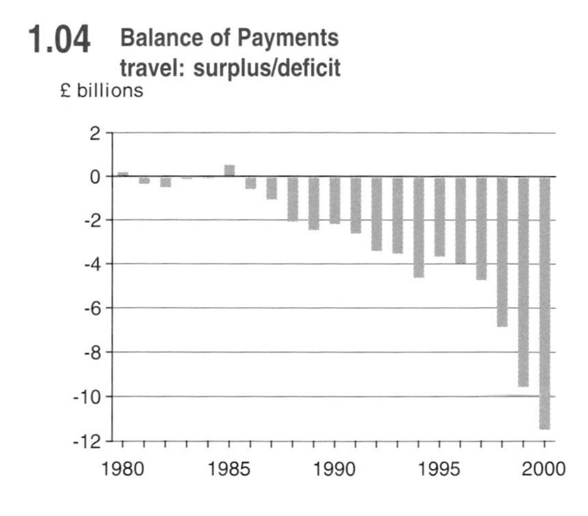

Between 1980 and 2000, overseas residents visiting the UK have spent more per visit, on average, than UK residents going abroad. In 2000, UK residents spent £426 per visit on average, nearly three times the average of £151 per visit spent in 1980. In comparison, overseas residents spent £236 on average in 1980, doubling to £503 in 2000.

Visits by purpose of visit

Tables 1.03 and **1.04** show the number of visits and spending of overseas residents visiting the UK and by UK residents travelling abroad broken down by their purpose of visit. The widening gap in the number of visits made by UK residents abroad and overseas residents to the UK is largely attributable to the difference in the number of holiday visits made by each group (**figure 1.05**). In 2000, UK residents made 36.7 million holiday visits abroad, four times the number made by overseas residents to the UK. Similar trends have been observed in holiday spending. In contrast, the number of business trips and associated spending of UK residents and overseas residents have remained broadly similar year on year over the last 20 years.

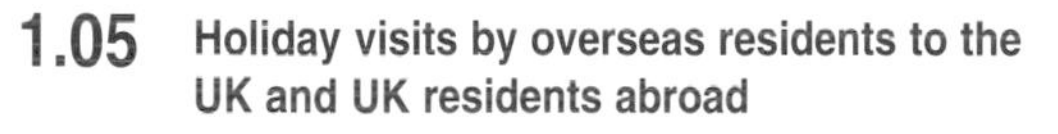

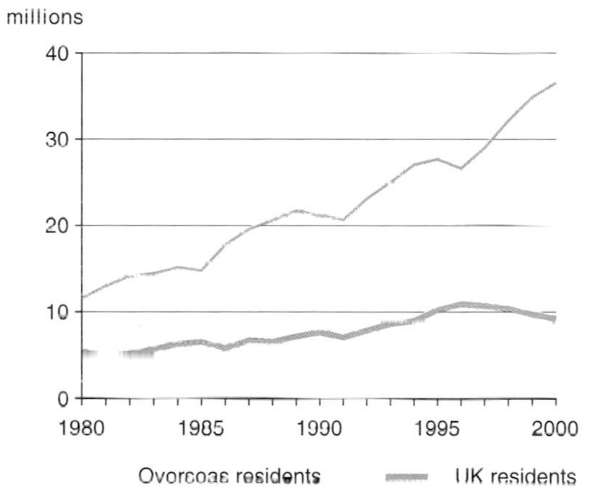

Figure 1.06 shows the trend in overseas residents' visits by their purpose of visit. Despite slight year on year declines in the early eighties and early nineties, the number of business trips made by

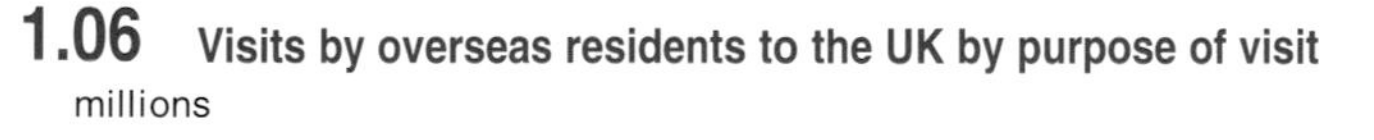

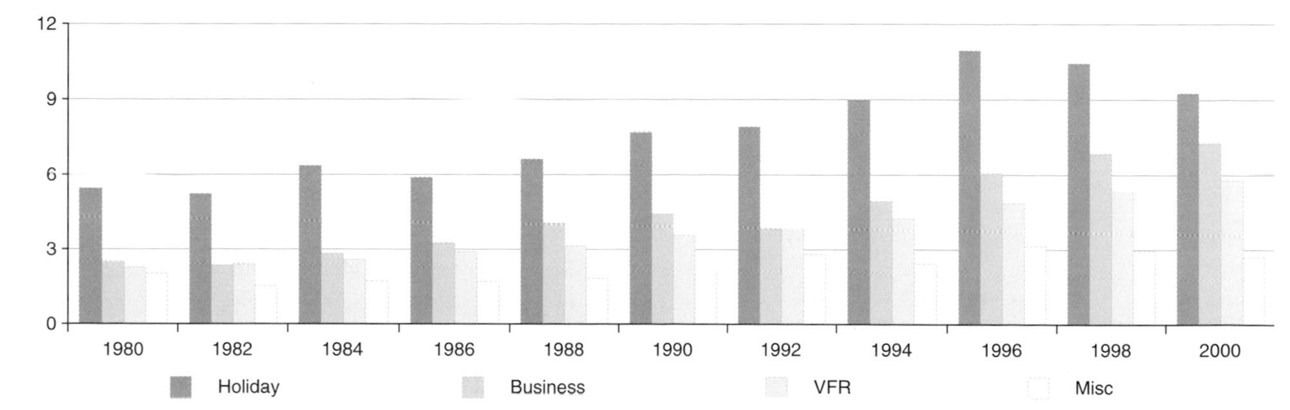

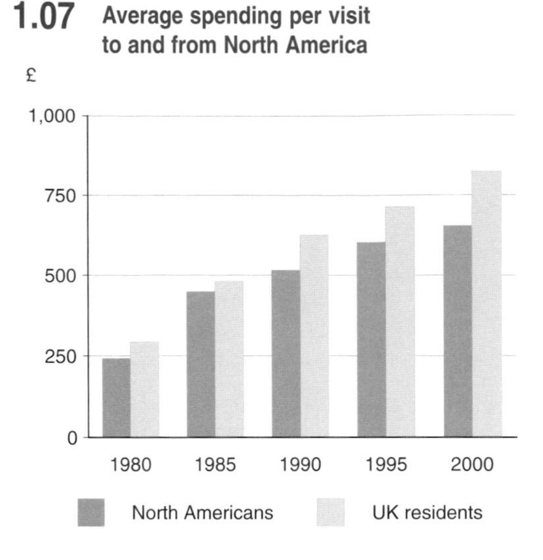

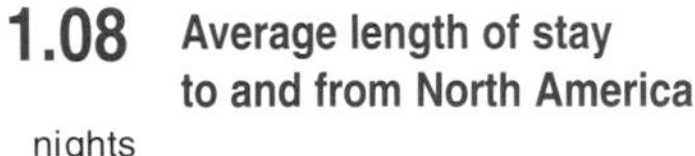

1.08 Average length of stay to and from North America

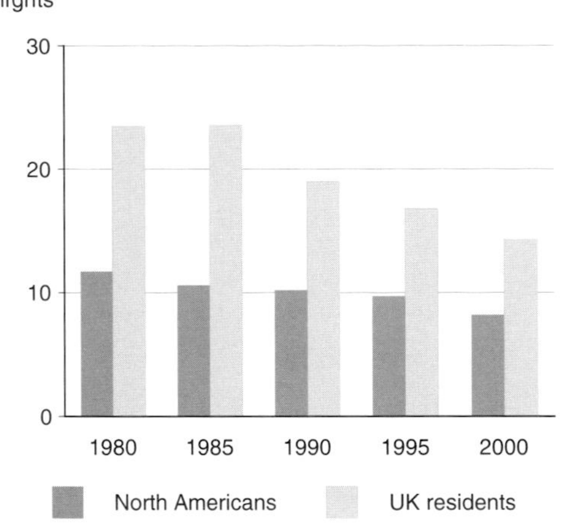

1.09 Average spending per day to and from North America

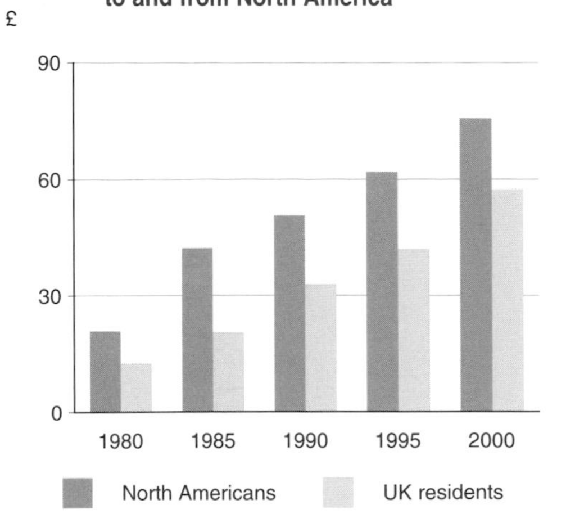

overseas residents to the UK increased between 1980 and 2000 at an average annual rate of 5.4 per cent, the largest increase among all purpose groups and significantly above the growth rate of 3.6 per cent for all overseas visits to the UK. Business visits also showed the largest increase in absolute terms. In 1980, 2.6 million business trips were made to the UK compared with 7.3 million in 2000. Overseas residents' visits to friends or relatives showed the next highest growth over the twenty year period. In 2000, overseas residents made 3.8 million more holiday visits to the UK than in 1980. Since the peak of 11.0 million visits in 1996, holiday visits from abroad have fallen by 1.7 million.

In contrast, holiday visits, business visits and visits to friends or relatives by UK residents travelling abroad all increased at an average annual rate of six per cent. The largest absolute increase was seen in holiday visits. In 2000, UK residents made 25.0 million more holiday visits abroad, compared with the 11.7 million made in 1980.

Visits by area of residence or visit

Tables 1.05 and **1.06** provide the breakdown in the number of visits and levels of spending of overseas residents travelling to the UK by their main area of residence, and UK residents travelling abroad by area of visit. The largest absolute increases between 1980 and 2000 were in visits and spending by visitors to and from Europe. However, in terms of proportional increases over this period, the number of visits to the UK by residents of North America showed the highest average annual growth rate of 4.3 per cent. This was followed closely by visits from residents of Europe, which increased at an average annual rate of 3.6 per cent. Spending by area of residence or visit showed a similar pattern.

In contrast, for UK residents travelling abroad the largest increase was in visits to 'Other Countries', an average annual growth rate of 7.4 per cent. This was closely followed by visits to North America, which increased at an average annual rate of 6.7 per cent.

Comparing the average spending per visit between 1980 and 2000, residents of Europe and 'Other Countries' visiting the UK continued to spend more per visit, on average, than UK residents travelling to these regions over the same period. Conversely, **figure 1.07** shows that residents of North America coming to the UK have continued to spend less per visit than UK residents during their visits to North America. **Figure 1.08** shows that this was largely due to UK residents staying approximately twice as long in North America, on average, as North Americans visiting the UK. However, average spending per day among North American residents visiting the UK was in fact higher than UK residents visiting North America (**figure 1.09**).

Visits by mode of travel

Tables 1.07 and **1.08** give the number of visits and levels of spending of overseas residents visiting the UK and UK residents travelling abroad broken down by their mode of travel. **Figures 1.10** and **1.11** show that in 2000, overseas residents made 17.8 million visits to the UK by air, nearly two and a half times the 7.3 million made in 1980, whilst UK residents made 41.4 million visits abroad by air – nearly four times the number in 1980. Overseas residents' visits to the UK by sea remained relatively stable during the 1980s and then increased during the early 1990s to 6.3 million. Since 1996, there has been a downward trend in visits by sea, largely due to the opening of the Channel Tunnel in 1994. UK residents' visits abroad by sea increased from 6.8 million in 1980 to 9.6 million in 2000, peaking at 12.0 million in 1994.

Air travel accounted for around 60 per cent of all overseas residents' visits to the UK and all UK residents' visits abroad in 1980, compared with over 70 per cent in 2000, a rise of more than 10 percentage points.

In 1995, overseas residents visiting the UK and UK residents travelling abroad each made nearly two million visits via the Channel Tunnel, accounting for eight per cent of the visits to the UK by overseas residents and five per cent of visits by UK residents abroad. **Figure 1.12** shows that these visits peaked in 1998 when UK residents made 6.1 million visits, nearly twice the number made by overseas residents. Visits by UK residents via the Channel Tunnel increased at an average annual rate of 47 per cent between 1995 and 1998, more than twice the rate of increase for such visits by overseas residents (21 per cent). The Channel Tunnel accounted for around two-fifths of non-air visits by overseas residents travelling to the UK and by UK residents abroad in 2000.

1.10 Visits by overseas residents to the UK by air and sea

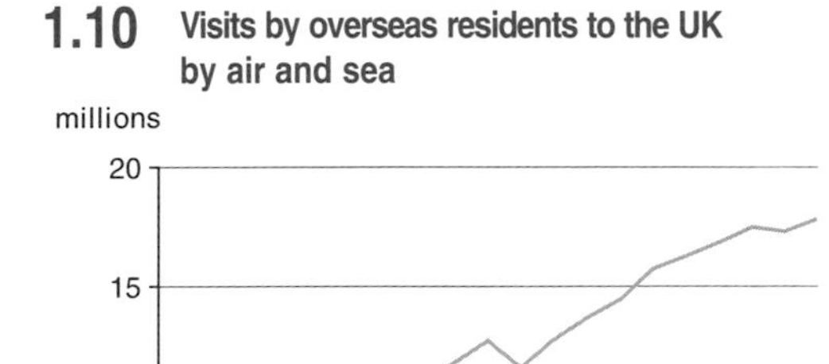

1.11 Visits by UK residents abroad by air and sea

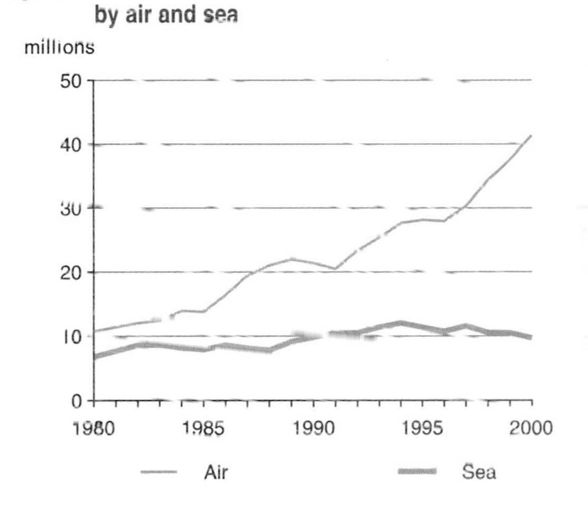

1.12 Visits via the Channel Tunnel

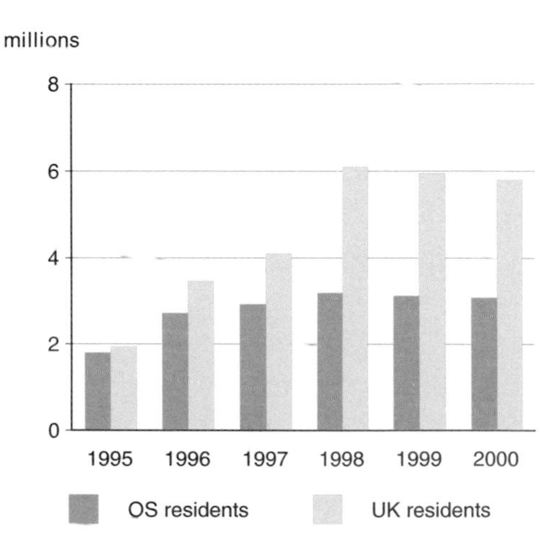

1.01 Overseas residents' visits, nights and spending in the UK 1980 to 2000

	Visits		Nights		Spending		Constant price spending (1995 constant prices)	
	thousands	*per cent change*	millions	*per cent change*	£ million	*per cent change*	£ million	*per cent change*
1980	12,421	*-0.5*	146.0	*-5.6*	2,961	*5.9*	8,085	*-10.5*
1981	11,452	*-7.8*	135.4	*-7.3*	2,970	*0.3*	7,177	*-11.2*
1982	11,636	*1.6*	136.3	*0.7*	3,188	*7.3*	7,059	*-1.6*
1983	12,464	*7.1*	145.0	*6.4*	4,003	*25.6*	8,323	*17.9*
1984	13,644	*9.5*	154.5	*6.6*	4,614	*15.3*	8,991	*8.0*
1985	14,449	*5.9*	167.0	*8.1*	5,442	*17.9*	9,876	*9.8*
1986	13,897	*-3.8*	158.2	*-5.3*	5,553	*2.0*	9,419	*-4.6*
1987	15,566	*12.0*	178.2	*12.6*	6,260	*12.7*	9,993	*6.1*
1988	15,799	*1.5*	172.9	*-3.0*	6,184	*-1.2*	9,142	*-8.5*
1989	17,338	*9.7*	186.5	*7.9*	6,945	*12.3*	9,567	*4.6*
1990	18,013	*3.9*	196.1	*5.1*	7,748	*11.6*	9,853	*3.0*
1991	17,125	*-4.9*	186.4	*-4.9*	7,386	*-4.7*	8,627	*-12.4*
1992	18,535	*8.2*	186.3	*-0.1*	7,891	*6.8*	8,784	*1.8*
1993	19,863	*7.2*	189.5	*1.7*	9,487	*20.2*	10,188	*16.0*
1994	20,794	*4.7*	191.8	*1.2*	9,786	*3.2*	10,050	*-1.3*
1995	23,537	*13.2*	220.3	*14.9*	11,763	*20.2*	11,763	*17.0*
1996	25,163	*6.9*	219.8	*-0.3*	12,290	*4.5*	11,954	*1.6*
1997	25,515	*1.4*	222.5	*1.3*	12,244	*-0.4*	11,542	*-3.4*
1998	25,745	*0.9*	230.8	*3.7*	12,671	*3.5*	11,573	*0.3*
1999	25,394	*-1.4*	211.7	*-8.3*	12,498	*-1.4*	11,133	*-3.8*
2000	25,209	*-0.7*	203.8	*-3.8*	12,805	*2.5*	11,102	*-0.3*
Average annual growth		*3.6*		*1.7*		*7.6*		*1.6*

Due to changes in the IPS sampling methodology introduced in 1999, care should be taken when comparing results for 1999 and 2000 with earlier years. See notes on page 9 relating to IPS interviewing on routes to the Irish Republic.

1.02 UK residents' visits, nights and spending abroad 1980 to 2000

	Visits		Nights		Spending		Constant price spending (1995 constant prices)	
	thousands	*per cent change*	millions	*per cent change*	£ million	*per cent change*	£ million	*per cent change*
1980	17,507	*13.2*	227.7	*11.1*	2,738	*29.8*	6,859	*27.4*
1981	19,046	*8.8*	251.1	*10.3*	3,272	*19.5*	7,345	*7.1*
1982	20,611	*8.2*	261.7	*4.2*	3,640	*11.2*	7,272	*-1.0*
1983	20,994	*1.9*	264.4	*1.0*	4,090	*12.4*	7,559	*3.9*
1984	22,072	*5.1*	277.5	*5.0*	4,663	*14.0*	7,755	*2.6*
1985	21,610	*-2.1*	270.0	*-2.7*	4,871	*4.5*	7,935	*2.3*
1986	24,949	*15.5*	310.2	*14.9*	6,083	*24.9*	8,916	*12.4*
1987	27,447	*10.0*	347.3	*12.0*	7,280	*19.7*	10,364	*16.2*
1988	28,828	*5.0*	366.9	*5.6*	8,216	*12.9*	12,515	*20.8*
1989	31,030	*7.6*	390.2	*6.4*	9,357	*13.9*	12,861	*2.8*
1990	31,150	*0.4*	382.7	*-1.9*	9,886	*5.7*	12,021	*-6.5*
1991	30,808	*-1.1*	377.8	*-1.3*	9,951	*0.7*	11,775	*-2.1*
1992	33,836	*9.8*	404.7	*7.1*	11,243	*13.0*	12,678	*7.7*
1993	36,720	*8.5*	427.7	*5.7*	12,972	*15.4*	13,184	*4.0*
1994	39,630	*7.9*	446.6	*4.4*	14,365	*10.7*	14,852	*12.7*
1995	41,345	*4.3*	450.8	*0.9*	15,386	*7.1*	15,386	*3.6*
1996	42,050	*1.7*	449.8	*-0.2*	16,223	*5.4*	15,897	*3.3*
1997	45,957	*9.3*	463.5	*3.1*	16,931	*4.4*	18,652	*17.3*
1998	50,872	*10.7*	509.2	*9.9*	19,489	*15.1*	21,847	*17.1*
1999	53,881	*5.9*	540.4	*6.1*	22,020	*13.0*	24,676	*12.9*
2000	56,837	*5.5*	566.9	*4.0*	24,251	*10.1*	27,281	*10.6*
Average annual growth		*6.1*		*4.7*		*11.5*		*7.1*

Due to changes in the IPS sampling methodology introduced in 1999, care should be taken when comparing results for 1999 and 2000 with earlier years. See notes on page 9 relating to IPS interviewing on routes to the Irish Republic.

1.03 Overseas residents' visits and spending in the UK by purpose of visit 1980 to 2000

	Holiday		Business		VFR		Miscellaneous		Total	
	visits thousands	spending £ million	visits thousands	spending £ million	visits thousands	spending £ million	visits thousands	spending £ million	visits thousands	spending £ million
1980	5,478	1,258	2,565	735	2,319	457	2,058	508	12,421	2,961
1981	5,037	1,276	2,453	763	2,287	442	1,675	484	11,452	2,970
1982	5,265	1,386	2,393	794	2,410	484	1,568	518	11,636	3,188
1983	5,818	1,711	2,556	961	2,560	639	1,530	687	12,464	4,003
1984	6,385	2,052	2,863	1,091	2,626	706	1,770	759	13,644	4,614
1985	6,666	2,379	3,014	1,293	2,880	852	1,890	908	14,449	5,442
1986	5,919	2,228	3,286	1,552	2,946	844	1,746	917	13,897	5,553
1987	6,828	2,695	3,564	1,644	3,179	910	1,996	1,001	15,566	6,260
1988	6,655	2,473	4,096	1,852	3,178	922	1,870	926	15,799	6,184
1989	7,286	2,757	4,363	2,032	3,497	1,049	2,193	1,094	17,338	6,945
1990	7,725	3,198	4,461	2,174	3,611	1,147	2,216	1,213	18,013	7,748
1991	7,169	2,849	4,219	2,077	3,591	1,148	2,147	1,293	17,125	7,386
1992	7,949	3,125	3,855	2,146	3,884	1,259	2,847	1,343	18,535	7,891
1993	8,729	3,925	4,706	2,420	4,109	1,467	2,319	1,654	19,863	9,487
1994	9,048	3,947	4,986	2,559	4,278	1,551	2,482	1,706	20,794	9,786
1995	10,323	4,567	5,763	3,219	4,602	1,739	2,849	2,214	23,537	11,763
1996	10,987	4,848	6,095	3,220	4,898	1,841	3,182	2,357	25,163	12,290
1997	10,803	4,555	6,347	3,501	5,155	1,941	3,209	2,223	25,515	12,244
1998	10,475	4,488	6,882	3,820	5,400	1,970	2,988	2,367	25,745	12,671
1999	9,826	4,251	7,044	3,967	5,640	2,133	2,884	2,108	25,394	12,498
2000	9,302	4,383	7,322	4,048	5,834	2,271	2,750	2,068	25,209	12,805
Average annual growth (%)	*2.7*	*6.4*	*5.4*	*8.9*	*4.7*	*8.3*	*1.5*	*7.3*	*3.6*	*7.6*

Due to changes in the IPS sampling methodology introduced in 1999, care should be taken when comparing results for 1999 and 2000 with earlier years. See notes on page 9 relating to IPS interviewing on routes to the Irish Republic.

1.04 UK residents' visits and spending abroad by purpose of visit 1980 to 2000

	Holiday		Business		VFR		Miscellaneous		Total	
	visits thousands	spending £ million	visits thousands	spending £ million	visits thousands	spending £ million	visits thousands	spending £ million	visits thousands	spending £ million
1980	11,666	1,851	2,690	521	2,317	263	834	103	17,507	2,738
1981	13,131	2,248	2,740	610	2,378	295	797	119	19,046	3,272
1982	14,224	2,477	2,768	683	2,529	350	1,090	130	20,611	3,640
1983	14,568	2,753	2,886	805	2,559	385	982	147	20,994	4,090
1984	15,246	3,111	3,155	984	2,689	407	982	161	22,072	4,663
1985	14,898	3,215	3,188	1,075	2,628	412	896	169	21,610	4,871
1986	17,896	4,287	3,249	1,131	2,774	505	1,029	160	24,949	6,083
1987	19,703	5,134	3,639	1,323	3,051	612	1,054	211	27,447	7,280
1988	20,700	5,893	3,957	1,448	3,182	629	990	246	28,828	8,216
1989	21,847	6,737	4,505	1,616	3,485	730	1,193	274	31,030	9,357
1990	21,273	6,810	4,769	1,836	3,952	930	1,156	310	31,150	9,886
1991	20,788	6,909	4,840	1,821	3,952	910	1,227	312	30,808	9,951
1992	23,236	7,987	5,162	1,932	4,100	978	1,338	346	33,836	11,243
1993	25,133	9,059	5,297	2,287	4,457	1,106	1,833	520	36,720	12,972
1994	27,187	10,026	5,614	2,565	4,674	1,270	2,155	504	39,630	14,365
1995	27,808	10,425	6,113	2,974	4,938	1,358	2,486	629	41,345	15,386
1996	26,765	10,610	6,879	3,359	5,502	1,533	2,904	721	42,050	16,223
1997	29,138	11,107	7,166	3,351	6,004	1,650	3,649	823	45,957	16,931
1998	32,306	12,495	8,033	4,124	6,452	1,869	4,082	1,001	50,872	19,489
1999	35,023	14,555	8,161	4,261	6,598	1,991	4,100	1,215	53,881	22,020
2000	36,685	15,784	8,872	4,732	7,178	2,258	4,102	1,477	56,837	24,251
Average annual growth (%)	*5.9*	*11.3*	*6.1*	*11.7*	*5.8*	*11.4*	*8.3*	*14.2*	*6.1*	*11.5*

Due to changes in the IPS sampling methodology introduced in 1999, care should be taken when comparing results for 1999 and 2000 with earlier years. See notes on page 9 relating to IPS interviewing on routes to the Irish Republic.

1.05 Overseas residents' visits and spending in the UK by area of residence 1980 to 2000

	North America		Europe		Other Countries		Total World	
	visits thousands	spending £ million	visits thousands	spending £ million	visits thousands	spending £ million	visits thousands	spending £ million
1980	2,082	508	7,984	1,263	2,355	1,190	12,421	2,961
1981	2,105	592	7,125	1,126	2,222	1,252	11,452	2,970
1982	2,135	686	7,122	1,175	2,379	1,327	11,636	3,188
1983	2,836	992	7,214	1,412	2,414	1,599	12,464	4,003
1984	3,330	1,271	7,608	1,573	2,706	1,770	13,644	4,614
1985	3,797	1,709	7,938	1,836	2,714	1,897	14,449	5,442
1986	2,843	1,464	8,421	2,227	2,633	1,862	13,897	5,553
1987	3,394	1,710	9,418	2,574	2,754	1,977	15,566	6,260
1988	3,272	1,579	9,791	2,665	2,736	1,940	15,799	6,184
1989	3,481	1,700	10,854	3,014	3,003	2,231	17,338	6,945
1990	3,685	1,907	11,060	3,452	3,268	2,389	18,013	7,748
1991	2,867	1,542	11,390	3,652	2,868	2,192	17,125	7,386
1992	3,377	1,743	12,034	3,777	3,124	2,371	18,535	7,891
1993	3,443	2,072	13,216	4,514	3,205	2,901	19,863	9,487
1994	3,469	2,022	13,766	4,594	3,559	3,169	20,794	9,786
1995	3,756	2,272	15,790	5,844	3,991	3,647	23,537	11,763
1996	3,675	2,277	17,615	6,488	3,872	3,525	25,163	12,290
1997	4,099	2,515	17,389	6,173	4,027	3,555	25,515	12,244
1998	4,553	2,801	17,383	6,303	3,809	3,566	25,745	12,671
1999	4,599	2,894	16,816	5,971	3,979	3,632	25,394	12,498
2000	4,869	3,197	16,086	5,749	4,253	3,859	25,209	12,805
Average annual growth (%)	*4.3*	*9.6*	*3.6*	*7.9*	*3.0*	*6.1*	*3.6*	*7.6*

Due to changes in the IPS sampling methodology introduced in 1999, care should be taken when comparing results for 1999 and 2000 with earlier years. See notes on page 9 relating to IPS interviewing on routes to the Irish Republic.

1.06 UK residents' visits and spending abroad by area of visit 1980 to 2000

	North America		Europe		Other Countries		Total World	
	visits thousands	spending £ million	visits thousands	spending £ million	visits thousands	spending £ million	visits thousands	spending £ million
1980	1,382	408	14,676	1,942	1,449	389	17,507	2,738
1981	1,514	518	16,063	2,265	1,469	490	19,046	3,272
1982	1,299	472	17,748	2,608	1,564	560	20,611	3,640
1983	1,023	417	18,377	3,021	1,594	652	20,994	4,090
1984	919	447	19,536	3,483	1,617	733	22,072	4,663
1985	914	440	19,181	3,687	1,515	744	21,610	4,871
1986	1,167	626	22,071	4,630	1,711	827	24,949	6,083
1987	1,559	805	23,903	5,441	1,985	1,034	27,447	7,280
1988	1,823	989	24,819	6,052	2,186	1,175	28,828	8,216
1989	2,218	1,325	26,451	6,608	2,361	1,424	31,030	9,357
1990	2,325	1,455	26,268	6,831	2,557	1,600	31,150	9,886
1991	2,370	1,539	26,057	6,888	2,381	1,525	30,808	9,951
1992	2,813	1,707	28,275	7,802	2,748	1,734	33,836	11,243
1993	3,052	2,063	30,506	8,734	3,162	2,175	36,720	12,972
1994	2,927	2,033	33,096	9,832	3,608	2,500	39,630	14,365
1995	3,120	2,229	34,418	10,422	3,808	2,736	41,345	15,386
1996	3,584	2,698	34,213	10,260	4,253	3,265	42,050	16,223
1997	3,594	2,713	37,745	10,879	4,618	3,338	45,957	16,931
1998	4,158	3,239	41,552	12,325	5,163	3,926	50,872	19,489
1999	4,733	3,694	43,620	13,940	5,529	4,386	53,881	22,020
2000	5,060	4,170	45,763	15,172	6,014	4,909	56,837	24,251
Average annual growth (%)	*6.7*	*12.3*	*5.9*	*10.8*	*7.4*	*13.5*	*6.1*	*11.5*

Due to changes in the IPS sampling methodology introduced in 1999, care should be taken when comparing results for 1999 and 2000 with earlier years. See notes on page 9 relating to IPS interviewing on routes to the Irish Republic.

1.07 Overseas residents' visits and spending in the UK by mode of travel 1980 to 2000

	Air		Sea		Tunnel		Total	
	visits thousands	spending £ million	visits thousands	spending £ million	visits thousands	spending £ million	visits thousands	spending £ million
1980	7,323	2,215	5,098	746	.	.	12,421	2,961
1981	6,889	2,313	4,563	657	.	.	11,452	2,970
1982	6,911	2,517	4,724	670	.	.	11,636	3,188
1983	7,661	3,148	4,803	855	.	.	12,464	4,003
1984	8,515	3,596	5,129	1,018	.	.	13,644	4,614
1985	9,413	4,430	5,036	1,011	.	.	14,449	5,442
1986	8,851	4,289	5,046	1,264	.	.	13,897	5,553
1987	10,335	5,014	5,231	1,247	.	.	15,566	6,260
1988	10,967	5,082	4,832	1,102	.	.	15,799	6,184
1989	11,829	5,721	5,509	1,224	.	.	17,338	6,945
1990	12,751	6,421	5,262	1,327	.	.	18,013	7,748
1991	11,614	6,035	5,511	1,351	.	.	17,125	7,386
1992	12,778	6,534	5,756	1,358	.	.	18,535	7,891
1993	13,694	7,857	6,169	1,631	.	.	19,863	9,487
1994	14,465	8,209	6,310	1,576	19	1	20,794	9,786
1995	15,754	9,628	5,990	1,590	1,794	544	23,537	11,763
1996	16,279	9,922	6,165	1,601	2,719	768	25,163	12,290
1997	16,858	9,900	5,734	1,360	2,922	983	25,515	12,244
1998	17,479	10,366	5,083	1,399	3,184	906	25,745	12,671
1999	17,284	10,451	4,993	1,280	3,117	767	25,394	12,498
2000	17,831	10,837	4,298	1,140	3,080	828	25,209	12,805
Average annual growth (%)	*4.5*	*8.3*	*-0.8*	*2.1*	.	.	*3.6*	*7.6*

Due to changes in the IPS sampling methodology introduced in 1999, care should be taken when comparing results for 1999 and 2000 with earlier years. See notes on page 9 relating to IPS interviewing on routes to the Irish Republic.

1.08 UK residents' visits and spending abroad by mode of travel 1980 to 2000

	Air		Sea		Tunnel		Total	
	visits thousands	spending £ million	visits thousands	spending £ million	visits thousands	spending £ million	visits thousands	spending £ million
1980	10,748	2,029	6,759	710	.	.	17,507	2,738
1981	11,374	2,361	7,672	911	.	.	19,046	3,272
1982	12,031	2,656	8,580	984	.	.	20,611	3,640
1983	12,361	2,959	8,634	1,131	.	.	20,994	4,090
1984	13,934	3,524	8,137	1,139	.	.	22,072	4,663
1985	13,732	3,695	7,878	1,176	.	.	21,610	4,871
1986	16,380	4,632	8,569	1,451	.	.	24,949	6,083
1987	19,369	5,739	8,077	1,541	.	.	27,447	7,280
1988	21,026	6,655	7,802	1,560	.	.	28,828	8,216
1989	21,925	7,457	9,105	1,900	.	.	31,030	9,357
1990	21,368	7,747	9,782	2,139	.	.	31,150	9,886
1991	20,408	7,740	10,401	2,211	.	.	30,808	9,951
1992	23,357	8,891	10,479	2,352	.	.	33,836	11,243
1993	25,354	10,316	11,366	2,656	.	.	36,720	12,972
1994	27,624	11,595	11,991	2,768	14	2	39,630	14,365
1995	28,097	12,250	11,311	2,718	1,937	419	41,345	15,386
1996	27,907	12,926	10,686	2,509	3,457	788	42,050	16,223
1997	30,341	13,402	11,522	2,791	4,095	739	45,957	16,931
1998	34,283	15,397	10,498	2,726	6,092	1,367	50,872	19,489
1999	37,510	17,623	10,427	2,958	5,944	1,439	53,881	22,020
2000	41,392	19,905	9,646	2,766	5,799	1,580	56,837	24,251
Average annual growth (%)	*7.0*	*12.1*	*1.8*	*7.0*	.	.	*6.1*	*11.5*

Due to changes in the IPS sampling methodology introduced in 1999, care should be taken when comparing results for 1999 and 2000 with earlier years. See notes on page 9 relating to IPS interviewing on routes to the Irish Republic.

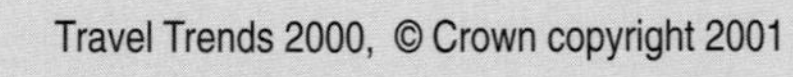

Chapter 2

Overseas residents' visits to the UK 1996 to 2000

- *Number of visits to the UK in 2000 same as in 1996 but spending up by half a billion, from £12.3 billion to £12.8 billion*

- *Visits by European residents down by one and a half million between 1996 and 2000, offset by an increase in visits from North America and 'Other Countries'*

- *Greatest increase in spending by North American visitors - up from £2.3 billion in 1996 to £3.2 billion in 2000*

- *Sea lost seven per cent of its market share between 1996 and 2000 - six per cent to air and one per cent to the Channel Tunnel*

- *UK attracting increasing number of visits from long-haul destinations - USA, Canada, Australia, India and South Africa. Visits down from France, Belgium and Germany*

2.01 **Number of visits 1996 to 2000**

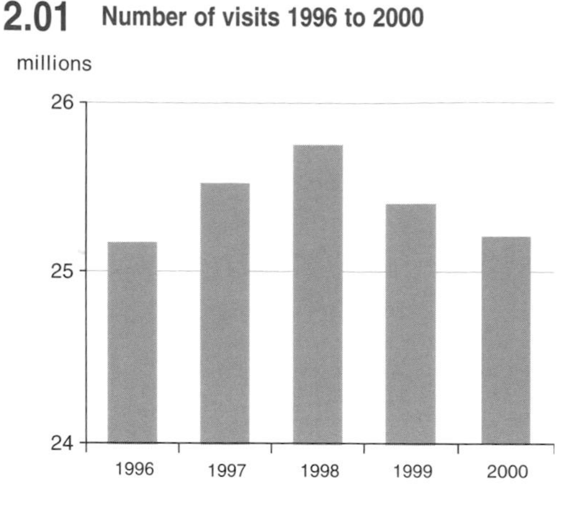

2.02 **Annual growth in spending 1996 to 2000**

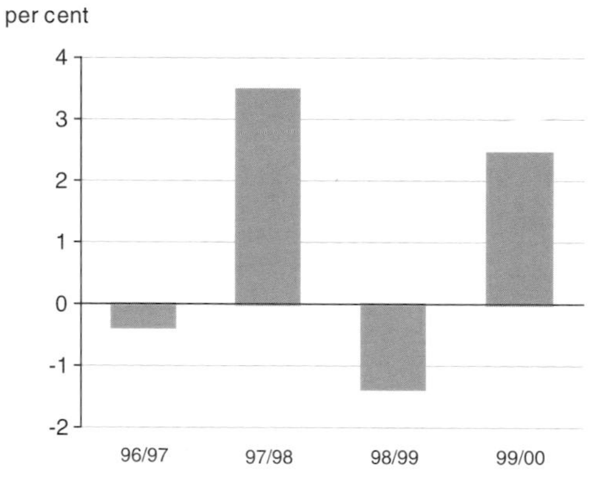

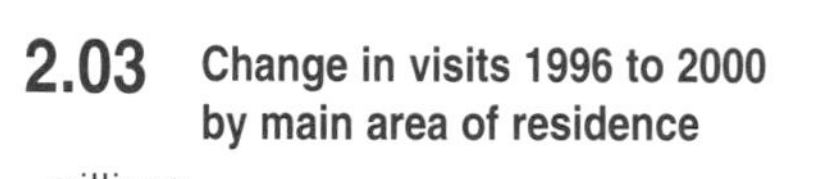
2.03 **Change in visits 1996 to 2000 by main area of residence**

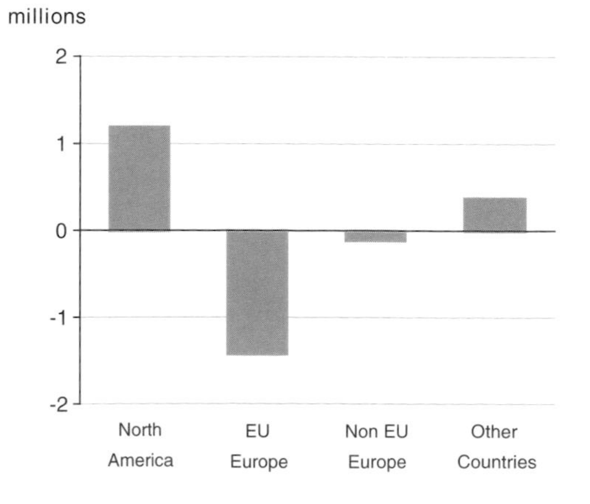

Chapter 2

Overseas residents' visits to the UK 1996 to 2000

This chapter examines the short-term trends in travel and tourism to the UK over the period 1996 to 2000.

The number of overseas residents' visits to the UK increased from 25.2 million in 1996 to 25.7 million in 1998. Since then visits by overseas residents have fallen back to 25.2 million in 2000 (**figure 2.01**).

Despite a fall of nearly 0.2 million visits between 1999 and 2000, accounting for 0.7 per cent of all visits, spending by overseas residents rose from £12.5 billion in 1999 to £12.8 billion in 2000. **Figure 2.02** shows that all of the growth since 1996, when spending was £12.3 billion, occurred between 1997 and 1998 (an increase of 3.5 per cent), and between 1999 and 2000 when spending increased by a further 2.5 per cent.

Visits, nights and spending by quarter

Table 2.01 provides a quarterly breakdown of visits and number of nights stayed by overseas residents in the UK over the period 1996 to 2000.

Table 2.02 gives the quarterly spending of overseas residents in the UK, both in current prices and 1995 constant prices (i.e. with the effects of inflation removed). Both non-seasonally adjusted current and constant price spending fell in the first quarter and rose in the second quarter of 2000 compared with the previous year. In quarter three current price spending rose by 3.3 per cent, whereas constant price spending remained almost unchanged. However, quarter four current price spending increased by 1.3 per cent, and constant price spending fell by 2.0 per cent.

Visits and spending by area of residence

Tables 2.03 and **2.04** show the annual breakdowns of overseas residents' visits and spending from 1996 to 2000 by the main area of residence. **Figure 2.03** shows that between 1996 and 2000 visits to the UK by residents of European countries fell by one and a half million. This decline, however, was offset by an increase in the number of visits by residents of North America and 'Other Countries' over the same period.

Between 1999 and 2000, visits by residents of 'Other Countries' showed the single largest percentage increase of 6.9 per cent, followed by a 5.9 per cent increase in the number of visits by North Americans. Visits by residents of European countries fell by 4.3 per cent. Since European residents made two-thirds of all visits to the UK in 1999, this fall in numbers accounted for the overall decline in visits to the UK in 2000.

Figure 2.04 illustrates that North American residents generated the greatest increase in spending, from £2.3 billion in 1996 to £3.2 billion in 2000, an average annual growth rate of 8.9 per cent. In comparison, spending by EU European residents decreased at an average annual rate of 3.8 per cent, from £5.3 billion in 1996 to £4.6 billion in 2000. This was due in part to the relative change in exchange rates seen over this period with the US dollar rising by three per cent in value against sterling, but EU currencies, such as the French franc, falling in value by over 30 per cent.

2.04 Levels of spending by area of residence and year

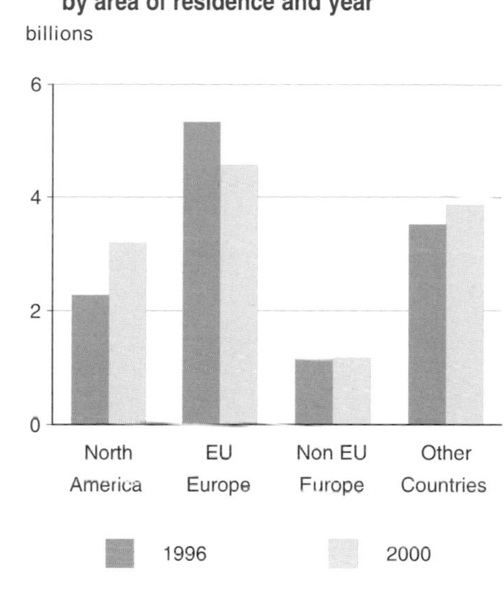

Visits and spending by purpose of visit

Tables 2.03 and 2.04 also show the annual breakdowns of overseas residents' visits and spending by purpose of visit. Between 1996 and 2000, the strongest growth was seen in the visits made by overseas residents for business which increased from 6.1 million in 1996 to 7.3 million in 2000, an average annual growth rate of 4.7 per cent. Visits to friends and family increased from 4.9 million to 5.8 million over the same period, an average annual growth rate of 4.5 per cent. In contrast, holiday visits and visits for miscellaneous purposes declined over this period. Inclusive tour holidays showed the largest average annual fall of 7.4 per cent.

Whilst there was an increase of nearly half a million in the number of holidaymakers from North America, between 1996 and 2000, holiday visits from all the other main regions of the world fell by over two million. In contrast, there was an increase in the number of business visits from all the main regions of the world, particularly North America which showed the largest percentage increase of 43 per cent.

Figure 2.05 compares the short-term trends in holiday and business visits, the two most popular reasons for visiting the UK, for European residents. Between 1996 and 2000, residents of European countries accounted for the largest fall in the number of holiday visits, a fall of two million, but also the greatest absolute increase in the number of business visits, an increase of 0.8 million. Their spending on holiday and business visits showed a similar pattern of change over time as visits.

2.05 Number of visits from Europe by purpose and year

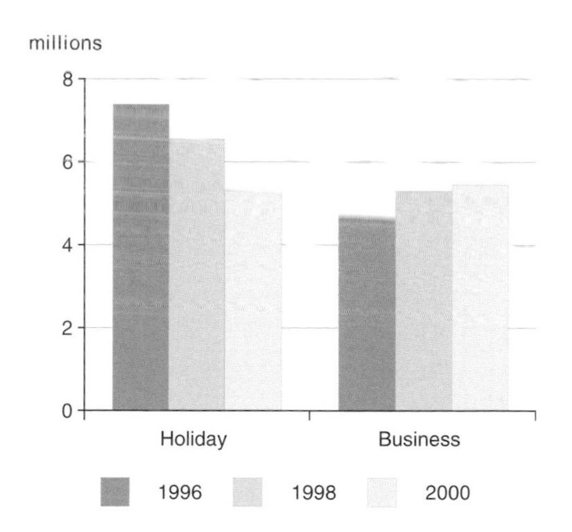

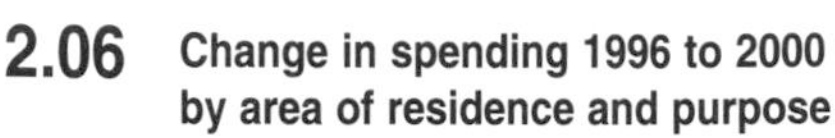

2.06 Change in spending 1996 to 2000 by area of residence and purpose

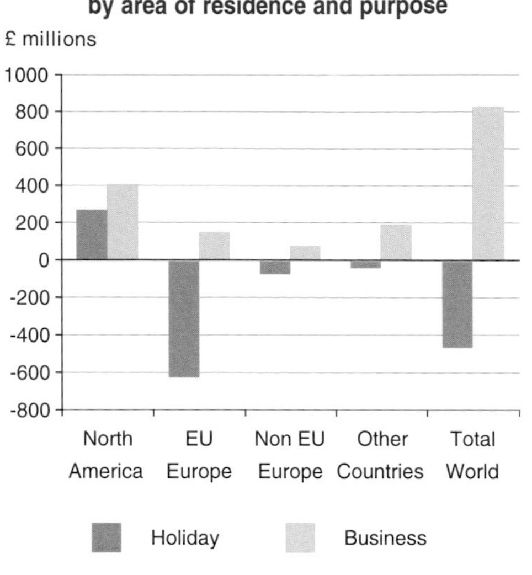

2.07 Average spending per day on business by area of residence

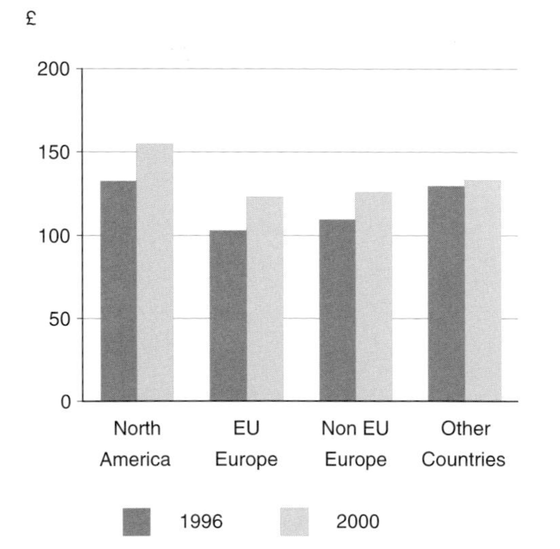

Figure 2.06 shows that in spite of the largest absolute increase in the number of business visits among European residents, it was North American residents who showed the greatest increase in business spending over the five-year period, both in absolute and percentage terms.

Average length of stay by purpose of visit

Table 2.05 shows the number of nights and average length of stay of overseas residents visiting the UK between 1996 and 2000 by main area of residence and purpose of visit. The average length of stay of overseas residents visiting the UK rose slightly from 8.7 nights in 1996 to 9.0 nights in 1998, but then fell to 8.1 nights in 2000. The average length of visits to friends or relatives showed a downward trend from an average of 12.3 nights in 1996 to 10.8 nights in 2000. For business visits, the average length of stay fell from 4.7 nights in 1998 to 4.1 nights in 2000.

Average spending by purpose of visit

Table 2.06 gives the average spending per visit and average spending per day of overseas residents visiting the UK between 1996 and 2000 by area of residence and purpose of visit. Despite a slight fall in their average length of stay, overseas residents visiting the UK spent on average £503 per visit in 2000, compared with only £484 in 1996. Although the average spend per visit fell between 1996 and 1997, it rose between 1997 and 1998 and then again between 1999 and 2000. Average spending per day remained at a similar level between 1996 and 1998, at around £55, and then increased to £62 in 2000 – an increase above the rate of inflation. Similar trends were shown in the spend per day for all reasons for visit except for those travelling on business. The average spending per visit by business travellers to the UK increased from £115 in 1996 to £134 in 2000, above the rate of inflation, although the majority of this rise was between 1998 and 1999. This was the largest increase for all purpose groups. **Figure 2.07** shows that the average spend per day for those on business trips increased for all the main regions of the world. The largest absolute increase of £22 was for business visits from North America, despite a fall of £9 between 1999 and 2000.

Visits and spending by mode of travel

Tables 2.07 and **2.08** give the breakdown of overseas residents' visits to the UK and spending by mode of travel and purpose of visit. In 1996, overseas residents' visits by air made up 65 per cent of all visits to the UK compared with 71 per cent in 2000. **Figure 2.08** shows that between 1996 and 2000, sea lost seven per cent of its market share, with one per cent going to the Channel Tunnel and six per cent to air. Between 1999 and 2000 alone, sea lost three per cent of its market share to air, falling from 20 per cent to 17 per cent, whilst the market share of the Channel Tunnel remained the same at 12 per cent.

2.08 Change in market share 1996 to 2000 by mode of travel

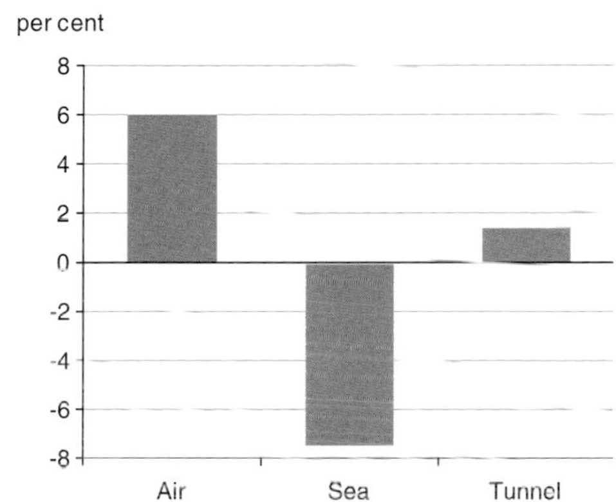

Overall, total air traffic increased by 10 per cent, from 16.3 million in 1996 to 17.8 million in 2000. Traffic via the Channel Tunnel increased until 1998, and since then has levelled off at 3.1 million, representing an increase of 13 per cent between 1996 and 2000. However, sea traffic over this five-year period fell by 30 per cent.

Visits and spending by country of residence

Tables 2.09 and **2.10** give the breakdown of overseas residents' visits to the UK and their spending by country of residence. **Figure 2.09** shows that residents of the USA made over a million more visits to the UK in 2000 than in 1996. After the USA, Canada, Australia, India and South Africa showed the highest number of additional visits to the UK, reflecting that the UK is increasingly attracting visitors from long-haul destinations. Visits by residents of the USA, Australia and South Africa have generally shown a steady increase over the five-year period, although there was a fall in visits by Australian residents between 1997 and 1998. There was a large absolute increase in visits by residents of India between 1996 and 1997 and then again between 1999 and 2000. Visits by residents of Canada, however, increased largely between 1999 and 2000, producing one of the largest increases in visits by country of residence both in absolute and percentage terms. Despite being amongst the top countries in terms of the number of visits made to the UK each year, there has been a particular decline in visits by residents of France, Belgium and Germany, a fall of 1.4 million between 1996 and 2000.

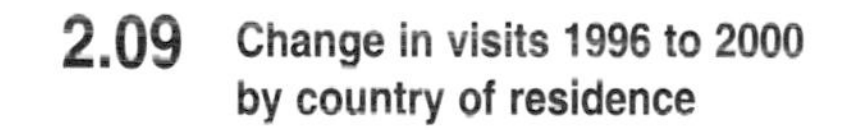
2.09 Change in visits 1996 to 2000 by country of residence

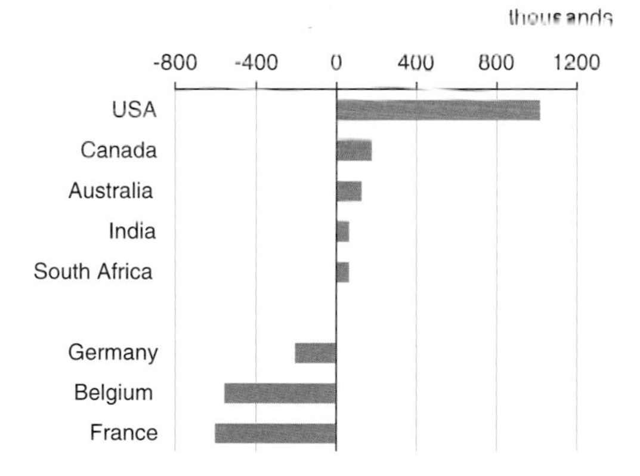

The largest absolute increase in spending was among residents of the USA, from £2 billion in 1996 to £2.8 billion in 2000, followed by spending among residents of 'Other Middle East' and Canada.

2.10 Average length of stay by area of residence and year

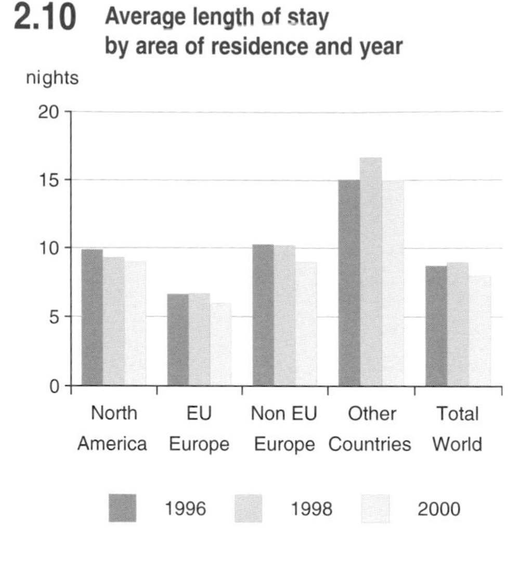

2.11 Average spending per day by area of residence and year

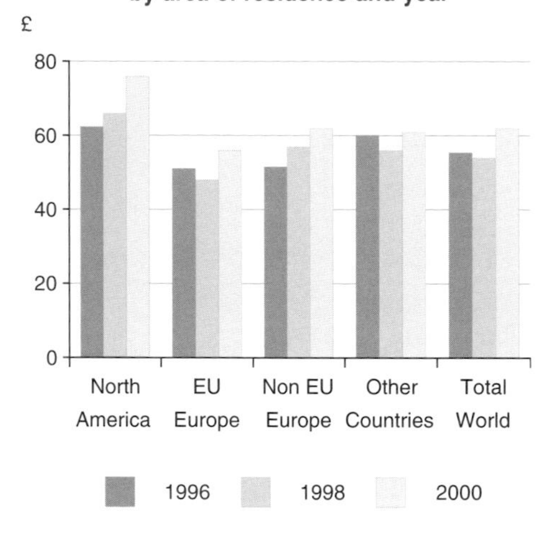

2.12 Number of visits by duration of stay and year

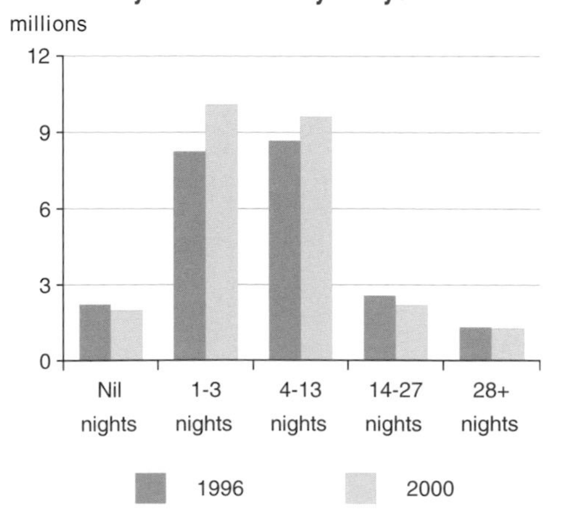

Average stay and spending by country of residence

Table 2.11 shows the breakdown of the number of nights and average length of stay of overseas residents' visits to the UK by country of residence. Compared with 1996, visitors from all the main regions of the world exhibited a trend for shorter stays in 2000 (**figure 2.10**). North America was the only region of the world showing a steady decline, from 9.9 days per visit in 1996 to 8.6 days per visit in 2000 (table 2.05). Over this period, visitors from Belgium stayed the least number of nights per visit on average.

Table 2.12 shows average spend per visit and average spend per day by overseas residents visiting the UK by country of residence. Residents of North America produced the largest increase in the average spend per day, from £62 in 1996 to £76 in 2000. **Figure 2.11** shows that the next largest absolute increase of £10 was for non-EU European residents. Despite the increases in average spending per day, there was relatively little change in the average spending per visit due to the decreases in the average length of stay.

Visits and spending by length of stay

Tables 2.13 and **2.14** give the breakdown of overseas residents' visits and spending by their length of stay. In the years up to and including 1998, estimates of visitor numbers from the Irish Republic and their characteristics were based on data provided by other sources. In 1999 the IPS commenced interviewing on routes to and from the Irish Republic. As a result of the change in methodology, care should be taken in making comparisons of 1999 and 2000 data with earlier years. Compared with 1996, overseas residents made fewer day trips to the UK and fewer visits lasting over two weeks. In contrast, they made more trips lasting 1-13 nights than in 1996. **Figure 2.12** shows that the largest absolute increase was in short stay visits lasting 1-3 nights. With visits from the Irish Republic removed, a similar trend is observed.

Between 1999 and 2000 the number of visits lasting 14-27 nights fell by 0.2 million, accounting for the majority of the fall in visitor numbers. Despite this fall, spending on these visits increased by £54 million.

Visits and spending by region of stay in the UK

Tables 2.15 and **2.16** show the breakdown of overnight visits by overseas residents and their spending by region of visit in the UK. As a single visit to the UK may include several regions, the sub-totals for each region will not add up to the overall total of overnight visits to the UK. Again, due to the change in methods of recording visitors from the Irish Republic, care should be taken when making comparisons of 1999 and 2000 data with earlier years. Between 1999 and 2000, there was very little change in the number of visits made to England, but as **figure 4.13** shows, spending on these visits increased by three per cent. In contrast, there was a fall in visits and spending to both Scotland and Wales.

2.13 Growth in spending 1999 to 2000 in major regions of UK

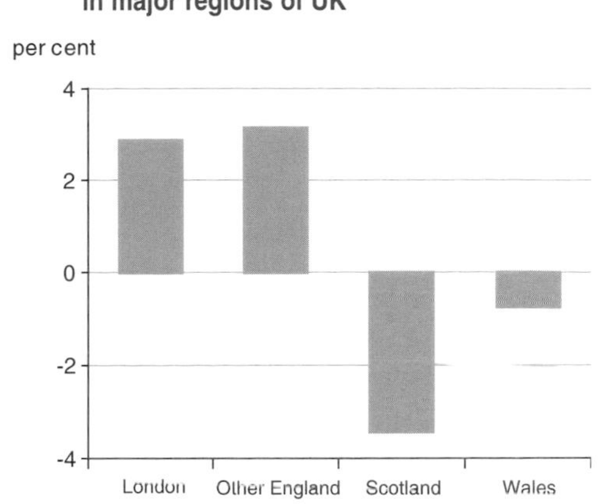

2.01 Visits and nights by quarter of year 1996 to 2000

	Quarter	Visits (thousands) not seasonally adjusted	*per cent change from year earlier*	seasonally adjusted	Nights (thousands) not seasonally adjusted	*per cent change from year earlier*
1996	1	4,719	*11.9*	6,200	37,121	*4.5*
	2	6,680	*12.2*	6,420	52,049	*5.4*
	3	8,132	*5.0*	6,300	85,123	*-1.5*
	4	5,632	*0.2*	6,240	45,472	*-7.3*
1997	1	4,940	*4.7*	6,370	38,433	*3.5*
	2	6,447	*-3.5*	6,310	49,650	*-4.6*
	3	8,168	*0.4*	6,250	89,238	*4.8*
	4	5,961	*5.8*	6,590	45,206	*-0.6*
1998	1	4,804	*-2.7*	6,360	37,858	*-1.5*
	2	6,834	*6.0*	6,480	57,220	*15.2*
	3	8,027	*-1.7*	6,330	84,985	*-4.8*
	4	6,080	*2.0*	6,580	50,714	*12.2*
1999	1	5,046	*5.0*	6,490	40,920	*8.1*
	2	6,799	*-0.5*	6,520	47,817	*-16.4*
	3	7,913	*-1.4*	6,210	80,418	*-5.4*
	4	5,636	*-7.3*	6,170	42,580	*-16.0*
2000	1	4,993	*-1.1*	6,360	36,575	*-10.6*
	2	6,733	*-1.0*	6,380	48,785	*2.0*
	3	7,943	*0.4*	6,300	75,928	*-5.6*
	4	5,540	*-1.7*	6,170	42,471	*-0.3*

Due to changes in the IPS sampling methodology introduced in 1999, care should be taken when comparing results for 1999 and 2000 with earlier years.
See notes on page 9 relating to IPS interviewing on routes to the Irish Republic.

2.02 Spending at current and 1995 constant prices by quarter of year 1996 to 2000

		Spending (£ million)			Constant price spending (£ million)		
	Quarter	not seasonally adjusted	*per cent change from year earlier*	seasonally adjusted	not seasonally adjusted	*per cent change from year earlier*	seasonally adjusted
1996	1	2,175	7.2	3,010	2,148	4.4	3,000
	2	3,021	9.1	3,120	2,948	6.2	3,030
	3	4,225	1.5	3,010	4,103	-1.1	2,930
	4	2,869	2.4	3,140	2,755	-0.9	3,000
1997	1	2,165	-0.5	2,980	2,078	-3.3	2,910
	2	2,979	-1.4	3,110	2,820	-4.3	2,880
	3	4,229	0.1	3,020	3,973	-3.2	2,860
	4	2,870	0.0	3,130	2,671	-3.0	2,900
1998	1	2,250	3.9	3,140	2,093	0.7	2,880
	2	3,200	7.4	3,210	2,941	4.3	2,970
	3	4,212	-0.4	3,070	3,830	-3.6	2,810
	4	3,009	4.8	3,250	2,709	1.4	2,910
1999	1	2,412	7.2	3,280	2,176	4.0	2,990
	2	3,064	-4.3	3,050	2,700	-7.2	2,720
	3	4,148	-1.5	3,050	3,687	-3.7	2,700
	4	2,874	-4.5	3,110	2,540	-6.2	2,720
2000	1	2,314	-4.1	3,120	2,047	-5.9	2,800
	2	3,297	7.6	3,300	2,870	5.1	2,830
	3	4,284	3.3	3,200	3,696	0.2	2,760
	4	2,911	1.3	3,180	2,489	-2.0	2,720

Due to changes in the IPS sampling methodology introduced in 1999, care should be taken when comparing results for 1999 and 2000 with earlier years. See notes on page 9 relating to IPS interviewing on routes to the Irish Republic.

2.03 Number of visits by main area of residence and purpose of visit 1996 to 2000

	Visits (thousands)					*Change 1999-00*	*Growth 1999-00*	*Average Annual Growth 1996-00*
	1996	1997	1998	1999	2000	*(000s)*	*(%)*	*(%)*
North America								
Holiday	1,700	1,903	2,169	2,122	2,168	*46*	*2.2*	*6.3*
of which inclusive tour	*415*	*458*	*472*	*523*	*549*	*26*	*5.0*	*7.2*
Business	742	809	905	935	1,059	*124*	*13.3*	*9.3*
Visiting friends or relatives	833	950	1,000	1,070	1,116	*46*	*4.3*	*7.6*
Miscellaneous	400	437	479	473	527	*54*	*11.4*	*7.1*
All visits	3,675	4,099	4,553	4,599	4,869	*270*	*5.9*	*7.3*
EU Europe								
Holiday	6,494	6,172	5,814	5,165	4,625	*-540*	*-10.5*	*-8.1*
of which inclusive tour	*1,941*	*1,751*	*1,652*	*1,524*	*1,315*	*-209*	*-13.7*	*-9.3*
Business	4,115	4,240	4,639	4,631	4,754	*123*	*2.7*	*3.7*
Visiting friends or relatives	2,887	2,946	3,093	3,176	3,223	*47*	*1.5*	*2.8*
Miscellaneous	1,945	1,942	1,665	1,611	1,418	*-193*	*-12.0*	*-7.6*
All visits	15,441	15,300	15,212	14,584	14,020	*-564*	*-3.9*	*-2.4*
Non EU Europe								
Holiday	898	766	739	801	679	*-122*	*-15.2*	*-6.8*
of which inclusive tour	*402*	*274*	*257*	*291*	*182*	*-109*	*-37.5*	*-18.0*
Business	559	579	661	696	698	*2*	*0.3*	*5.7*
Visiting friends or relatives	339	377	408	407	399	*-8*	*-2.0*	*4.2*
Miscellaneous	378	367	363	328	290	*-38*	*-11.6*	*-6.4*
All visits	2,174	2,090	2,171	2,232	2,066	*-166*	*-7.4*	*-1.3*
Other Countries								
Holiday	1,895	1,963	1,753	1,737	1,831	*94*	*5.4*	*-0.9*
of which inclusive tour	*603*	*592*	*444*	*397*	*421*	*24*	*6.0*	*-8.6*
Business	679	719	677	782	810	*28*	*3.6*	*4.5*
Visiting friends or relatives	839	883	898	988	1,097	*109*	*11.0*	*6.9*
Miscellaneous	459	463	480	472	516	*44*	*9.3*	*3.0*
All visits	3,872	4,027	3,809	3,979	4,253	*274*	*6.9*	*2.4*
Total World								
Holiday	10,987	10,803	10,475	9,826	9,302	*-524*	*-5.3*	*-4.1*
of which inclusive tour	*3,362*	*3,076*	*2,824*	*2,735*	*2,467*	*-268*	*-9.8*	*-7.4*
Business	6,095	6,347	6,882	7,044	7,322	*278*	*3.9*	*4.7*
Visiting friends or relatives	4,898	5,155	5,400	5,640	5,834	*194*	*3.4*	*4.5*
Miscellaneous	3,182	3,209	2,988	2,884	2,750	*-134*	*-4.6*	*-3.6*
All visits	25,163	25,515	25,745	25,394	25,209	*-185*	*-0.7*	*0.0*

Due to changes in the IPS sampling methodology introduced in 1999, care should be taken when comparing results for 1999 and 2000 with earlier years. See notes on page 9 relating to IPS interviewing on routes to the Irish Republic.

2.04 Spending by main area of residence and purpose of visit 1996 to 2000

	Spending (£million)					Change 1999-00	Growth 1999-00	Average Annual Growth 1996-00
	1996	1997	1998	1999	2000	(£million)	(%)	(%)
North America								
Holiday	1,018	1,103	1,260	1,195	1,288	*93*	*7.8*	*6.1*
of which inclusive tour	*200*	*216*	*239*	*209*	*250*	*41*	*19.6*	*5.7*
Business	630	715	806	896	1,037	*141*	*15.7*	*13.3*
Visiting friends or relatives	340	423	413	502	505	*3*	*0.6*	*10.4*
Miscellaneous	282	267	314	291	356	*65*	*22.3*	*6.0*
All visits	2,277	2,515	2,801	2,894	3,197	*303*	*10.5*	*8.9*
EU Europe								
Holiday	2,067	1,764	1,678	1,501	1,443	*-58*	*-3.9*	*-8.6*
of which inclusive tour	*592*	*481*	*447*	*422*	*346*	*-76*	*-18.0*	*-12.6*
Business	1,398	1,492	1,612	1,604	1,549	*-55*	*-3.4*	*2.6*
Visiting friends or relatives	710	660	706	722	738	*16*	*2.2*	*1.0*
Miscellaneous	1,153	1,057	1,042	932	827	*-105*	*-11.3*	*-8.0*
All visits	5,335	4,979	5,044	4,775	4,570	*-205*	*-4.3*	*-3.8*
Non EU Europe								
Holiday	376	321	305	331	304	*-27*	*-8.2*	*-5.2*
of which inclusive tour	*138*	*97*	*97*	*103*	*63*	*-40*	*-38.8*	*-17.8*
Business	365	355	484	425	442	*17*	*4.0*	*4.9*
Visiting friends or relatives	122	188	206	171	181	*10*	*5.8*	*10.4*
Miscellaneous	289	327	262	267	250	*-17*	*-6.4*	*-3.6*
All visits	1,154	1,194	1,259	1,197	1,180	*-17*	*-1.4*	*0.6*
Other Countries								
Holiday	1,387	1,367	1,245	1,223	1,347	*124*	*10.1*	*-0.7*
of which inclusive tour	*219*	*214*	*156*	*152*	*161*	*9*	*5.9*	*-7.4*
Business	828	938	918	1,042	1,020	*-22*	*-2.1*	*5.1*
Visiting friends or relatives	669	670	646	737	847	*110*	*14.9*	*6.1*
Miscellaneous	632	572	749	620	635	*15*	*2.4*	*0.1*
All visits	3,525	3,555	3,566	3,632	3,859	*227*	*6.3*	*2.3*
Total World								
Holiday	4,848	4,555	4,488	4,251	4,383	*132*	*3.1*	*-2.5*
of which inclusive tour	*1,149*	*1,009*	*940*	*886*	*820*	*-66*	*-7.4*	*-8.1*
Business	3,220	3,501	3,820	3,967	4,048	*81*	*2.0*	*5.9*
Visiting friends or relatives	1,841	1,941	1,970	2,133	2,271	*138*	*6.5*	*5.4*
Miscellaneous	2,357	2,223	2,367	2,108	2,068	*-40*	*-1.9*	*-3.2*
All visits	12,290	12,244	12,671	12,498	12,805	*307*	*2.5*	*1.0*

Due to changes in the IPS sampling methodology introduced in 1999, care should be taken when comparing results for 1999 and 2000 with earlier years. See notes on page 9 relating to IPS interviewing on routes to the Irish Republic.

2.05 Number of nights and average length of stay by main area of residence 1996 to 2000

	Nights (thousands)					Average length of stay (nights)				
	1996	1997	1998	1999	2000	1996	1997	1998	1999	2000
North America										
Holiday	15,474	15,828	18,786	16,798	16,683	9.1	8.3	8.7	7.9	7.7
of which inclusive tour	*2,899*	*2,915*	*3,324*	*2,950*	*3,171*	*7.0*	*6.4*	*7.0*	*5.6*	*5.8*
Business	4,736	5,207	5,432	5,452	6,673	6.4	6.4	6.0	5.8	6.3
Visiting friends or relatives	11,468	12,966	12,637	12,854	13,001	13.8	13.7	12.6	12.0	11.6
Miscellaneous	4,679	5,566	5,516	4,834	5,751	11.7	12.7	11.5	10.2	10.9
All visits	36,358	39,567	42,371	39,938	42,108	9.9	9.7	9.3	8.7	8.6
EU Europe										
Holiday	36,364	35,889	34,298	28,927	23,916	5.6	5.8	5.9	5.6	5.2
of which inclusive tour	*9,188*	*8,291*	*7,877*	*7,184*	*5,783*	*4.7*	*4.7*	*4.8*	*4.7*	*4.4*
Business	13,514	14,422	*15,901*	13,432	*12,530*	3.3	3.4	3.4	2.9	2.6
Visiting friends or relatives	25,018	23,266	24,729	22,877	22,590	8.7	7.9	8.0	7.2	7.0
Miscellaneous	27,803	26,756	27,718	25,315	20,869	14.3	13.8	16.6	15.7	14.7
All visits	102,699	100,333	102,645	90,552	79,904	6.7	6.6	6.7	6.2	5.7
Non EU Europe										
Holiday	6,840	6,156	4,996	5,145	5,048	7.6	8.0	6.8	6.4	7.4
of which inclusive tour	*1,883*	*1,399*	*1,240*	*1,413*	*901*	*4.7*	*5.1*	*4.8*	*4.9*	*5.0*
Business	3,316	2,951	3,827	2,978	3,497	5.9	5.1	5.8	4.3	5.0
Visiting friends or relatives	4,660	4,956	*6,113*	4,877	*4,470*	13.8	13.1	15.0	12.0	11.2
Miscellaneous	7,505	8,504	7,121	7,512	5,942	19.9	23.2	19.6	22.9	20.5
All visits	22,321	22,567	22,057	20,511	18,956	10.3	10.8	10.2	9.2	9.2
Other Countries										
Holiday	21,366	22,076	21,437	20,326	20,905	11.3	11.3	12.2	11.7	11.4
of which inclusive tour	*2,777*	*3,100*	*2,188*	*2,116*	*1,990*	*4.6*	*5.2*	*4.9*	*5.3*	*4.7*
Business	6,367	7,296	7,105	8,638	7,628	9.4	10.2	10.5	11.0	9.4
Visiting friends or relatives	18,839	19,416	20,211	20,143	23,214	22.5	22.0	22.5	20.4	21.2
Miscellaneous	11,814	11,271	*14,950*	11,627	*11,044*	25.7	24.4	31.1	24.6	21.4
All visits	58,386	60,060	63,703	60,734	62,791	15.1	14.9	16.7	15.3	14.8
Total World										
Holiday	80,045	79,949	79,517	71,196	66,552	7.3	7.4	7.6	7.2	7.2
of which inclusive tour	*16,747*	*15,705*	*14,629*	*13,664*	*11,846*	*5.0*	*5.1*	*5.2*	*5.0*	*4.8*
Business	27,933	29,877	32,265	30,501	30,327	4.6	4.7	4.7	4.3	4.1
Visiting friends or relatives	59,985	60,605	63,691	60,751	63,274	12.3	11.8	11.8	10.8	10.8
Miscellaneous	51,801	52,097	55,305	49,288	43,605	16.3	16.2	18.5	17.1	15.9
All visits	219,764	222,527	230,777	211,735	203,759	8.7	8.7	9.0	8.3	8.1

Due to changes in the IPS sampling methodology introduced in 1999, care should be taken when comparing results for 1999 and 2000 with earlier years. See notes on page 9 relating to IPS interviewing on routes to the Irish Republic.

2.06 Average spending per visit and spending per day by main area of residence 1996 to 2000

	Average spending per visit (£)					Average spending per day (£)				
	1996	1997	1998	1999	2000	1996	1997	1998	1999	2000
North America										
Holiday	599	580	581	563	594	66	70	67	71	77
of which inclusive tour	*481*	*472*	*506*	*400*	*455*	*69*	*74*	*72*	*71*	*79*
Business	849	884	891	958	980	133	137	148	164	155
Visiting friends or relatives	407	445	413	470	452	30	33	33	39	39
Miscellaneous	706	610	657	614	676	60	48	57	60	62
All visits	618	612	614	627	654	62	63	66	72	76
EU Europe										
Holiday	306	271	272	273	291	55	47	46	49	56
of which inclusive tour	*305*	*275*	*271*	*277*	*263*	*64*	*58*	*57*	*59*	*60*
Business	340	352	347	346	326	103	103	101	119	124
Visiting friends or relatives	246	224	228	227	229	28	28	29	32	33
Miscellaneous	593	544	626	578	583	41	40	38	37	40
All visits	340	319	325	320	318	51	49	48	52	56
Non EU Europe										
Holiday	418	419	413	413	448	55	52	61	64	60
of which inclusive tour	*345*	*356*	*379*	*353*	*349*	*74*	*70*	*78*	*73*	*70*
Business	652	613	732	611	634	110	120	126	143	127
Visiting friends or relatives	360	498	505	421	454	26	38	34	35	41
Miscellaneous	765	890	722	815	863	39	38	37	36	42
All visits	530	570	579	535	570	52	53	57	58	62
Other Countries										
Holiday	732	697	710	704	736	65	62	58	60	64
of which inclusive tour	*363*	*362*	*352*	*383*	*382*	*79*	*69*	*71*	*72*	*81*
Business	1,220	1,306	1,355	1,332	1,250	130	129	129	121	134
Visiting friends or relatives	798	759	719	746	773	36	35	32	37	37
Miscellaneous	1,376	1,237	1,559	1,312	1,231	54	51	50	53	58
All visits	908	881	934	910	905	60	59	56	60	61
Total World										
Holiday	434	413	410	424	461	60	56	55	58	64
of which inclusive tour	*342*	*328*	*333*	*324*	*332*	*69*	*64*	*64*	*65*	*69*
Business	628	552	555	563	553	115	117	118	130	134
Visiting friends or relatives	376	376	365	378	389	31	32	31	35	30
Miscellaneous	741	693	792	731	752	45	43	43	43	47
All visits	484	475	487	487	503	55	55	54	58	62

Due to changes in the IPS sampling methodology introduced in 1999, care should be taken when comparing results for 1999 and 2000 with earlier years. See notes on page 9 relating to IPS interviewing on routes to the Irish Republic.

2.07 Number of visits by mode of travel and purpose of visit 1996 to 2000

	Visits (thousands)					*Change 1999-00*	*Growth 1999-00*	*Average Annual Growth 1996-00*
	1996	1997	1998	1999	2000	*(000s)*	*(%)*	*(%)*
Air								
Holiday	5,852	5,924	5,956	5,738	5,604	*-134*	*-2.3*	*-1.1*
of which inclusive tour	*1,681*	*1,567*	*1,466*	*1,343*	*1,225*	*-118*	*-8.8*	*-7.6*
Business	4,869	5,200	5,555	5,480	5,776	*296*	*5.4*	*4.4*
Visiting friends or relatives	3,502	3,719	3,920	4,088	4,459	*371*	*9.1*	*6.2*
Miscellaneous	2,056	2,015	2,048	1,979	1,992	*13*	*0.7*	*-0.8*
All visits	16,279	16,858	17,479	17,284	17,831	*547*	*3.2*	*2.3*
Sea								
Holiday	3,667	3,390	2,891	2,671	2,295	*-376*	*-14.1*	*-11.1*
of which inclusive tour	*1,304*	*1,124*	*918*	*1,040*	*886*	*-154*	*-14.8*	*-9.2*
Business	745	679	756	822	741	*-81*	*-9.9*	*-0.1*
Visiting friends or relatives	899	878	876	878	780	*-98*	*-11.2*	*-3.5*
Miscellaneous	855	787	559	622	481	*-141*	*-22.7*	*-13.4*
All visits	6,165	5,734	5,083	4,993	4,298	*-695*	*-13.9*	*-8.6*
Tunnel								
Holiday	1,468	1,489	1,628	1,416	1,403	*-13*	*-0.9*	*-1.1*
of which inclusive tour	*376*	*385*	*440*	*352*	*356*	*4*	*1.1*	*-1.4*
Business	481	468	571	743	804	*61*	*8.2*	*13.7*
Visiting friends or relatives	498	558	604	675	595	*-80*	*-11.9*	*4.5*
Miscellaneous	271	407	380	283	278	*-5*	*-1.8*	*0.6*
All visits	2,719	2,922	3,184	3,117	3,080	*-37*	*-1.2*	*3.2*
Total								
Holiday	10,987	10,803	10,475	9,826	9,302	*-524*	*-5.3*	*-4.1*
of which inclusive tour	*3,362*	*3,076*	*2,824*	*2,735*	*2,467*	*-268*	*-9.8*	*-7.4*
Business	6,095	6,347	6,882	7,044	7,322	*278*	*3.9*	*4.7*
Visiting friends or relatives	4,898	5,155	5,400	5,640	5,834	*194*	*3.4*	*4.5*
Miscellaneous	3,182	3,209	2,988	2,884	2,750	*-134*	*-4.6*	*-3.6*
All visits	25,163	25,515	25,745	25,394	25,209	*-185*	*-0.7*	*0.0*

Due to changes in the IPS sampling methodology introduced in 1999, care should be taken when comparing results for 1999 and 2000 with earlier years. See notes on page 9 relating to IPS interviewing on routes to the Irish Republic.

2.08 Spending by mode of travel and purpose of visit 1996 to 2000

	Spending (£million)					Change 1999-00	Growth 1999-00	Average Annual Growth 1996-00
	1996	1997	1998	1999	2000	*(million)*	*(%)*	*(%)*
Air								
Holiday	3,583	3,414	3,404	3,243	3,413	*170*	*5.2*	*-1.2*
of which inclusive tour	*760*	*688*	*645*	*585*	*580*	*-5*	*-0.9*	*-6.5*
Business	2,968	3,208	3,544	3,623	3,748	*125*	*3.5*	*6.0*
Visiting friends or relatives	1,547	1,599	1,577	1,780	1,971	*191*	*10.7*	*6.2*
Miscellaneous	1,802	1,657	1,818	1,771	1,673	*-98*	*-5.5*	*-1.8*
All visits	9,922	9,900	10,366	10,451	10,837	*386*	*3.7*	*2.2*
Sea								
Holiday	861	756	677	637	579	*-58*	*-9.1*	*-9.4*
of which inclusive tour	*297*	*228*	*201*	*219*	*169*	*-50*	*-22.8*	*-13.1*
Business	143	114	114	191	134	*-57*	*-29.8*	*-1.6*
Visiting friends or relatives	198	188	270	219	163	*-56*	*-25.6*	*-4.7*
Miscellaneous	398	301	336	229	261	*32*	*14.0*	*-10.0*
All visits	1,601	1,360	1,399	1,280	1,140	*-140*	*-10.9*	*-8.1*
Tunnel								
Holiday	404	385	407	371	390	*19*	*5.1*	*-0.9*
of which inclusive tour	*93*	*93*	*94*	*82*	*72*	*-10*	*-12.2*	*6.2*
Business	109	178	162	153	166	*13*	*8.5*	*11.1*
Visiting friends or relatives	97	155	124	134	137	*3*	*2.2*	*9.0*
Miscellaneous	156	264	213	109	134	*25*	*22.9*	*-3.7*
All visits	768	983	906	767	828	*61*	*8.0*	*1.9*
Total								
Holiday	4,848	4,555	4,488	4,251	4,383	*132*	*3.1*	*-2.5*
of which inclusive tour	*1,149*	*1,009*	*940*	*886*	*820*	*-66*	*-7.4*	*-8.1*
Business	3,220	3,501	3,820	3,967	4,048	*81*	*2.0*	[illegible]
Visiting friends or relatives	1,841	1,941	1,970	2,133	2,271	*138*	*6.5*	*5.4*
Miscellaneous	2,357	2,223	2,367	2,108	2,068	*-40*	*-1.9*	*-3.2*
All visits	12,290	12,244	12,671	12,498	12,805	*307*	*2.5*	*1.0*

Due to changes in the IPS sampling methodology introduced in 1999, care should be taken when comparing results for 1999 and 2000 with earlier years. See notes on page 9 relating to IPS interviewing on routes to the Irish Republic.

2.09 Number of visits by country of residence 1996 to 2000

	Visits (thousands)					*Change 1999-00*	*Growth 1999-00*	*Average Annual Growth 1996-00*
	1996	1997	1998	1999	2000	*(000s)*	*(%)*	*(%)*
Canada	595	667	673	660	772	*112*	*17.0*	*6.7*
USA	3,080	3,432	3,880	3,939	4,097	*158*	*4.0*	*7.4*
North America	3,675	4,099	4,553	4,599	4,869	*270*	*5.9*	*7.3*
Austria	259	218	242	242	227	*-15*	*-6.2*	*-3.2*
Belgium	1,554	1,345	1,183	1,077	997	*-80*	*-7.4*	*-10.5*
Denmark	445	415	433	458	421	*-37*	*-8.1*	*-1.4*
Finland	143	144	145	137	154	*17*	*12.4*	*1.9*
France	3,690	3,586	3,274	3,223	3,087	*-136*	*-4.2*	*-4.4*
Germany	2,963	2,911	2,830	2,794	2,758	*-36*	*-1.3*	*-1.8*
Greece	184	155	195	202	224	*22*	*10.9*	*5.0*
Irish Republic*	2,078	2,232	2,310	2,075	2,087	*12*	*0.6*	*0.1*
Italy	924	990	1,090	1,076	949	*-127*	*-11.8*	*0.7*
Luxembourg	55	58	60	53	51	*-2*	*-3.8*	*-1.9*
Netherlands	1,539	1,653	1,718	1,617	1,440	*-177*	*-10.9*	*-1.6*
Portugal	161	154	177	174	174	*0*	*0.0*	*2.0*
Spain	807	825	879	829	849	*20*	*2.4*	*1.3*
Sweden	639	616	676	628	602	*-26*	*-4.1*	*-1.5*
EU Europe	15,441	15,300	15,212	14,584	14,020	*-564*	*-3.9*	*-2.4*
Cyprus	77	88	74	76	66	*-10*	*-13.2*	*-3.8*
Gibraltar	20	23	20	23	24	*1*	*4.3*	*4.7*
Iceland	50	44	75	41	47	*6*	*14.6*	*-1.5*
Malta	53	52	42	57	49	*-8*	*-14.0*	*-1.9*
Norway	406	453	509	507	455	*-52*	*-10.3*	*2.9*
Switzerland	578	567	583	616	579	*-37*	*-6.0*	*0.0*
Turkey	86	89	75	103	78	*-25*	*-24.3*	*-2.4*
Central & Eastern Europe	601	469	493	551	504	*-47*	*-8.5*	*-4.3*
Former USSR	253	245	249	183	204	*21*	*11.5*	*-5.2*
Former Yugoslavia	50	58	50	74	60	*-14*	*-18.9*	*4.7*
Non EU Europe	2,174	2,090	2,171	2,232	2,066	*-166*	*-7.4*	*-1.3*
North Africa	68	92	86	81	87	*6*	*7.4*	*6.4*
South Africa	240	262	284	300	304	*4*	*1.3*	*6.1*
Rest of Africa	238	225	246	257	277	*20*	*7.8*	*3.9*
Israel	241	252	198	230	220	*-10*	*-4.3*	*-2.3*
Other Middle East	356	377	374	377	394	*17*	*4.5*	*2.6*
Hong Kong	189	167	165	150	183	*33*	*22.0*	*-0.8*
India	141	184	175	183	206	*23*	*12.6*	*9.9*
Japan	584	570	545	495	557	*62*	*12.5*	*-1.2*
Rest of Asia	686	647	456	579	645	*66*	*11.4*	*-1.5*
Australia	650	684	603	728	777	*49*	*6.7*	*4.6*
New Zealand	132	148	166	193	174	*-19*	*-9.8*	*7.2*
Caribbean	62	77	95	101	101	*0*	*0.0*	*13.0*
Central & South America	279	334	404	300	317	*17*	*5.7*	*3.2*
Rest of the World	7	7	12	8	11	*3*	*37.5*	*12.0*
Other Countries	3,872	4,027	3,809	3,979	4,253	*274*	*6.9*	*2.4*
Total World	25,163	25,515	25,745	25,394	25,209	*-185*	*-0.7*	*0.0*

* Due to changes in the IPS sampling methodology introduced in 1999, care should be taken when comparing results for 1999 and 2000 with earlier years. See notes on page 9 relating to IPS interviewing on routes to the Irish Republic.

2.10 Spending by country of residence 1996 to 2000

	Spending (£million)					*Change 1999-00*	*Growth 1999-00*	*Average Annual Growth 1996-00*
	1996	1997	1998	1999	2000	*(£million)*	*(%)*	*(%)*
Canada	307	351	319	356	445	*89*	*25.0*	*9.7*
USA	1,970	2,164	2,482	2,538	2,752	*214*	*8.4*	*8.7*
North America	2,277	2,515	2,801	2,894	3,197	*303*	*10.5*	*8.9*
Austria	134	94	101	100	89	*-11*	*-11.0*	*-9.7*
Belgium	261	217	225	216	219	*3*	*1.4*	*-4.3*
Denmark	161	169	163	198	170	*-28*	*-14.1*	*1.4*
Finland	135	70	66	54	65	*11*	*20.4*	*-16.7*
France	708	649	750	710	684	*-26*	*-3.7*	*-0.9*
Germany	1,068	1,071	882	927	887	*-40*	*-4.3*	*-4.5*
Greece	140	152	157	163	167	*4*	*2.5*	*4.5*
Irish Republic*	940	856	824	594	570	*-24*	*-4.0*	*-11.8*
Italy	476	471	555	560	472	*-88*	*-15.7*	*-0.2*
Luxembourg	16	21	27	16	15	*-1*	*-6.3*	*-1.6*
Netherlands	390	409	407	389	374	*-15*	*-3.9*	*-1.0*
Portugal	77	70	94	105	73	*-32*	*-30.5*	*-1.3*
Spain	456	380	384	381	409	*28*	*7.3*	*-2.7*
Sweden	290	263	310	271	276	*5*	*1.8*	*-1.2*
EU Europe	5,335	4,979	5,044	4,775	4,570	*-205*	*-4.3*	*-3.8*
Cyprus	50	72	56	63	79	*16*	*25.4*	*12.1*
Gibraltar	16	13	12	9	12	*3*	*33.3*	*-6.9*
Iceland	37	41	38	20	27	*7*	*35.0*	*-7.6*
Malta	23	26	24	29	23	*-6*	*-20.7*	*0.0*
Norway	193	196	218	238	183	*-55*	*-23.1*	*-1.3*
Switzerland	333	286	287	321	289	*-32*	*-10.0*	*-3.5*
Turkey	76	75	71	125	91	*-34*	*-27.2*	*4.6*
Central & Eastern Europe	197	196	251	205	180	*-25*	*-12.2*	*-2.2*
Former USSR	195	228	276	157	232	*75*	*47.8*	*4.4*
Former Yugoslavia	35	60	27	30	63	*33*	*110.0*	*15.8*
Non EU Europe	1,154	1,194	1,259	1,197	1,180	*-17*	*-1.4*	*0.6*
North Africa	101	187	149	144	108	*-36*	*-25.0*	*1.7*
South Africa	180	202	216	257	215	*-42*	*16.3*	*4.5*
Rest of Africa	320	287	373	345	345	*0*	*0.0*	*1.9*
Israel	122	136	113	112	132	*20*	*17.9*	*2.0*
Other Middle East	486	545	515	613	696	*83*	*13.5*	*9.4*
Hong Kong	202	175	135	123	154	*31*	*25.2*	*-6.6*
India	90	127	140	143	134	*-9*	*-6.3*	*10.5*
Japan	439	361	429	365	456	*91*	*24.9*	*1.0*
Rest of Asia	654	580	512	549	574	*25*	*4.6*	*-3.2*
Australia	502	525	424	516	517	*1*	*0.2*	*0.7*
New Zealand	104	107	120	141	129	*-12*	*-8.5*	*5.5*
Caribbean	48	61	89	68	100	*32*	*47.1*	*20.1*
Central & South America	264	259	344	253	283	*30*	*11.9*	*1.8*
Rest of the World	12	5	8	5	14	*9*	*180.0*	*3.9*
Other Countries	3,525	3,555	3,566	3,632	3,859	*227*	*6.3*	*2.3*
Total World	12,290	12,244	12,671	12,498	12,805	*307*	*2.5*	*1.0*

* Due to changes in the IPS sampling methodology introduced in 1999, care should be taken when comparing results for 1999 and 2000 with earlier years. See notes on page 9 relating to IPS interviewing on routes to the Irish Republic.

2.11 Number of nights and average length of stay by country of residence 1996 to 2000

	Nights (thousands)					Average length of stay (nights)				
	1996	1997	1998	1999	2000	1996	1997	1998	1999	2000
Canada	8,266	8,876	8,584	8,930	8,885	14	13	13	14	12
USA	28,092	30,691	33,788	31,008	33,223	9	9	9	8	8
North America	36,358	39,567	42,371	39,938	42,108	10	10	9	9	9
Austria	2,351	2,162	1,916	1,960	1,812	9	10	8	8	8
Belgium	3,765	3,640	3,474	3,345	2,695	2	3	3	3	3
Denmark	2,618	2,762	2,674	2,712	2,494	6	7	6	6	6
Finland	1,735	1,231	1,303	872	1,150	12	9	9	6	7
France	18,514	17,071	18,010	18,105	16,196	5	5	6	6	5
Germany	21,454	21,028	18,901	18,744	17,120	7	7	7	7	6
Greece	2,453	2,306	2,085	2,735	2,823	13	15	11	14	13
Irish Republic*	15,528	16,619	17,243	8,080	7,847	7	7	8	4	4
Italy	10,188	9,627	12,442	11,791	8,073	11	10	11	11	9
Luxembourg	283	234	303	234	206	5	4	5	4	4
Netherlands	6,460	7,644	7,335	7,140	5,931	4	5	4	4	4
Portugal	1,289	1,173	1,613	1,311	1,105	8	8	9	8	6
Spain	11,637	10,776	10,201	8,983	8,624	14	13	12	11	10
Sweden	4,423	4,061	5,145	4,542	3,829	7	7	8	7	6
EU Europe	102,699	100,333	102,645	90,552	79,904	7	7	7	6	6
Cyprus	1,286	1,755	927	1,174	1,403	17	20	13	15	21
Gibraltar	210	189	122	179	172	10	8	6	8	7
Iceland	371	402	449	186	219	7	9	6	5	5
Malta	390	500	458	507	577	7	10	11	9	12
Norway	2,579	2,261	2,474	2,358	2,542	6	5	5	5	6
Switzerland	4,543	4,132	3,963	3,919	3,488	8	7	7	6	6
Turkey	1,449	1,288	1,051	1,653	1,363	17	14	14	16	18
Central & Eastern Europe	7,091	7,409	8,162	6,214	5,317	12	16	17	11	11
Former USSR	3,323	3,676	3,798	2,619	2,965	13	15	15	14	15
Former Yugoslavia	1,079	954	652	1,703	912	21	16	13	23	15
Non EU Europe	22,321	22,567	22,057	20,511	18,956	10	11	10	9	9
North Africa	1,179	1,768	2,104	1,515	1,186	17	19	24	19	14
South Africa	3,687	4,542	4,587	4,971	4,381	15	17	16	17	14
Rest of Africa	4,567	4,252	5,392	5,391	5,041	19	19	22	21	18
Israel	1,884	1,851	1,371	1,617	1,704	8	7	7	7	8
Other Middle East	5,377	6,460	5,784	6,331	6,543	15	17	16	17	17
Hong Kong	2,382	2,185	1,629	1,526	1,984	13	13	10	10	11
India	2,509	3,266	3,563	3,640	4,118	18	18	20	20	20
Japan	5,305	4,937	6,992	5,735	6,084	9	9	13	12	11
Rest of Asia	8,976	9,936	9,088	8,683	9,745	13	15	20	15	15
Australia	13,126	12,876	11,292	11,197	12,170	20	19	19	15	16
New Zealand	3,379	2,837	4,397	3,565	3,496	26	19	27	18	20
Caribbean	1,442	1,267	2,057	1,841	2,005	23	16	22	18	20
Central & South America	4,373	3,763	5,320	4,603	4,125	16	11	13	15	13
Rest of the World	199	119	127	116	209	30	17	11	15	18
Other Countries	58,386	60,060	63,703	60,734	62,791	15	15	17	15	15
Total World	219,764	222,527	230,777	211,735	203,759	9	9	9	8	8

* Due to changes in the IPS sampling methodology introduced in 1999, care should be taken when comparing results for 1999 and 2000 with earlier years. See notes on page 9 relating to IPS interviewing on routes to the Irish Republic.

2.12 Average spending per visit and spending per day by country of residence 1996 to 2000

	Average spending per visit (£)					Average spending per day (£)				
	1996	1997	1998	1999	2000	1996	1997	1998	1999	2000
Canada	514	525	472	537	574	37	39	37	40	50
USA	638	629	638	642	670	70	70	73	82	83
North America	618	612	614	627	654	62	63	66	72	76
Austria	515	428	418	412	392	57	43	53	51	49
Belgium	168	161	190	201	219	69	59	65	65	81
Denmark	360	407	376	432	403	61	61	61	73	68
Finland	943	484	453	392	422	77	57	50	62	57
France	192	181	229	220	221	38	38	42	39	42
Germany	360	368	311	331	321	50	51	47	49	52
Greece	760	976	802	809	745	57	66	75	60	59
Irish Republic*	452	384	357	283	270	61	52	48	73	72
Italy	514	475	509	520	497	47	49	45	47	58
Luxembourg	295	364	447	310	301	57	89	88	70	75
Netherlands	253	247	237	240	260	60	53	55	54	63
Portugal	478	450	533	602	420	60	59	58	80	66
Spain	563	460	436	458	480	39	35	38	42	47
Sweden	452	427	458	430	459	65	65	60	59	72
EU Europe	340	319	325	320	318	51	49	48	52	56
Cyprus	853	817	757	830	1,192	39	41	60	54	56
Gibraltar	811	573	569	396	480	78	69	95	50	68
Iceland	724	929	499	489	577	99	102	84	109	123
Malta	429	504	572	510	472	58	53	53	57	40
Norway	475	430	426	468	401	75	86	88	101	72
Switzerland	575	504	491	520	499	73	69	72	82	83
Turkey	878	838	940	1,215	1,174	52	58	67	76	67
Central & Eastern Europe	326	416	509	371	357	28	26	31	33	34
Former USSR	768	930	1,107	856	1,133	59	62	72	60	78
Former Yugoslavia	694	1,038	541	402	1,053	32	63	42	18	69
Non EU Europe	530	570	579	535	570	52	53	57	58	62
North Africa	1,496	2,026	1,719	1,701	1,244	86	106	71	95	91
South Africa	745	767	754	853	704	49	44	47	51	49
Rest of Africa	1,335	1,269	1,512	1,333	1,239	70	67	69	63	68
Israel	506	537	569	485	598	65	73	82	69	77
Other Middle East	1,362	1,443	1,375	1,623	1,765	90	84	89	97	106
Hong Kong	1,067	1,044	817	817	841	85	80	83	80	77
India	637	687	795	780	645	36	39	39	39	32
Japan	751	633	786	736	817	83	73	61	64	75
Rest of Asia	952	895	1,121	947	890	73	58	56	63	59
Australia	771	765	703	707	664	38	41	38	46	42
New Zealand	790	723	721	729	740	31	38	27	39	37
Caribbean	778	785	931	675	991	33	48	43	37	50
Central & South America	945	773	849	839	890	60	69	64	55	68
Rest of the World	1,793	752	723	667	1,246	60	44	66	44	68
Other Countries	908	881	934	910	905	60	59	56	60	61
Total World	484	475	487	487	503	55	55	54	58	62

* Due to changes in the IPS sampling methodology introduced in 1999, care should be taken when comparing results for 1999 and 2000 with earlier years. See notes on page 9 relating to IPS interviewing on routes to the Irish Republic.

2.13 Number of visits by length of stay and purpose of visit 1996 to 2000

	Visits (thousands)					Spending (£million)				
	1996	1997	1998	1999*	2000	1996	1997	1998	1999*	2000
Nil nights										
Holiday	969	941	735	595	530	34	27	31	27	26
of which inclusive tour	*0*	*0*	*0*	*0*	*0*	*0*	*0*	*0*	*0*	*0*
Business	841	867	953	1,144	1,227	46	45	47	56	65
Visiting friends or relatives	43	42	50	69	61	2	3	2	4	4
Miscellaneous	375	451	298	245	179	27	29	22	14	15
All visits	2,228	2,301	2,036	2,053	1,997	133	127	127	139	145
1-3 nights										
Holiday	3,401	3,145	3,148	3,350	3,215	837	726	731	800	776
of which inclusive tour	*1,561*	*1,391*	*1,266*	*1,228*	*1,150*	*357*	*290*	*265*	*249*	*221*
Business	2,734	2,824	3,125	3,752	3,938	889	959	1,073	1,314	1,373
Visiting friends or relatives	960	1,060	1,078	1,647	1,648	164	202	197	294	294
Miscellaneous	1,162	1,168	1,130	1,298	1,305	278	339	206	265	271
All visits	8,258	8,198	8,482	10,046	10,106	2,168	2,227	2,208	2,672	2,715
4-13 nights										
Holiday	4,574	4,604	4,547	4,566	4,429	2,164	2,095	2,128	2,049	2,179
of which inclusive tour	*1,631*	*1,531*	*1,401*	*1,383*	*1,220*	*666*	*597*	*550*	*525*	*495*
Business	1,553	1,620	1,733	1,805	1,813	1,306	1,367	1,451	1,666	1,655
Visiting friends or relatives	2,039	2,123	2,314	2,683	2,841	688	689	722	902	926
Miscellaneous	524	540	487	569	542	335	361	314	376	322
All visits	8,690	8,887	9,080	9,623	9,625	4,493	4,512	4,614	4,993	5,083
14-27 nights										
Holiday	1,176	1,193	1,109	1,005	820	933	924	807	796	733
of which inclusive tour	*157*	*142*	*145*	*112*	*91*	*111*	*107*	*114*	*96*	*93*
Business	200	207	212	202	213	307	330	369	318	363
Visiting friends or relatives	781	775	790	806	834	399	418	395	442	490
Miscellaneous	419	349	350	350	331	381	322	300	306	331
All visits	2,576	2,524	2,461	2,363	2,198	2,019	1,994	1,870	1,862	1,916
28 nights or more										
Holiday	323	338	335	310	309	520	442	448	490	571
of which inclusive tour	*13*	*11*	*11*	*11*	*6*	*15*	*14*	*11*	*16*	*11*
Business	114	122	129	142	131	357	513	603	613	592
Visiting friends or relatives	412	444	432	435	450	395	453	485	490	557
Miscellaneous	484	469	482	422	393	1,183	1,031	1,391	1,148	1,129
All visits	1,332	1,373	1,377	1,308	1,283	2,455	2,439	2,928	2,742	2,848
All Visits										
Holiday	10,987	10,803	10,475	9,826	9,302	4,848	4,555	4,488	4,251	4,383
of which inclusive tour	*3,362*	*3,076*	*2,824*	*2,735*	*2,467*	*1,149*	*1,009*	*940*	*886*	*820*
Business	6,095	6,347	6,882	7,044	7,322	3,220	3,501	3,820	3,967	4,048
Visiting friends or relatives	4,898	5,155	5,400	5,640	5,834	1,841	1,941	1,970	2,133	2,271
Miscellaneous	3,182	3,209	2,988	2,884	2,750	2,357	2,223	2,367	2,108	2,068
All visits	25,163	25,515	25,745	25,394	25,209	12,290	12,244	12,671	12,498	12,805

Due to changes in the IPS sampling methodology introduced in 1999, care should be taken when comparing results for 1999 and 2000 with earlier years. See notes on page 9 relating to IPS interviewing on routes to the Irish Republic.

2.14 Number of visits by length of stay and area of residence 1996 to 2000

	Visits (thousands)					Spending (£million)				
	1996	1997	1998	1999*	2000	1996	1997	1998	1999*	2000
Nil nights										
North America	43	41	45	65	59	11	11	12	15	19
EU Europe	2,098	2,118	1,832	1,840	1,764	103	90	88	101	99
Non EU Europe	54	102	110	107	121	6	12	13	9	9
Other Countries	33	40	49	41	53	13	14	15	14	18
Total World	2,228	2,301	2,036	2,053	1,997	133	127	127	139	145
1-3 nights										
North America	1,103	1,288	1,388	1,538	1,623	306	354	405	472	516
EU Europe	5,174	5,024	5,174	6,484	6,412	1,204	1,193	1,144	1,498	1,453
Non EU Europe	791	697	888	914	850	264	256	279	278	287
Other Countries	1,189	1,188	1,031	1,111	1,221	393	424	380	425	460
Total World	8,258	8,198	8,482	10,046	10,106	2,168	2,227	2,208	2,672	2,715
4-13 nights										
North America	1,768	1,942	2,254	2,237	2,405	1,126	1,254	1,463	1,471	1,630
EU Europe	4,505	4,485	4,485	4,905	4,675	1,661	1,600	1,550	1,773	1,714
Non EU Europe	933	893	839	884	805	468	458	449	503	434
Other Countries	1,484	1,567	1,502	1,598	1,740	1,238	1,200	1,152	1,246	1,303
Total World	8,690	8,887	9,080	9,623	9,625	4,493	4,512	4,614	4,993	5,083
14-27 nights										
North America	562	604	626	550	569	471	509	499	489	586
EU Europe	1,132	1,003	992	937	794	648	546	531	526	483
Non EU Europe	235	233	187	186	162	192	191	145	151	125
Other Countries	648	684	656	690	672	708	747	695	696	721
Total World	2,576	2,524	2,461	2,363	2,198	2,019	1,994	1,870	1,862	1,916
28 nights or more										
North America	199	224	240	300	213	364	386	422	448	446
EU Europe	455	437	420	419	375	696	605	808	707	721
Non EU Europe	160	164	147	141	127	222	276	373	256	324
Other Countries	519	548	571	610	567	1,174	1,171	1,324	1,251	1,356
Total World	1,332	1,373	1,377	1,308	1,283	2,455	2,439	2,928	2,742	2,848
All visits										
North America	3,675	4,099	4,553	4,599	4,869	2,277	2,515	2,801	2,894	3,197
EU Europe	15,441	15,300	15,212	14,584	14,020	5,335	4,979	5,044	4,775	4,570
Non EU Europe	2,174	2,090	2,171	2,232	2,066	1,154	1,194	1,259	1,197	1,180
Other Countries	3,872	4,027	3,809	3,979	4,253	3,525	3,555	3,566	3,632	3,859
Total World	25,163	25,515	25,745	25,394	25,209	12,290	12,244	12,671	12,498	12,805

Due to changes in the IPS sampling methodology introduced in 1999, care should be taken when comparing results for 1999 and 2000 with earlier years. See notes on page 9 relating to IPS interviewing on routes to the Irish Republic.

2.15 Number of visits and spending by UK area of visit and area of residence 1996 to 2000

	Visits (thousands)					Spending (£million) 1				
	1996	1997	1998	1999*	2000	1996	1997	1998	1999*	2000
London										
North America	2,423	2,693	2,976	3,077	3,282	1,291	1,423	1,602	1,698	1,910
EU Europe	5,709	5,474	5,458	6,089	5,815	2,016	1,942	1,941	2,195	2,066
Non EU Europe	1,299	1,204	1,167	1,266	1,110	596	639	678	699	650
Other Countries	2,835	2,913	2,668	2,737	2,939	2,105	1,990	2,072	2,116	2,275
Total World	12,266	12,284	12,269	13,168	13,145	6,007	5,993	6,293	6,708	6,901
Other England										
North America	1,624	1,779	1,993	1,900	2,007	665	738	828	842	915
EU Europe	5,450	5,253	5,401	6,088	5,922	1,736	1,572	1,665	1,871	1,810
Non EU Europe	930	866	898	889	897	454	448	482	389	448
Other Countries	1,536	1,656	1,582	1,671	1,799	1,137	1,275	1,201	1,220	1,285
Total World	9,540	9,554	9,873	10,548	10,624	3,991	4,033	4,175	4,322	4,458
Total England										
North America	3,409	3,790	4,211	4,249	4,509	1,956	2,161	2,430	2,540	2,825
EU Europe	10,361	10,037	10,203	11,475	11,066	3,751	3,514	3,606	4,065	3,875
Non EU Europe	2,004	1,890	1,903	1,994	1,844	1,049	1,086	1,160	1,088	1,098
Other Countries	3,729	3,889	3,627	3,788	4,064	3,241	3,265	3,272	3,337	3,560
Total World	19,503	19,606	19,944	21,506	21,484	9,998	10,026	10,468	11,030	11,359
Scotland										
North America	536	572	606	570	561	249	267	299	278	282
EU Europe	781	778	799	795	644	327	280	318	289	280
Non EU Europe	157	161	174	131	135	80	73	71	84	56
Other Countries	363	402	368	360	348	183	180	195	166	171
Total World	1,837	1,912	1,947	1,856	1,689	839	799	882	817	789
Wales										
North America	182	200	203	186	206	39	47	37	44	54
EU Europe	371	418	312	574	538	85	79	53	132	119
Non EU Europe	44	42	43	41	51	10	16	11	9	11
Other Countries	164	180	159	209	185	65	68	64	83	83
Total World	760	840	718	1,010	980	198	210	164	269	267
All Areas										
North America	3,675	4,099	4,553	4,599	4,869	2,270	2,508	2,793	2,884	3,186
EU Europe	13,363	13,068	12,902	14,584	14,020	4,305	4,028	4,115	4,669	4,459
Non EU Europe	2,174	2,091	2,168	2,232	2,066	1,152	1,193	1,258	1,195	1,178
Other Countries	3,872	4,026	3,812	3,979	4,253	3,517	3,546	3,557	3,622	3,849
Total World	23,085	23,283	23,435	25,394	25,209	11,244	11,275	11,723	12,370	12,672

1 Channel Islands and transit passengers are excluded from spending figures

Due to changes in the IPS sampling methodology introduced in 1999, care should be taken when comparing results for 1999 and 2000 with earlier years. See notes on page 9 relating to IPS interviewing on routes to the Irish Republic.

* From 1999 figures include residents from the Irish Republic

2.16 Number of visits and spending by UK area and purpose of visit 1996 to 2000

	Visits (thousands)					Spending (£million) 1				
	1996	1997	1998	1999*	2000	1996	1997	1998	1999*	2000
London										
Holiday	6,520	6,402	6,194	6,303	6,189	2,723	2,526	2,472	2,542	2,646
of which inclusive tour	*2,696*	*2,437*	*2,155*	*2,148*	*1,917*	*829*	*708*	*625*	*613*	*558*
Business	2,479	2,546	2,725	3,005	3,129	1,703	1,758	2,080	2,333	2,311
Visiting friends or relatives	1,877	1,960	2,061	2,474	2,498	675	734	735	882	951
Miscellaneous	1,390	1,376	1,289	1,386	1,329	907	975	1,007	952	993
All visits	12,266	12,284	12,269	13,168	13,145	6,007	5,993	6,293	6,708	6,901
Other England										
Holiday	3,469	3,366	3,332	3,286	3,045	1,154	1,062	1,051	1,051	1,055
of which inclusive tour	*785*	*750*	*738*	*644*	*614*	*198*	*166*	*175*	*159*	*138*
Business	2,311	2,361	2,622	2,886	3,022	982	1,210	1,184	1,263	1,428
Visiting friends or relatives	2,536	2,671	2,737	3,149	3,369	764	837	864	1,007	1,068
Miscellaneous	1,224	1,157	1,182	1,227	1,188	1,091	923	1,076	1,001	907
All visits	9,540	9,554	9,873	10,548	10,624	3,991	4,033	4,175	4,322	4,458
Total England										
Holiday	8,872	8,685	8,454	8,543	8,142	3,877	3,588	3,522	3,593	3,701
of which inclusive tour	*3,218*	*2,947*	*2,678*	*2,558*	*2,298*	*1,027*	*875*	*801*	*772*	*696*
Business	4,318	4,457	4,894	5,450	5,720	2,685	2,968	3,264	3,595	3,739
Visiting friends or relatives	3,893	4,112	4,278	5,071	5,274	1,439	1,572	1,599	1,800	2,019
Miscellaneous	2,420	2,352	2,317	2,442	2,348	1,997	1,898	2,083	1,952	1,900
All visits	19,503	19,606	19,944	21,506	21,484	9,998	10,026	10,468	11,030	11,359
Scotland										
Holiday	1,086	1,110	1,149	1,041	898	456	448	489	409	416
of which inclusive tour	*285*	*287*	*318*	*266*	*239*	*105*	*107*	*119*	*90*	*95*
Business	255	292	299	339	266	109	140	171	194	148
Visiting friends or relatives	374	379	381	397	418	143	127	138	150	161
Miscellaneous	123	131	118	79	108	131	84	84	63	64
All visits	1,837	1,912	1,947	1,856	1,689	839	799	882	817	789
Wales										
Holiday	400	426	366	453	483	80	97	63	97	111
of which inclusive tour	*106*	*108*	*97*	*124*	*160*	*14*	*18*	*14*	*24*	*25*
Business	103	124	99	157	166	46	37	37	63	53
Visiting friends or relatives	192	211	210	304	244	44	44	41	71	57
Miscellaneous	66	79	44	95	86	28	32	23	39	46
All visits	760	840	718	1,010	980	198	210	164	269	267
All Areas										
Holiday	10,446	10,222	9,874	9,831	9,300	4,493	4,213	4,146	4,170	4,288
of which inclusive tour	*3,365*	*3,076*	*2,824*	*2,765*	*2,493*	*1,154*	*1,009*	*940*	*894*	*827*
Business	5,441	5,641	6,151	7,042	7,325	2,907	3,214	3,544	3,953	4,051
Visiting friends or relatives	4,236	4,444	4,663	5,642	5,837	1,648	1,765	1,801	2,139	2,273
Miscellaneous	2,961	2,976	2,747	2,879	2,746	2,196	2,083	2,233	2,108	2,061
All visits	23,085	23,283	23,435	25,394	25,209	11,244	11,275	11,723	12,370	12,672

1 Channel Islands and transit passengers are excluded from spending figures

Due to changes in the IPS sampling methodology introduced in 1999, care should be taken when comparing results for 1999 and 2000 with earlier years. See notes on page 9 relating to IPS interviewing on routes to the Irish Republic.

* From 1999 figures include residents from the Irish Republic

Chapter *3*

UK residents' visits abroad 1996 to 2000

- *Visits abroad up from 42.1 million to 56.8 million between 1996 and 2000*

- *Spending up from £16.2 billion in 1996 to £24.3 billion in 2000*

- *Holiday visits up by over a third from 26.8 million in 1996 to 36.7 million in 2000*

- *Visits by air up from 27.9 million in 1996 to 41.4 million in 2000 and by tunnel from 3.5 million to 5.8 million. Visits by sea down from 10.7 million to 9.6 million*

- *Spain saw the largest increase in number of visits between 1996 and 2000 of 3.6 million*

Chapter 3

UK residents' visits abroad 1996 to 2000

3.01 Visits by year and quarter 1996-2000

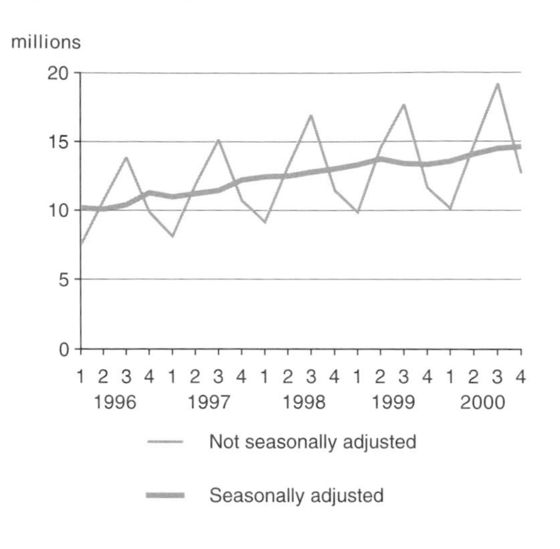

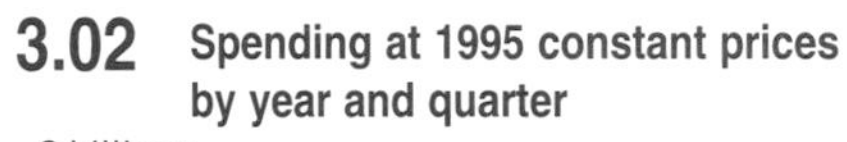

3.02 Spending at 1995 constant prices by year and quarter

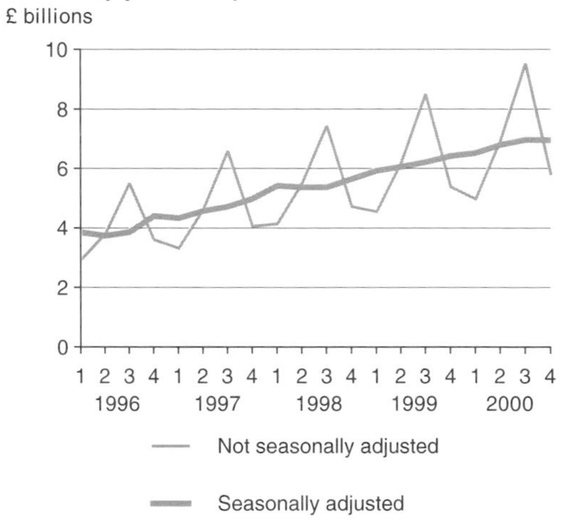

3.03 Growth in visits by purpose

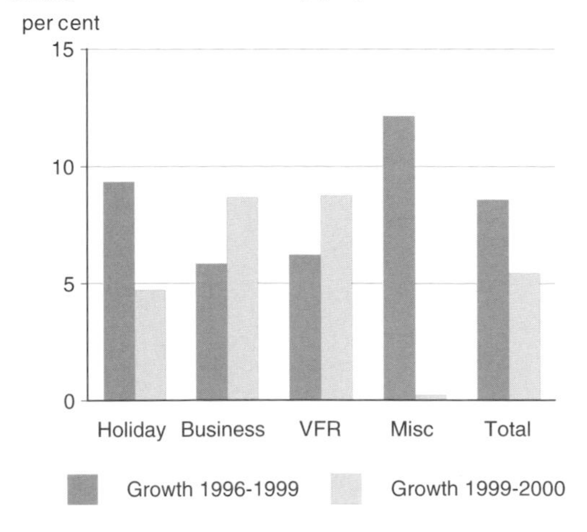

This chapter looks at the short-term trends of UK residents travelling abroad between 1996 and 2000. During this period, the number of visits abroad increased from 42.1 million to 56.8 million, an average annual growth rate of 7.8 per cent. In comparison, growth between 1999 and 2000 was only 5.5 per cent. Spending by UK residents abroad rose from £16.2 billion in 1996 to £24.3 billion in 2000, an average annual growth of 10.6 per cent. Between 1999 and 2000, spending increased by £2.2 billion, an increase of 10.1 per cent.

Visits, nights and spending by quarter

Table 3.01 gives the number of visits made and nights spent by UK residents abroad, broken down by time of year of travel. For visits, both non-seasonally adjusted and seasonally adjusted figures are shown, along with the percentage growth from the same quarter in the previous year.

Figure 3.01 and **3.02** show a clear seasonal pattern in the number of visits and spending abroad. The highest number of visits were made in quarter three of each year, with a record 19.2 million being made in quarter three of 2000. The relative proportion of visits made in each quarter of the year have remained constant since 1996. The seasonally adjusted figures show the underlying trend in growth between 1996 and 2000 and indicate a slower rate of increase in more recent years. As expected, the number of nights spent abroad also peaks in quarter three of each year, with a total of 221.8 million nights being spent abroad by UK residents in quarter three of 2000.

Table 3.02 provides details of spending, both in current prices and 1995 constant prices (ie. with effects of inflation removed), by UK residents abroad between 1996 and 2000. Constant price spending showed steady growth during the early part of the period, followed by a period of more rapid growth during 1997 and 1998 before again displaying a more steady increase in the last two years.

Visits and spending by main area and purpose of visit

Tables 3.03 and **3.04** show the number of UK residents' visits and related levels of spending to the different areas of the world by purpose of visit. The increase of 3.0 million visits between 1999 and 2000 was due to 1.7 million more holidays, 0.7 million more business trips and 0.6 million more visits to friends or relatives than in the previous year. Over half of the £2.2 billion increase in spending abroad in this period was spent on holiday trips (£1.2 billion) compared with 21 per cent on business trips (£0.5 billion) and 12 per cent on visits to friends or relatives (£0.3 billion).

Figure 3.03 compares the average annual growth in visits abroad between 1996 and 1999 with growth between 1999 and 2000. Growth in the number of business visits and visits to friends or relatives has been more rapid between 1999 and 2000 than in the previous few years. In contrast, the growth in holidays and visits for miscellaneous reasons has slowed down. A slow down in growth can also be seen in visits to North America and EU Europe. However, visits to non-EU Europe increased by 12.2 per cent between 1999 and 2000 compared with an average annual growth of 4.4 per cent between 1996 and 1999. Overall, growth in visits and spending is slowing. Growth in spending between 1999 and 2000 was 10.1 per cent, while growth in visits was 5.5 per cent.

Average stay and spending by purpose of visit

Tables 3.05 and **3.06** provide details of the number of nights spent by UK residents abroad between 1996 and 2000, together with the average length of stay, the average spend per visit and the average spend per day by region of the world and purpose of visit. Although the number of nights spent abroad increased from 450 million in 1996 to 567 million in 2000, a rise of 26 per cent, the average length of stay remained constant. This reflects the increase in number of visits described earlier. **Figure 3.04** shows the similarities in average length of stay between 1996 and 2000.

Figures 3.05 and **3.06** show that the average spending per visit and the average spending per day were higher for all purpose groups in 2000 compared with 1996. Average spending per visit increased by 11 per cent overall from £385 to £426. A large increase was seen in average spending on visits made for miscellaneous reasons, from £248 per visit in 1996 to £360 per visit in 2000, an increase of 45 per cent. Increases in average spending per day for all visits were greater than increases in average spending per visit, rising from £36 in 1996 to £43 in 2000, an increase of 19 per cent. The number of holiday visits increased by over a third from 26.8 million in 1996 to 36.7 million in 2000. Spend per visit on holidays increased by nine per cent, while spend per visit on inclusive tour holidays was almost the same in 2000 as it was in 1996.

3.04 Average length of stay by purpose and year

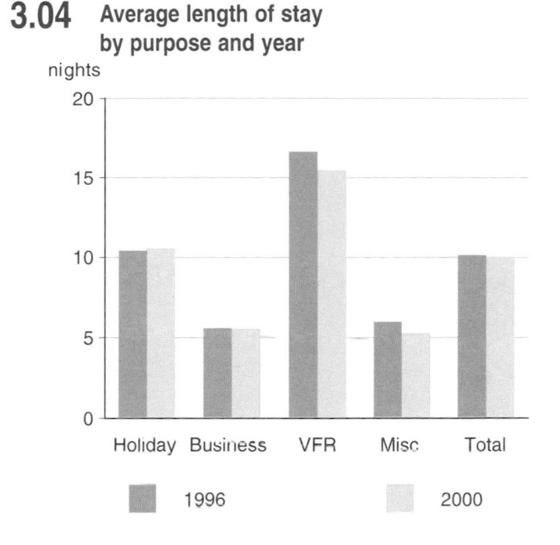

3.05 Average spending per visit by purpose and year

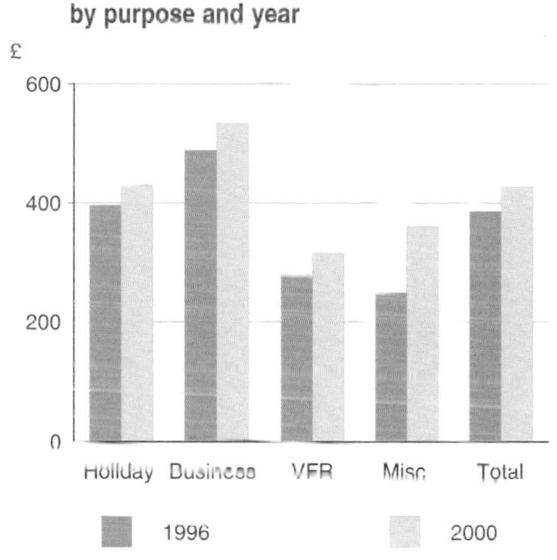

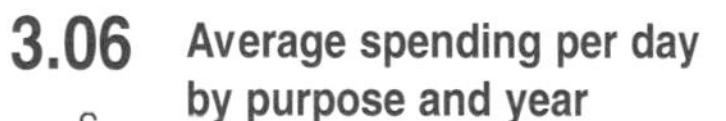

3.06 Average spending per day by purpose and year

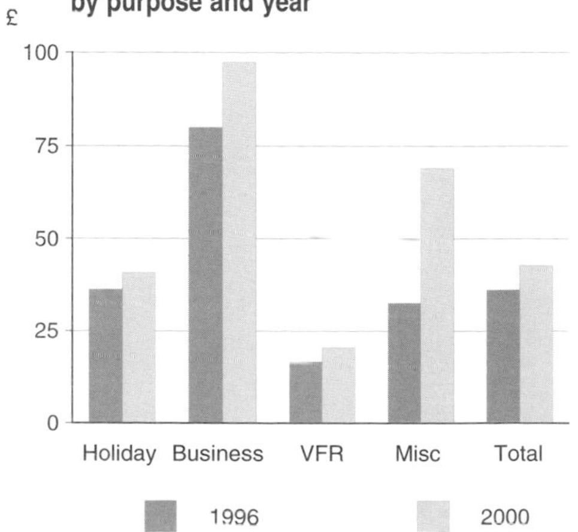

3.07 Number of visits by year and mode of travel

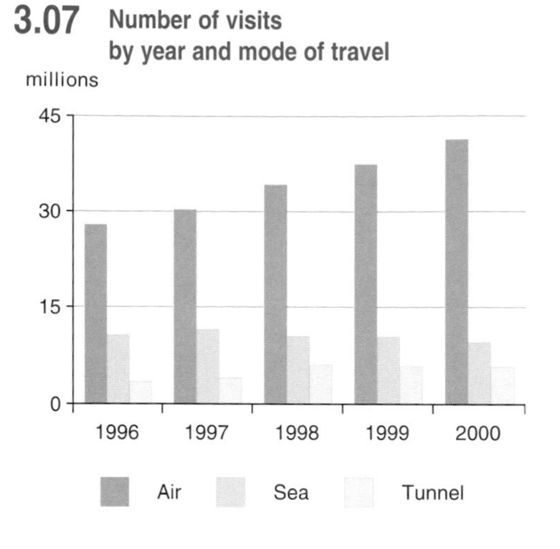

3.08 Increase in number of visits by country of visit 1996 to 2000

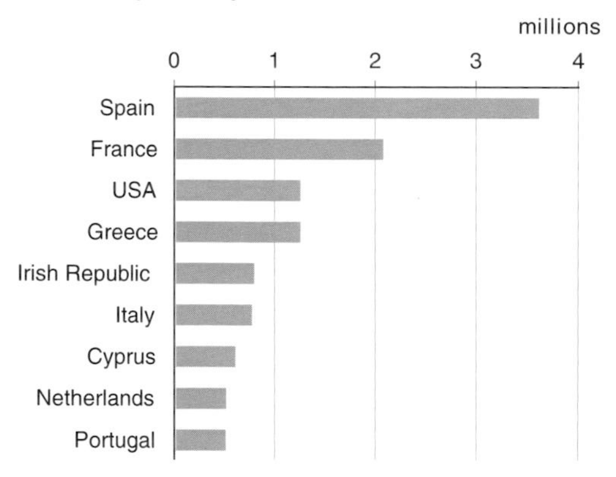

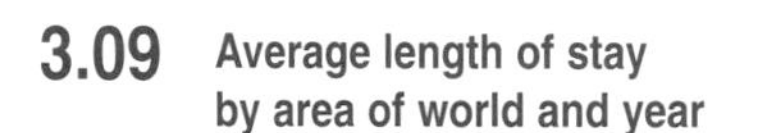

3.09 Average length of stay by area of world and year

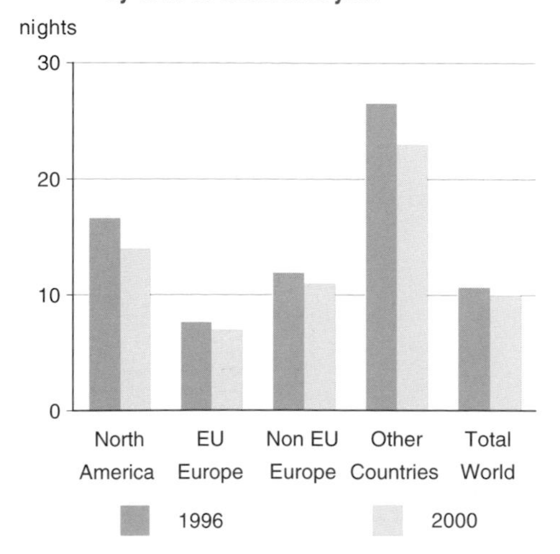

Visits and spending by mode of travel

Table 3.07 and **3.08** provide a breakdown of UK residents' visits and spending abroad by mode of travel and purpose of visit between 1996 and 2000. **Figure 3.07** shows the steady rise in the number of visits made by air over the period, an average annual increase of 10.4 per cent. In contrast, visits by sea have fallen by 10 per cent since 1996, an annual average decrease of 2.5 per cent. Visits by tunnel were 68 per cent higher in 2000 (5.8 million) than in 1996 (3.5 million), with an average annual increase of 13.8 per cent. Between 1999 and 2000, visits by tunnel decreased by 2.4 per cent and visits by sea fell by 7.5 per cent. While the number of visits by sea and tunnel may be falling, spending has increased across all modes since 1996, with visits made via the Tunnel showing the greatest average annual increase of 19.0 per cent.

Visits and spending by country of visit

Tables 3.09 and **3.10** give details of the number of visits and spending of UK residents abroad by country of visit between 1996 and 2000. **Figure 3.08** shows the nine countries where the number of visits has increased by half a million or more since 1996. Spain saw the largest increase in number of visits over the period (3.6 million), an average annual growth rate of 10.3 per cent. Visits to France, the most popular country visited in 2000, increased by 2.1 million between 1996 and 2000, an annual growth of 4.9 per cent, but decreased by 43 thousand visits between 1999 and 2000. The number of visits to both the USA and Greece have increased by over a million since 1996. Greece has one of the largest annual average growth rates for spending at 17 per cent, an increase of £0.5 billion since 1996. The largest increase in spending was on visits to Spain, with £1.4 billion more spent in 2000 than in 1996. Spending in the USA increased by £1.3 billion and in France by £1.2 billion over the same period.

Of those countries featured in Table 3.09, Iceland showed the largest average annual increase in visits between 1996 and 2000 at 37.9 per cent. Visits to this country have more than trebled from 21 thousand in 1996 to 76 thousand in 2000. By comparison, visits to Turkey showed an average annual decrease of 6.9 per cent, reflecting a fall from 1.0 million visits in 1996 to 0.8 million in 2000.

Average stay and spending by country of visit

Tables 3.11 and **3.12** provide a breakdown of the number of nights spent abroad by UK residents, together with their average length of stay, average spending per visit and average spending per day by country of visit.

Figure 3.09 shows the average length of stay for visits to the main regions of the world in 1996 and in 2000. North America and 'Other Countries' saw the greatest decline in average length of stay, with visits to North America falling from an average of 17 nights in 1996 to 14 nights in 2000 and trips to 'Other Countries' falling from 27 nights on average in 1996 to 23 nights in 2000. The length of trips to Australia fell by over a week from 51 days to 43 days. There was little variation over time, in average length of stay, for visits to Europe.

The increases in average spend per day can be seen in **figure 3.10**. North America saw an increase in average daily spending of 29 per cent between 1996 and 2000, from £45 per day to £58 per day, while increases in Europe and elsewhere were smaller.

Visits and spending by length of stay

Table 3.13 gives a breakdown of UK residents' visits and spending abroad by length of stay and purpose of visit, while **table 3.14** gives the same breakdown by length of stay and main area of the visit. **Figure 3.11** shows that the largest average annual increases between 1996 and 2000 were for trips lasting between 1 and 3 nights and those lasting between 4 and 13 nights (average growth rates of 15 per cent and 13 per cent respectively). In comparison, day trips showed only a small increase over this period of 1.5 per cent, although large increases were seen in this category in the mid 1990s, coinciding with the opening of the Channel Tunnel.

While holidays and business trips still account for 80 per cent of visits lasting between 1 and 3 nights, **figure 3.12** shows that the greatest annual average growth in these short visits has been seen among visits to friends or family and visits for miscellaneous reasons (24 per cent each).

EU Europe is still the most popular destination for trips lasting between 1 and 3 nights but the largest average annual increase between 1996 and 2000 for these short visits was seen to 'Other countries' (18.3 per cent).

3.10 Average spend per day by area of world and year

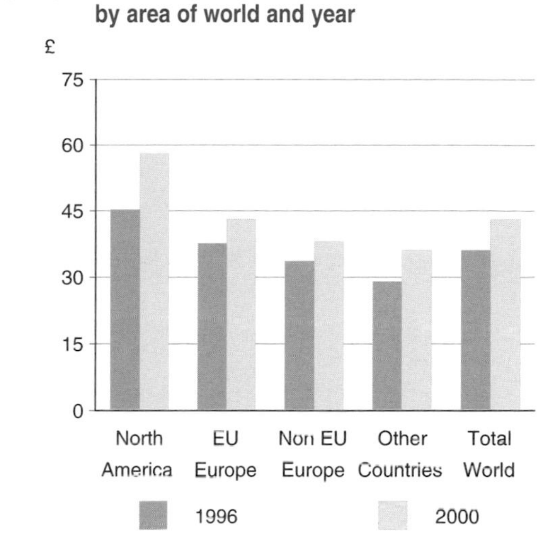

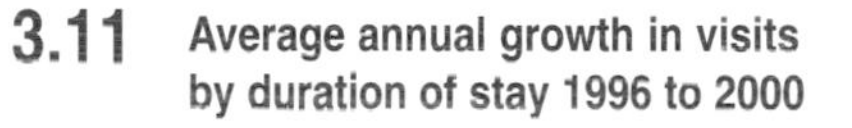
3.11 Average annual growth in visits by duration of stay 1996 to 2000

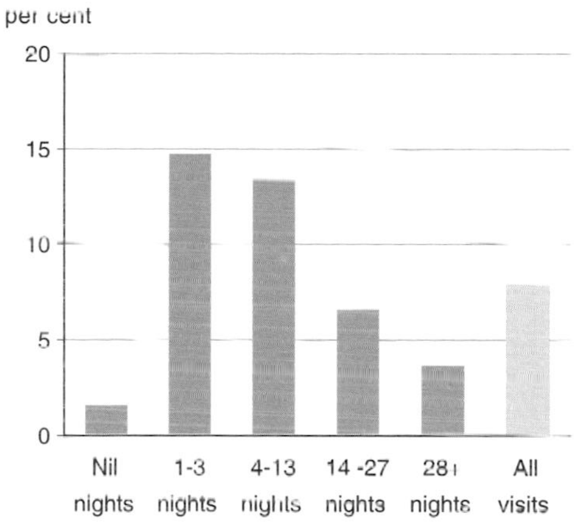

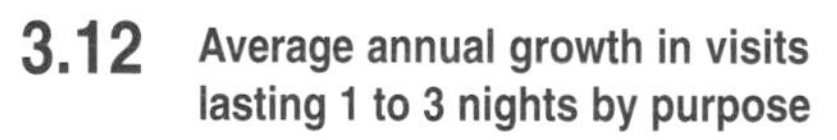
3.12 Average annual growth in visits lasting 1 to 3 nights by purpose

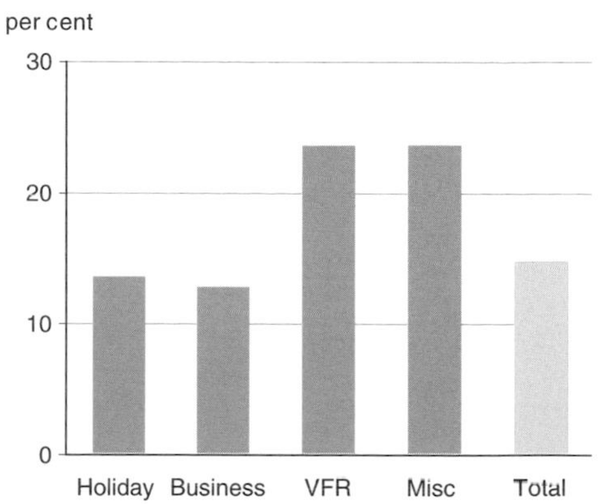

3.01 Visits and nights by quarter of year 1996 to 2000

		Visits (thousands)			Nights (thousands)	
	Quarter	not seasonally adjusted	*per cent change from year earlier*	seasonally adjusted	not seasonally adjusted	*per cent change from year earlier*
1996	1	7,531	*4.8*	10,210	84,450	*14.0*
	2	10,743	*-2.3*	10,120	110,961	*-4.1*
	3	13,889	*-1.0*	10,420	169,623	*-4.2*
	4	9,888	*8.2*	11,300	84,743	*1.0*
1997	1	8,153	*8.3*	11,000	84,549	*0.1*
	2	11,889	*10.7*	11,240	115,836	*4.4*
	3	15,181	*9.3*	11,470	177,166	*4.4*
	4	10,734	*8.6*	12,250	85,975	*1.5*
1998	1	9,178	*12.6*	12,480	88,998	*5.3*
	2	13,242	*11.4*	12,520	130,569	*12.7*
	3	16,974	*11.8*	12,810	191,054	*7.8*
	4	11,479	*6.9*	13,060	98,586	*14.7*
1999	1	9,879	*7.6*	13,360	91,565	*2.9*
	2	14,575	*10.1*	13,760	135,510	*3.8*
	3	17,738	*4.5*	13,430	208,833	*9.3*
	4	11,690	*1.8*	13,340	104,536	*6.0*
2000	1	10,142	*2.7*	13,570	95,795	*4.6*
	2	14,792	*1.5*	14,110	141,929	*4.7*
	3	19,236	*8.4*	14,520	221,755	*6.2*
	4	12,666	*8.3*	14,630	107,404	*2.7*

Due to changes in the IPS sampling methodology introduced in 1999, care should be taken when comparing results for 1999 and 2000 with earlier years.
See notes on page 9 relating to IPS interviewing on routes to the Irish Republic.

3.02 Spending at current and 1995 constant prices by quarter of year 1996 to 2000

		Spending (£ million)			Constant price spending (£ million)		
	Quarter	not seasonally adjusted	*per cent change from year earlier*	seasonally adjusted	not seasonally adjusted	*per cent change from year earlier*	seasonally adjusted
1996	1	3,064	*15.5*	4,020	2,955	*7.5*	3,860
	2	3,962	*0.4*	3,920	3,810	*-4.1*	3,750
	3	5,681	*2.3*	3,980	5,516	*0.2*	3,870
	4	3,516	*8.7*	4,290	3,616	*14.4*	4,420
1997	1	3,129	*2.1*	4,050	3,333	*12.8*	4,340
	2	4,266	*7.7*	4,230	4,640	*21.8*	4,590
	3	5,899	*3.8*	4,190	6,607	*19.8*	4,730
	4	3,637	*3.4*	4,460	4,072	*12.6*	5,000
1998	1	3,646	*16.5*	4,800	4,151	*24.5*	5,430
	2	4,885	*14.5*	4,730	5,513	*18.8*	5,380
	3	6,617	*12.2*	4,800	7,448	*12.7*	5,380
	4	4,341	*19.3*	5,160	4,735	*16.3*	5,660
1999	1	4,109	*12.7*	5,340	4,569	*10.1*	5,940
	2	5,578	*14.2*	5,500	6,194	*12.4*	6,070
	3	7,571	*14.4*	5,590	8,512	*14.3*	6,230
	4	4,762	*9.7*	5,800	5,401	*14.1*	6,440
2000	1	4,339	*5.6*	5,710	4,981	*9.0*	6,530
	2	6,146	*10.2*	6,040	6,950	*12.2*	6,810
	3	8,503	*12.3*	6,170	9,548	*12.2*	6,980
	4	5,263	*10.5*	6,320	5,802	*7.4*	6,970

Due to changes in the IPS sampling methodology introduced in 1999, care should be taken when comparing results for 1999 and 2000 with earlier years. See notes on page 9 relating to IPS interviewing on routes to the Irish Republic.

3.03 Number of visits by main area and purpose of visit 1996 to 2000

	Visits (thousands)					*Change 1999-00*	*Growth 1999-00*	*Average Annual Growth 1996-00*
	1996	1997	1998	1999	2000	*(000s)*	*(%)*	*(%)*
North America								
Holiday	2,267	2,244	2,591	2,964	3,052	*88*	*3.0*	*7.7*
of which inclusive tour	*866*	*806*	*952*	*1,058*	*1,131*	*73*	*6.9*	*6.9*
Business	668	646	771	810	965	*155*	*19.1*	*9.6*
Visiting friends or relatives	588	629	690	838	924	*86*	*10.3*	*12.0*
Miscellaneous	61	76	105	121	120	*-1*	*-0.8*	*18.4*
All visits	3,584	3,594	4,158	4,733	5,060	*327*	*6.9*	*9.0*
EU Europe								
Holiday	19,428	21,594	23,510	25,978	26,768	*790*	*3.0*	*8.3*
of which inclusive tour	*9,570*	*11,043*	*12,328*	*14,134*	*14,544*	*410*	*2.9*	*11.0*
Business	5,034	5,226	5,878	5,871	6,420	*549*	*9.4*	*6.3*
Visiting friends or relatives	3,540	3,816	4,129	3,971	4,262	*291*	*7.3*	*4.7*
Miscellaneous	2,588	3,316	3,719	3,680	3,691	*11*	*0.3*	*9.3*
All visits	30,591	33,952	37,237	39,500	41,140	*1,640*	*4.2*	*7.7*
Non EU Europe								
Holiday	2,593	2,684	3,058	2,769	3,193	*424*	*15.3*	*5.3*
of which inclusive tour	*1,955*	*1,981*	*2,203*	*1,980*	*2,226*	*246*	*12.4*	*3.3*
Business	570	636	725	787	778	*-9*	*-1.1*	*8.1*
Visiting friends or relatives	369	404	454	472	567	*95*	*20.1*	*11.3*
Miscellaneous	90	69	78	93	84	*-9*	*-9.7*	*-1.7*
All visits	3,622	3,793	4,315	4,120	4,623	*503*	*12.2*	*6.3*
Other Countries								
Holiday	2,477	2,616	3,147	3,312	3,671	*359*	*10.8*	*10.3*
of which inclusive tour	*1,509*	*1,562*	*1,953*	*1,905*	*2,154*	*249*	*13.1*	*9.3*
Business	608	659	657	693	709	*16*	*2.3*	*3.9*
Visiting friends or relatives	1,004	1,155	1,179	1,318	1,426	*108*	*8.2*	*9.2*
Miscellaneous	164	188	180	206	207	*1*	*0.5*	*6.0*
All visits	4,253	4,618	5,163	5,529	6,014	*485*	*8.8*	*9.0*
Total World								
Holiday	26,765	29,138	32,306	35,023	36,685	*1,662*	*4.7*	*8.2*
of which inclusive tour	*13,901*	*15,393*	*17,437*	*19,077*	*20,055*	*978*	*5.1*	*9.6*
Business	6,879	7,166	8,033	8,161	8,872	*711*	*8.7*	*6.6*
Visiting friends or relatives	5,502	6,004	6,452	6,598	7,178	*580*	*8.8*	*6.9*
Miscellaneous	2,904	3,649	4,082	4,100	4,102	*2*	*0.0*	*9.0*
All visits	42,050	45,957	50,872	53,881	56,837	*2,956*	*5.5*	*7.8*

Due to changes in the IPS sampling methodology introduced in 1999, care should be taken when comparing results for 1999 and 2000 with earlier years. See notes on page 9 relating to IPS interviewing on routes to the Irish Republic.

3.04 Spending by main area and purpose of visit 1996 to 2000

	Spending (£million)					*Change 1999-00*	*Growth 1999-00*	*Average Annual Growth 1996-00*
	1996	1997	1998	1999	2000	*(£million)*	*(%)*	*(%)*
North America								
Holiday	1,713	1,747	1,998	2,316	2,512	*196*	*8.5*	*10.0*
of which inclusive tour	*716*	*668*	*804*	*879*	*1,013*	*134*	*15.2*	*9.1*
Business	662	604	815	834	1,017	*183*	*21.9*	*11.3*
Visiting friends or relatives	244	282	316	373	450	*86*	*23.1*	*17.1*
Miscellaneous	79	80	109	171	182	*11*	*6.4*	*23.2*
All visits	2,698	2,713	3,239	3,694	4,170	*476*	*12.9*	*11.5*
EU Europe								
Holiday	6,033	6,492	7,157	8,666	9,067	*401*	*4.6*	*10.7*
of which inclusive tour	*3,430*	*3,767*	*4,104*	*5,026*	*5,192*	*166*	*3.3*	*10.9*
Business	1,638	1,702	2,014	2,133	2,390	*257*	*12.0*	*9.9*
Visiting friends or relatives	661	689	815	757	842	*85*	*11.2*	*6.2*
Miscellaneous	474	568	667	780	995	*215*	*27.6*	*20.4*
All visits	8,806	9,451	10,653	12,335	13,294	*959*	*7.8*	*10.8*
Non EU Europe								
Holiday	1,028	1,011	1,086	1,057	1,290	*233*	*22.0*	*5.8*
of which inclusive tour	*786*	*741*	*766*	*750*	*907*	*157*	*20.9*	*3.6*
Business	309	293	446	375	404	*29*	*7.7*	*6.9*
Visiting friends or relatives	84	95	100	124	138	*14*	*11.3*	*13.2*
Miscellaneous	32	29	39	49	46	*-3*	*-6.1*	*9.5*
All visits	1,453	1,428	1,672	1,605	1,878	*273*	*17.0*	*6.6*
Other Countries								
Holiday	1,836	1,856	2,254	2,516	2,915	*399*	*15.9*	*12.3*
of which inclusive tour	*1,061*	*1,034*	*1,2[illegible]*	*1,290*	*1,511*	*221*	*17.1*	*9.2*
Business	749	751	849	919	922	*3*	*0.3*	*5.3*
Visiting friends or relatives	543	584	636	737	819	*82*	*11.1*	*10.8*
Miscellaneous	136	147	186	214	254	*40*	*18.7*	*16.9*
All visits	3,265	3,338	3,926	4,386	4,909	*523*	*11.9*	*10.7*
Total World								
Holiday	10,610	11,107	12,495	14,555	15,784	*1,229*	*8.4*	*10.4*
of which inclusive tour	*5,993*	*6,210*	*6,913*	*7,945*	*8,623*	*678*	*8.5*	*9.5*
Business	3,359	3,351	4,124	4,261	4,732	*471*	*11.1*	*8.9*
Visiting friends or relatives	1,533	1,650	1,869	1,991	2,258	*267*	*13.4*	*10.2*
Miscellaneous	721	823	1,001	1,215	1,477	*262*	*21.6*	*19.6*
All visits	16,223	16,931	19,489	22,020	24,251	*2,231*	*10.1*	*10.6*

Due to changes in the IPS sampling methodology introduced in 1999, care should be taken when comparing results for 1999 and 2000 with earlier years. See notes on page 9 relating to IPS interviewing on routes to the Irish Republic.

3.05 Number of nights and average length of stay by main area and purpose of visit 1996 to 2000

	Nights (thousands)					Average length of stay (nights)				
	1996	1997	1998	1999	2000	1996	1997	1998	1999	2000
North America										
Holiday	37,385	36,313	39,347	43,768	44,189	16.5	16.2	15.2	14.8	14.5
of which inclusive tour	*12,294*	*11,421*	*12,851*	*14,016*	*14,589*	*14.2*	*14.2*	*13.5*	*13.2*	*12.9*
Business	7,454	6,282	8,077	8,000	8,326	11.2	9.7	10.5	9.9	8.6
Visiting friends or relatives	12,865	12,706	14,609	17,004	17,435	21.9	20.2	21.2	20.3	18.9
Miscellaneous	2,059	2,608	2,846	2,885	2,465	33.5	34.2	27.0	23.8	20.6
All visits	59,762	57,909	64,878	71,657	72,415	16.7	16.1	15.6	15.1	14.3
EU Europe										
Holiday	169,555	183,439	200,917	229,380	235,886	8.7	8.5	8.5	8.8	8.8
of which inclusive tour	*92,424*	*104,356*	*114,119*	*132,382*	*134,825*	*9.7*	*9.5*	*9.3*	*9.4*	*9.3*
Business	20,603	18,270	22,124	22,759	*25,928*	4.1	3.5	3.8	3.9	4.0
Visiting friends or relatives	33,221	34,609	37,935	35,016	37,897	9.4	9.1	9.2	8.8	8.9
Miscellaneous	10,435	9,137	11,253	8,006	8,511	4.0	2.8	3.0	2.2	2.3
All visits	233,813	245,455	272,228	295,159	308,221	7.6	7.2	7.3	7.5	7.5
Non EU Europe										
Holiday	32,023	29,713	34,568	30,855	35,599	12.4	11.1	11.3	11.1	11.1
of which inclusive tour	*22,938*	*21,550*	*24,281*	*21,505*	*24,144*	*11.7*	*10.9*	*11.0*	*10.9*	*10.8*
Business	3,979	4,466	4,303	4,667	4,298	7.0	7.0	5.9	5.9	5.5
Visiting friends or relatives	6,357	6,598	6,934	6,818	*7,946*	17.3	16.3	15.3	14.4	14.0
Miscellaneous	965	1,102	1,563	1,265	1,203	10.7	16.0	20.1	13.6	14.3
All visits	43,324	41,879	47,368	43,605	49,046	12.0	11.0	11.0	10.6	10.6
Other Countries										
Holiday	53,975	52,991	61,775	63,476	70,585	21.8	20.3	19.6	19.2	19.2
of which inclusive tour	*20,978*	*21,040*	*25,406*	*25,253*	*28,162*	*13.9*	*13.5*	*13.0*	*13.3*	*13.1*
Business	10,028	10,775	10,591	10,200	10,097	16.5	16.4	16.1	14.7	14.2
Visiting friends or relatives	40,128	45,698	43,049	46,500	47,266	40.0	39.6	36.5	35.3	33.2
Miscellaneous	8,746	8,819	9,317	9,847	*9,254*	53.5	46.9	51.7	47.8	44.6
All visits	112,878	118,283	124,732	130,024	137,202	26.5	25.6	24.2	23.5	22.8
Total World										
Holiday	292,938	302,456	336,606	367,479	386,258	10.9	10.4	10.4	10.5	10.5
of which inclusive tour	*148,634*	*158,367*	*176,658*	*193,156*	*201,720*	*10.7*	*10.3*	*10.1*	*10.1*	*10.1*
Business	42,064	39,793	45,095	45,626	48,648	6.1	5.6	5.6	5.6	5.5
Visiting friends or relatives	92,571	99,610	102,527	105,337	110,544	16.8	16.6	15.9	16.0	15.4
Miscellaneous	22,205	21,667	24,978	22,003	21,433	7.7	5.9	6.1	5.4	5.2
All visits	449,778	463,526	509,206	540,445	*566,884*	10.7	10.1	10.0	10.0	10.0

Due to changes in the IPS sampling methodology introduced in 1999, care should be taken when comparing results for 1999 and 2000 with earlier years. See notes on page 9 relating to IPS interviewing on routes to the Irish Republic.

3.06 Average spending per visit and spending per day by main area and purpose of visit 1996 to 2000

	Average spending per visit (£)					Average spending per day (£)				
	1996	1997	1998	1999	2000	1996	1997	1998	1999	2000
North America										
Holiday	756	779	771	781	823	46	48	51	53	57
of which inclusive tour	*827*	*828*	*845*	*830*	*896*	*58*	*58*	*63*	*63*	*69*
Business	991	936	1,057	1,029	1,054	89	96	101	104	122
Visiting friends or relatives	415	449	458	445	498	19	22	22	22	26
Miscellaneous	1,278	1,045	1,035	1,416	1,519	38	31	38	59	74
All visits	753	755	779	780	824	45	47	50	52	58
EU Europe										
Holiday	310	300	303	333	338	35	35	36	38	38
of which inclusive tour	*358*	*341*	*333*	*356*	*357*	*37*	*36*	*36*	*38*	*39*
Business	325	326	343	363	372	80	93	91	94	92
Visiting friends or relatives	187	181	197	191	198	20	20	21	22	22
Miscellaneous	183	171	179	212	270	45	62	59	97	117
All visits	287	278	286	312	323	38	38	39	42	43
Non EU Europe										
Holiday	396	377	355	382	404	32	34	31	34	36
of which inclusive tour	*402*	*374*	*348*	*379*	*408*	*34*	*34*	*32*	*35*	*38*
Business	543	461	615	477	519	78	66	104	80	94
Visiting friends or relatives	227	236	221	263	244	13	14	14	18	17
Miscellaneous	357	414	499	533	546	33	26	25	39	38
All visits	401	377	388	390	406	34	34	35	37	38
Other Countries										
Holiday	741	710	716	760	794	34	35	36	40	41
of which inclusive tour	*703*	*662*	*634*	*677*	*702*	*51*	*49*	*49*	*51*	*54*
Business	1,233	1,141	1,291	1,326	1,299	75	70	80	90	91
Visiting friends or relatives	541	505	540	559	574	14	13	15	16	17
Miscellaneous	834	780	1,032	1,041	1,227	16	17	20	22	28
All visits	768	723	760	793	816	29	28	31	34	36
Total World										
Holiday	396	381	386	415	430	36	37	37	40	41
of which inclusive tour	*431*	*403*	*396*	*416*	*430*	*40*	*39*	*39*	*41*	*43*
Business	488	468	513	522	533	80	84	91	93	97
Visiting friends or relatives	279	275	290	302	315	17	17	18	19	20
Miscellaneous	248	226	245	296	360	32	38	40	55	69
All visits	385	368	383	408	426	36	36	38	41	43

Due to changes in the IPS sampling methodology introduced in 1999, care should be taken when comparing results for 1999 and 2000 with earlier years. See notes on page 9 relating to IPS interviewing on routes to the Irish Republic.

3.07 Number of visits by mode of travel and purpose of visit 1996 to 2000

	Visits (thousands)					*Change 1999-00*	*Growth 1999-00*	*Average Annual Growth 1996-00*
	1996	1997	1998	1999	2000	*(000s)*	*(%)*	*(%)*
Air								
Holiday	18,375	19,937	22,945	25,282	27,901	*2,619*	*10.4*	*11.0*
of which inclusive tour	*11,239*	*12,203*	*13,897*	*14,998*	*16,411*	*1,413*	*9.4*	*9.9*
Business	5,152	5,575	6,077	6,400	6,946	*546*	*8.5*	*7.8*
Visiting friends or relatives	3,744	4,094	4,449	4,974	5,643	*669*	*13.4*	*10.8*
Miscellaneous	636	734	812	854	902	*48*	*5.6*	*9.1*
All visits	27,907	30,341	34,283	37,510	41,392	*3,882*	*10.3*	*10.4*
Sea								
Holiday	6,481	6,984	6,216	6,843	6,106	*-737*	*-10.8*	*-1.5*
of which inclusive tour	*2,200*	*2,582*	*2,260*	*2,923*	*2,561*	*-362*	*-12.4*	*3.9*
Business	1,061	1,018	955	875	933	*58*	*6.6*	*-3.2*
Visiting friends or relatives	1,459	1,567	1,549	1,069	1,042	*-27*	*-2.5*	*-8.1*
Miscellaneous	1,685	1,952	1,778	1,640	1,565	*-75*	*-4.6*	*-1.8*
All visits	10,686	11,522	10,498	10,427	9,646	*-781*	*-7.5*	*-2.5*
Tunnel								
Holiday	1,910	2,217	3,145	2,898	2,677	*-221*	*-7.6*	*8.8*
of which inclusive tour	*463*	*608*	*1,280*	*1,155*	*1,083*	*-72*	*-6.2*	*23.7*
Business	666	572	1,000	886	993	*107*	*12.1*	*10.5*
Visiting friends or relatives	299	343	454	554	494	*-60*	*-10.8*	*13.4*
Miscellaneous	583	963	1,492	1,605	1,635	*30*	*1.9*	*29.4*
All visits	3,457	4,095	6,092	5,944	5,799	*-145*	*-2.4*	*13.8*
Total								
Holiday	26,765	29,138	32,306	35,023	36,685	*1,662*	*4.7*	*8.2*
of which inclusive tour	*13,901*	*15,393*	*17,437*	*19,077*	*20,055*	*978*	*5.1*	*9.6*
Business	6,879	7,166	8,033	8,161	8,872	*711*	*8.7*	*6.6*
Visiting friends or relatives	5,502	6,004	6,452	6,598	7,178	*580*	*8.8*	*6.9*
Miscellaneous	2,904	3,649	4,082	4,100	4,102	*2*	*0.0*	*9.0*
All visits	42,050	45,957	50,872	53,881	56,837	*2,956*	*5.5*	*7.8*

Due to changes in the IPS sampling methodology introduced in 1999, care should be taken when comparing results for 1999 and 2000 with earlier years. See notes on page 9 relating to IPS interviewing on routes to the Irish Republic.

3.08 Spending by mode of travel and purpose of visit 1996 to 2000

	Spending (£million)					*Change 1999-00*	*Growth 1999-00*	*Average Annual Growth 1996-00*
	1996	1997	1998	1999	2000	*(£million)*	*(%)*	*(%)*
Air								
Holiday	8,587	8,868	10,003	11,695	13,079	*1,384*	*11.8*	*11.1*
of which inclusive tour	*5,110*	*5,135*	*5,684*	*6,501*	*7,252*	751	11.6	9.1
Business	2,772	2,834	3,414	3,615	3,960	*345*	*9.5*	*9.3*
Visiting friends or relatives	1,190	1,298	1,497	1,710	1,979	*260*	*15.1*	*13.6*
Miscellaneous	377	402	482	594	888	*294*	*49.5*	*23.9*
All visits	12,926	13,402	15,397	17,623	19,905	*2,282*	*12.9*	*11.4*
Sea								
Holiday	1,559	1,794	1,720	2,092	1,927	*-165*	*-7.9*	*5.4*
of which inclusive tour	*756*	*916*	*885*	*1,113*	*1,032*	-81	-7.3	8.1
Business	393	381	416	355	373	*18*	*5.1*	*-1.3*
Visiting friends or relatives	292	299	286	189	188	*-1*	*-0.5*	*-10.4*
Miscellaneous	266	317	304	323	278	*-45*	*-13.9*	*1.1*
All visits	2,509	2,791	2,726	2,958	2,766	*-192*	*-6.5*	*2.5*
Tunnel								
Holiday	465	444	773	768	778	*10*	*1.3*	*13.7*
of which inclusive tour	*128*	*159*	*345*	*331*	*338*	7	2.1	27.5
Business	195	137	293	291	399	*108*	*37.1*	*19.6*
Visiting friends or relatives	50	53	86	83	92	*9*	*10.8*	*16.5*
Miscellaneous	78	104	215	298	311	*13*	*4.4*	*41.3*
All visits	788	739	1,367	1,439	1,580	*141*	*9.8*	*19.0*
Total								
Holiday	10,610	11,107	12,495	14,555	15,784	*1,229*	*8.4*	*10.4*
of which inclusive tour	*5,000*	*6,210*	*6,913*	*7,945*	*8,623*	678	8.5	9.5
Business	3,359	3,351	4,124	4,261	4,732	*471*	*11.1*	*8.9*
Visiting friends or relatives	1,533	1,650	1,869	1,991	2,258	*267*	*13.4*	*10.2*
Miscellaneous	721	823	1,001	1,215	1,477	*262*	*21.6*	*19.6*
All visits	16,223	16,931	19,489	22,020	24,251	*2,231*	*10.1*	*10.6*

Due to changes in the IPS sampling methodology introduced in 1999, care should be taken when comparing results for 1999 and 2000 with earlier years. See notes on page 9 relating to IPS interviewing on routes to the Irish Republic.

3.09 Number of visits by country of visit 1996 to 2000

	Visits (thousands)					*Change 1999-00*	*Growth 1999-00*	*Average Annual Growth 1996-00*
	1996	1997	1998	1999	2000	*(000s)*	*(%)*	*(%)*
Canada	506	566	616	674	729	*55*	*8.2*	*9.6*
USA	3,079	3,028	3,542	4,058	4,331	*273*	*6.7*	*8.9*
North America	3,584	3,594	4,158	4,733	5,060	*327*	*6.9*	*9.0*
Austria	415	425	535	471	467	*-4*	*-0.8*	*3.0*
Belgium	1,421	1,419	1,699	1,602	1,657	*55*	*3.4*	*3.9*
Denmark	248	264	231	276	299	*23*	*8.3*	*4.8*
Finland	95	80	108	125	152	*27*	*21.6*	*12.5*
France	9,834	11,149	11,518	11,946	11,903	*-43*	*-0.4*	*4.9*
Germany	1,898	2,023	2,062	2,101	2,411	*310*	*14.8*	*6.2*
Greece	1,460	1,512	1,860	2,444	2,709	*265*	*10.8*	*16.7*
Irish Republic*	3,169	3,613	3,937	4,233	3,961	*-272*	*-6.4*	*5.7*
Italy	1,558	1,801	2,012	2,114	2,327	*213*	*10.1*	*10.5*
Luxembourg	33	53	61	93	69	*-24*	*-25.8*	*20.2*
Netherlands	1,532	1,756	1,952	1,943	2,044	*101*	*5.2*	*7.5*
Portugal	1,102	1,304	1,299	1,453	1,612	*159*	*10.9*	*10.0*
Spain	7,545	8,281	9,650	10,373	11,154	*781*	*7.5*	*10.3*
Sweden	280	273	313	328	377	*49*	*14.9*	*7.7*
EU Europe	30,591	33,952	37,237	39,500	41,140	*1,640*	*4.2*	*7.7*
Cyprus	709	713	952	958	1,310	*352*	*36.7*	*16.6*
Gibraltar	31	40	39	46	35	*-11*	*-23.9*	*3.1*
Iceland	21	27	43	32	76	*44*	*137.5*	*37.9*
Malta	395	374	457	386	428	*42*	*10.9*	*2.0*
Norway	208	262	254	233	271	*38*	*16.3*	*6.8*
Switzerland	509	580	652	690	768	*78*	*11.3*	*10.8*
Turkey	1,032	998	1,037	851	775	*-76*	*-8.9*	*-6.9*
Central & Eastern Europe	521	548	616	692	700	*8*	*1.2*	*7.7*
Former USSR	126	138	144	136	142	*6*	*4.4*	*3.0*
Former Yugoslavia	71	113	122	96	117	*21*	*21.9*	*13.3*
Non EU Europe	3,622	3,793	4,315	4,120	4,623	*503*	*12.2*	*6.3*
North Africa	536	577	651	625	758	*133*	*21.3*	*9.1*
South Africa	202	230	277	261	325	*64*	*24.5*	*12.6*
Rest of Africa	349	406	310	376	356	*-20*	*-5.3*	*0.5*
Israel	145	149	160	153	168	*15*	*9.8*	*3.7*
Other Middle East	241	265	281	318	366	*48*	*15.1*	*11.0*
Hong Kong	153	180	162	152	175	*23*	*15.1*	*3.4*
India	413	402	439	455	474	*19*	*4.2*	*3.5*
Japan	99	95	129	100	111	*11*	*11.0*	*2.9*
Rest of Asia	788	787	890	1,040	1,129	*89*	*8.6*	*9.4*
Australia	287	339	407	461	470	*9*	*2.0*	*13.1*
New Zealand	89	86	97	112	107	*-5*	*-4.5*	*4.7*
Caribbean	534	626	705	783	794	*11*	*1.4*	*10.4*
Central & South America	206	257	364	388	427	*39*	*10.1*	*20.0*
Rest of the World	210	219	293	303	355	*52*	*17.2*	*14.0*
Other Countries	4,253	4,618	5,163	5,529	6,014	*485*	*8.8*	*9.0*
Total World	42,050	45,957	50,872	53,881	56,837	*2,956*	*5.5*	*7.8*

* Due to changes in the IPS sampling methodology introduced in 1999, care should be taken when comparing results for 1999 and 2000 with earlier years. See notes on page 9 relating to IPS interviewing on routes to the Irish Republic.

3.10 Spending by country of visit 1996 to 2000

	Spending (£million)					*Change 1999-00*	*Growth 1999-00*	*Average Annual Growth 1996-00*
	1996	1997	1998	1999	2000	*(£million)*	*(%)*	*(%)*
Canada	333	374	412	453	510	*57*	*12.6*	*11.2*
USA	2,366	2,339	2,827	3,241	3,660	*419*	*12.9*	*11.5*
North America	2,698	2,713	3,239	3,694	4,170	*476*	*12.9*	*11.5*
Austria	207	180	241	198	205	*7*	*3.5*	*-0.2*
Belgium	255	284	311	384	347	*-37*	*-9.6*	*8.0*
Denmark	84	86	69	78	82	*4*	*5.1*	*-0.6*
Finland	39	28	40	56	59	*3*	*5.4*	*10.9*
France	2,015	2,256	2,663	2,990	3,198	*208*	*7.0*	*12.2*
Germany	562	597	597	600	728	*128*	*21.3*	*6.7*
Greece	576	588	651	938	1,080	*142*	*15.1*	*17.0*
Irish Republic*	705	764	749	1,021	941	*-80*	*-7.8*	*7.5*
Italy	733	828	1,025	978	1,159	*181*	*18.5*	*12.1*
Luxembourg	11	13	12	21	14	*-7*	*-33.3*	*6.2*
Netherlands	352	398	474	491	550	*59*	*12.0*	*11.8*
Portugal	452	492	468	615	597	*-18*	*-2.9*	*7.2*
Spain	2,704	2,825	3,236	3,830	4,127	*297*	*7.8*	*11.1*
Sweden	93	94	96	114	182	*68*	*59.6*	*18.3*
EU Europe	8,806	9,451	10,653	12,335	13,294	*959*	*7.8*	*10.8*
Cyprus	285	296	391	415	585	*170*	*41.0*	*19.7*
Gibraltar	8	10	13	16	9	*-7*	*-43.8*	*3.0*
Iceland	12	11	17	11	50	*39*	*354.5*	*42.9*
Malta	118	107	114	120	128	*8*	*6.7*	*2.1*
Norway	75	89	115	85	91	*6*	*7.1*	*5.0*
Switzerland	210	218	300	287	318	*31*	*10.8*	*10.9*
Turkey	406	369	328	310	319	*9*	*2.9*	*-5.9*
Central & Eastern Europe	176	197	229	235	246	*11*	*4.7*	*8.7*
Former USSR	114	88	119	79	95	*16*	*20.3*	*-4.5*
Former Yugoslavia	50	45	47	46	38	*-8*	*-17.4*	*-6.6*
Non EU Europe	1,453	1,428	1,672	1,605	1,878	*273*	*17.0*	*6.6*
North Africa	216	231	234	242	319	*77*	*31.8*	*10.2*
South Africa	194	188	250	216	245	*29*	*13.4*	*6.0*
Rest of Africa	236	241	213	295	276	*-19*	*-6.4*	*4.0*
Israel	75	68	82	87	90	*3*	*3.4*	*4.7*
Other Middle East	146	147	171	213	244	*31*	*14.6*	*13.7*
Hong Kong	146	129	91	135	147	*12*	*8.9*	*0.2*
India	230	228	242	319	331	*12*	*3.8*	*9.5*
Japan	101	84	120	99	111	*12*	*12.1*	*2.4*
Rest of Asia	665	636	746	852	1,007	*155*	*18.2*	*10.9*
Australia	409	491	542	587	692	*105*	*17.9*	*14.1*
New Zealand	125	106	123	137	148	*11*	*8.0*	*4.3*
Caribbean	336	388	480	545	563	*18*	*3.3*	*13.8*
Central & South America	175	184	336	322	331	*9*	*2.8*	*17.3*
Rest of the World	212	217	296	337	406	*69*	*20.5*	*17.6*
Other Countries	3,265	3,338	3,926	4,386	4,909	*523*	*11.9*	*10.7*
Total World	16,223	16,931	19,489	22,020	24,251	*2,231*	*10.1*	*10.6*

* Due to changes in the IPS sampling methodology introduced in 1999, care should be taken when comparing results for 1999 and 2000 with earlier years. See notes on page 9 relating to IPS interviewing on routes to the Irish Republic.

3.11 Number of nights and average length of stay by country of visit 1996 to 2000

	Nights (thousands)					Average length of stay (nights)				
	1996	1997	1998	1999	2000	1996	1997	1998	1999	2000
Canada	10,367	10,613	11,083	11,639	11,406	21	19	18	17	16
USA	49,395	47,295	53,795	60,018	61,010	16	16	15	15	14
North America	59,762	57,909	64,878	71,657	72,415	17	16	16	15	14
Austria	3,302	3,488	4,403	4,091	3,937	8	8	8	9	8
Belgium	3,832	4,001	4,098	4,664	4,148	3	3	2	3	3
Denmark	2,051	1,701	1,675	1,580	1,426	8	6	7	6	5
Finland	769	558	986	993	802	8	7	9	8	5
France	46,383	48,534	50,860	56,779	60,306	5	4	4	5	5
Germany	12,714	12,579	12,797	11,933	13,529	7	6	6	6	6
Greece	19,969	20,286	24,027	30,153	33,160	14	13	13	12	12
Irish Republic*	19,843	21,208	22,409	22,474	21,287	6	6	6	5	5
Italy	15,232	15,749	18,158	19,268	20,370	10	9	9	9	9
Luxembourg	133	378	408	375	302	4	7	7	4	4
Netherlands	7,360	7,144	7,758	8,505	8,461	5	4	4	4	4
Portugal	12,911	14,948	14,792	15,995	16,366	12	11	11	11	10
Spain	87,310	92,944	107,620	116,245	121,985	12	11	11	11	11
Sweden	2,003	1,938	2,238	2,105	2,143	7	7	7	6	6
EU Europe	233,813	245,455	272,228	295,159	308,221	8	7	7	7	7
Cyprus	9,614	9,382	12,009	11,631	15,983	14	13	13	12	12
Gibraltar	254	430	573	331	346	8	11	15	7	10
Iceland	172	279	442	375	630	8	11	10	12	8
Malta	4,766	4,262	5,148	4,509	4,882	12	11	11	12	11
Norway	2,652	2,089	2,384	1,914	2,780	13	8	9	8	10
Switzerland	3,678	4,399	4,242	4,449	4,769	7	8	7	6	6
Turkey	13,808	12,400	13,068	11,325	10,413	13	12	13	13	13
Central & Eastern Europe	5,323	5,264	5,856	6,284	6,082	10	10	10	9	9
Former USSR	1,494	2,110	2,195	1,440	1,660	12	15	15	11	12
Former Yugoslavia	1,562	1,263	1,451	1,347	1,501	22	11	12	14	13
Non EU Europe	43,324	41,879	47,368	43,605	49,046	12	11	11	11	11
North Africa	6,658	7,608	7,911	7,208	10,396	12	13	12	12	14
South Africa	5,854	5,395	6,429	5,751	6,762	29	23	23	22	21
Rest of Africa	8,819	11,019	7,869	9,554	8,915	25	27	25	25	25
Israel	2,567	2,133	2,137	1,936	2,140	18	14	13	13	13
Other Middle East	4,476	5,987	6,413	6,085	6,223	19	23	23	19	17
Hong Kong	3,561	4,630	2,936	4,057	3,808	23	26	18	27	22
India	14,116	13,286	12,678	13,592	13,936	34	33	29	30	29
Japan	1,926	2,082	2,607	1,872	2,041	19	22	20	19	18
Rest of Asia	28,332	26,582	28,623	31,249	33,119	36	34	32	30	29
Australia	14,569	15,395	18,707	20,083	20,410	51	45	46	44	43
New Zealand	3,708	4,255	4,687	3,806	5,058	42	49	48	34	47
Caribbean	9,936	11,556	12,894	12,735	12,622	19	18	18	16	16
Central & South America	5,088	5,484	7,238	8,264	7,394	25	21	20	21	17
Rest of the World	3,267	2,870	3,603	3,832	4,378	16	13	12	13	12
Other Countries	112,878	118,283	124,732	130,024	137,202	27	26	24	24	23
Total World	449,778	463,526	509,206	540,445	566,884	11	10	10	10	10

* Due to changes in the IPS sampling methodology introduced in 1999, care should be taken when comparing results for 1999 and 2000 with earlier years. See notes on page 9 relating to IPS interviewing on routes to the Irish Republic.

3.12 Average spending per visit and spending per day by country of visit 1996 to 2000

	Average spending per visit (£)					Average spending per day (£)				
	1996	1997	1998	1999	2000	1996	1997	1998	1999	2000
Canada	658	661	669	672	700	32	35	37	39	45
USA	768	772	798	799	845	48	49	53	54	60
North America	753	755	779	780	824	45	47	50	52	58
Austria	498	422	450	420	439	63	52	55	48	52
Belgium	179	200	183	240	209	67	71	76	82	84
Denmark	340	327	300	282	276	41	51	41	49	58
Finland	412	349	375	451	390	51	50	41	57	74
France	205	202	231	250	269	43	46	52	53	53
Germany	296	295	289	285	302	44	47	47	50	54
Greece	394	389	350	384	399	29	29	27	31	33
Irish Republic*	223	211	190	241	238	36	36	33	45	44
Italy	471	460	510	463	498	48	53	56	51	57
Luxembourg	328	239	194	224	201	81	33	29	56	46
Netherlands	229	227	243	253	269	48	56	61	58	65
Portugal	410	377	360	424	371	35	33	32	38	37
Spain	358	341	335	369	370	31	30	30	33	34
Sweden	334	345	307	348	484	47	48	43	54	85
EU Europe	287	278	286	312	323	38	38	39	42	43
Cyprus	402	415	411	433	447	30	32	33	36	37
Gibraltar	263	257	325	361	252	32	24	22	50	28
Iceland	584	406	389	355	655	70	39	38	30	79
Malta	300	286	249	311	299	25	25	22	27	26
Norway	358	338	451	366	335	28	42	48	45	33
Switzerland	412	376	460	416	414	57	50	71	64	67
Turkey	394	370	317	304	412	29	30	25	27	31
Central & Eastern Europe	337	359	372	340	351	33	37	39	37	40
Former USSR	907	637	827	578	670	76	42	54	55	57
Former Yugoslavia	697	395	384	484	[illegible]	32	35	32	34	25
Non EU Europe	401	377	388	390	406	34	34	35	37	38
North Africa	402	401	360	387	421	32	30	30	34	31
South Africa	960	815	904	828	755	33	35	39	38	36
Rest of Africa	678	593	688	785	775	27	22	27	31	31
Israel	521	456	511	568	536	29	32	38	45	42
Other Middle East	606	555	610	671	665	33	25	27	35	39
Hong Kong	955	715	560	887	839	41	28	31	33	39
India	557	568	551	700	698	16	17	19	23	24
Japan	1,012	882	931	988	1,002	52	40	46	53	54
Rest of Asia	843	808	838	819	892	23	24	26	27	30
Australia	1,423	1,450	1,332	1,274	1,472	28	32	29	29	34
New Zealand	1,399	1,226	1,260	1,221	1,383	34	25	26	36	29
Caribbean	628	620	680	696	710	34	34	37	43	45
Central & South America	853	717	924	829	774	34	34	46	39	45
Rest of the World	1,006	991	1,010	1,109	1,143	65	76	82	88	93
Other Countries	768	723	760	793	816	29	28	31	34	36
Total World	385	368	383	408	426	36	36	38	41	43

* Due to changes in the IPS sampling methodology introduced in 1999, care should be taken when comparing results for 1999 and 2000 with earlier years. See notes on page 9 relating to IPS interviewing on routes to the Irish Republic.

3.13 Number of visits and spending by length of stay and purpose of visit 1996 to 2000

	Visits (thousands)					Spending (£million)				
	1996	1997	1998	1999	2000	1996	1997	1998	1999	2000
Nil nights										
Holiday	2,037	2,050	1,683	1,517	1,220	94	100	97	102	84
of which inclusive tour	*0*	*0*	*0*	*0*	*1*	*0*	*0*	*0*	*0*	*0*
Business	699	721	784	870	987	28	32	39	58	70
Visiting friends or relatives	33	43	34	65	66	3	1	3	6	6
Miscellaneous	1,582	2,185	2,329	2,230	2,303	157	204	282	302	427
All visits	4,351	4,999	4,830	4,682	4,576	283	337	421	468	587
1-3 nights										
Holiday	2,812	3,407	3,723	4,311	4,657	485	597	695	886	970
of which inclusive tour	*1,033*	*1,382*	*1,619*	*1,693*	*1,703*	*214*	*285*	*335*	*371*	*366*
Business	2,807	2,937	3,322	4,141	4,502	740	758	926	1,163	1,364
Visiting friends or relatives	593	621	726	1,161	1,310	69	64	92	148	177
Miscellaneous	445	580	691	1,054	975	95	144	126	238	212
All visits	6,657	7,545	8,463	10,668	11,443	1,388	1,563	1,839	2,434	2,722
4-13 nights										
Holiday	10,602	11,936	14,032	16,396	17,695	3,647	4,014	4,636	5,681	6,356
of which inclusive tour	*6,657*	*7,636*	*8,776*	*9,824*	*10,537*	*2,333*	*2,555*	*2,844*	*3,347*	*3,740*
Business	2,105	2,131	2,401	2,539	2,699	1,550	1,555	1,810	1,799	2,015
Visiting friends or relatives	1,587	1,774	1,904	2,830	3,228	312	351	429	603	745
Miscellaneous	373	352	477	487	515	147	134	174	223	231
All visits	14,667	16,193	18,814	22,251	24,137	5,655	6,053	7,049	8,306	9,347
14-27 nights										
Holiday	9,388	9,792	10,758	11,703	12,012	5,053	5,167	5,744	6,559	7,016
of which inclusive tour	*6,067*	*6,260*	*6,887*	*7,382*	*7,679*	*3,252*	*3,260*	*3,588*	*4,069*	*4,385*
Business	342	350	359	372	437	429	458	566	555	652
Visiting friends or relatives	1,182	1,237	1,294	1,603	1,596	434	458	482	622	665
Miscellaneous	134	117	141	166	152	79	76	93	133	121
All visits	11,046	11,496	12,552	13,845	14,197	5,995	6,160	6,885	7,870	8,453
28 nights or more										
Holiday	998	904	973	1,096	1,100	1,063	941	1,036	1,305	1,334
of which inclusive tour	*144*	*115*	*156*	*178*	*135*	*194*	*110*	*146*	*157*	*132*
Business	223	202	252	239	247	473	394	635	686	631
Visiting friends or relatives	791	842	883	938	978	437	478	569	612	665
Miscellaneous	150	164	169	162	157	204	222	283	319	487
All visits	2,161	2,112	2,278	2,435	2,483	2,178	2,035	2,524	2,922	3,118
All Visits										
Holiday	26,765	29,138	32,306	35,023	36,685	10,610	11,107	12,495	14,555	15,784
of which inclusive tour	*13,901*	*15,393*	*17,437*	*19,077*	*20,055*	*5,993*	*6,210*	*6,913*	*7,945*	*8,623*
Business	6,879	7,166	8,033	8,161	8,872	3,359	3,351	4,124	4,261	4,732
Visiting friends or relatives	5,502	6,004	6,452	6,598	7,178	1,533	1,650	1,869	1,991	2,258
Miscellaneous	2,904	3,649	4,082	4,100	4,102	721	823	1,001	1,215	1,477
All visits	42,050	45,957	50,872	53,881	56,837	16,223	16,931	19,489	22,020	24,251

Due to changes in the IPS sampling methodology introduced in 1999, care should be taken when comparing results for 1999 and 2000 with earlier years. See notes on page 9 relating to IPS interviewing on routes to the Irish Republic.

3.14 Number of visits and spending by length of stay and area of visit 1996 to 2000

	Visits (thousands)					Spending (£million)				
	1996	1997	1998	1999	2000	1996	1997	1998	1999	2000
Nil nights										
North America	0	0	0	0	1	0	0	0	0	3
EU Europe	4,316	4,948	4,778	4,616	4,515	282	335	418	463	578
Non EU Europe	33	45	49	62	54	1	2	2	4	4
Other Countries	1	6	3	4	5	0	0	0	0	2
Total World	4,351	4,999	4,830	4,682	4,576	283	337	421	468	587
1-3 nights										
North America	131	130	155	187	223	43	45	66	74	91
EU Europe	6,018	6,822	7,683	9,772	10,373	1,198	1,371	1,592	2,162	2,368
Non EU Europe	440	510	544	620	718	125	122	156	162	198
Other Countries	69	83	81	88	129	23	24	26	36	65
Total World	6,657	7,545	8,463	10,668	11,443	1,388	1,563	1,839	2,434	2,722
4-13 nights										
North America	1,252	1,375	1,706	2,051	2,381	858	895	1,147	1,343	1,675
EU Europe	10,558	11,729	13,466	16,497	17,563	3,413	3,756	4,288	5,214	5,628
Non EU Europe	1,534	1,695	2,000	1,914	2,150	546	577	707	677	775
Other Countries	1,323	1,394	1,642	1,790	2,043	838	825	906	1,072	1,269
Total World	14,667	16,193	18,814	22,251	24,137	5,655	6,053	7,049	8,306	9,347
14-27 nights										
North America	1,914	1,792	1,974	2,137	2,133	1,430	1,403	1,603	1,731	1,901
EU Europe	5,857	6,257	6,689	7,880	7,927	2,620	2,697	2,912	3,642	3,740
Non EU Europe	1,452	1,406	1,566	1,358	1,522	647	628	675	609	731
Other Countries	1,823	2,040	2,324	2,469	2,615	1,298	1,431	1,696	1,887	2,082
Total World	11,046	11,496	12,552	13,846	14,197	5,995	6,160	6,885	7,870	8,453
28 nights or more										
North America	287	297	322	357	323	366	369	423	546	501
EU Europe	673	584	684	735	761	571	509	672	832	955
Non EU Europe	163	136	157	165	179	134	99	131	153	170
Other Countries	1,038	1,095	1,114	1,178	1,220	1,105	1,059	1,298	1,392	1,492
Total World	2,161	2,112	2,278	2,435	2,483	2,178	2,035	2,524	2,922	3,118
All visits										
North America	3,584	3,594	4,158	4,733	5,060	2,698	2,713	3,239	3,694	4,170
EU Europe	30,591	33,952	37,237	39,500	41,140	8,806	9,451	10,653	12,335	13,294
Non EU Europe	3,622	3,793	4,315	4,120	4,623	1,453	1,428	1,672	1,605	1,878
Other Countries	4,253	4,618	5,163	5,529	6,014	3,265	3,338	3,926	4,386	4,909
Total World	42,050	45,957	50,872	53,881	56,837	16,223	16,931	19,489	22,020	24,251

Due to changes in the IPS sampling methodology introduced in 1999, care should be taken when comparing results for 1999 and 2000 with earlier years. See notes on page 9 relating to IPS interviewing on routes to the Irish Republic.

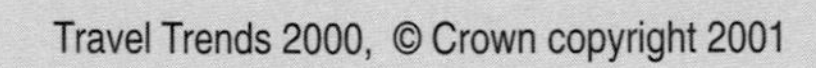

Chapter *4*

Overseas residents' visits to the UK 2000

- *Over 25 million visits in 2000 with spending of £12.8 billion*
- *Over 14 million visits from within EU Europe accounting for 56 per cent of all visits to the UK but only 36 per cent of total spending*
- *Over nine million holiday trips to the UK accounting for 37 per cent of all visits and 34 per cent of spending*
- *Over 13 million overnight visits to London with spending of nearly £7 billion*
- *Residents of the USA topped the league table of visits with over four million visits and £2.8 billion spending*

Overseas residents' visits to the UK in 2000 by country or area of residence

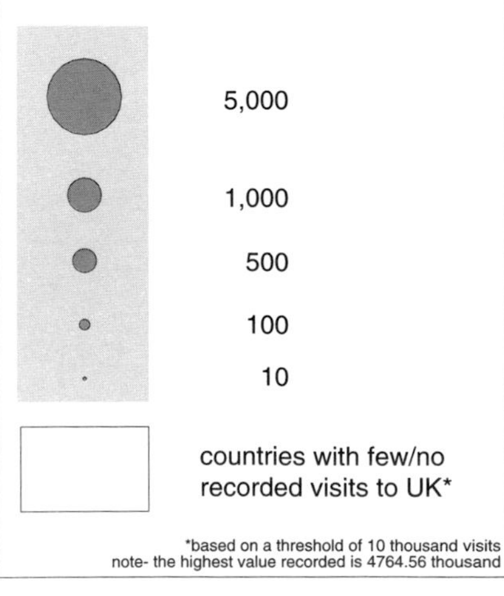

See Inset
Inset - Mainland Europe

Chapter 4

Overseas residents' visits to the UK 2000

4.01 Proportion of visits and spending by mode of travel

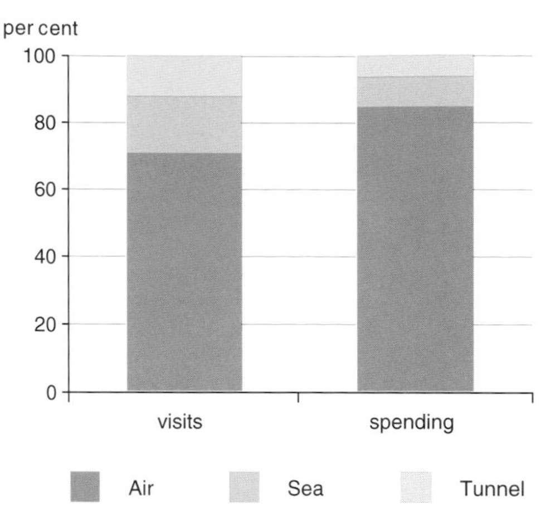

4.02 Average spending per visit by mode of travel

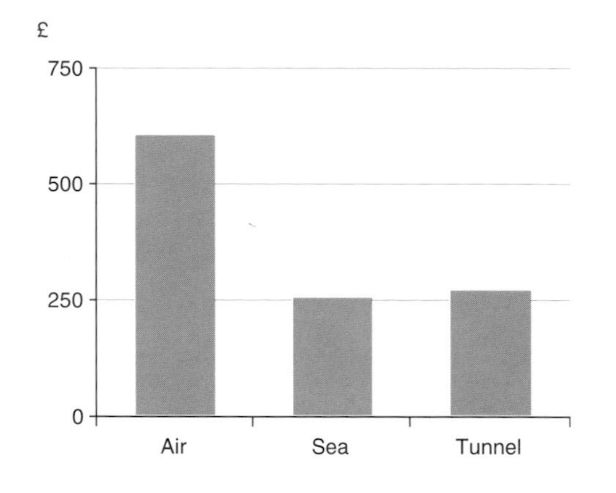

4.03 Average spending per visit by area of residence

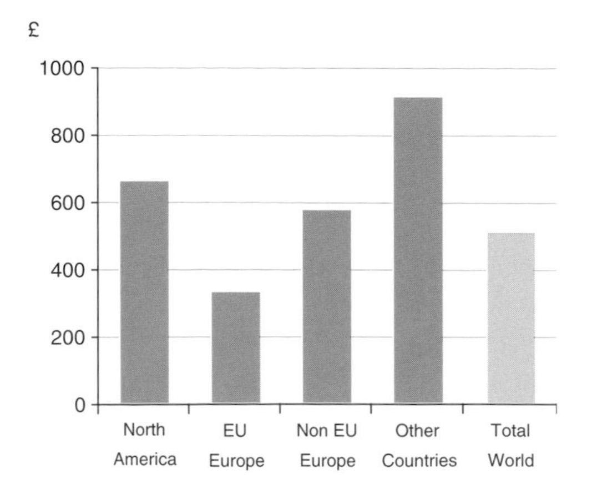

During 2000, overseas residents made 25.2 million visits to the UK spending £12.8 billion. This chapter considers the variety of characteristics exhibited by these visitors.

Visits and spending by mode of travel

Table 4.01 gives details of visits and spending in the UK by overseas residents from each of four main regions of the world, broken down by mode of travel and purpose of visit. **Figure 4.01** shows that the largest proportion of overseas visitors to the UK in 2000 arrived by air (71 per cent), 17 per cent arrived by sea and 12 per cent via the Channel Tunnel.

Those travelling by air accounted for an even greater proportion of spending (85 per cent), whereas visitors by sea accounted for nine per cent and those via the Channel Tunnel six per cent. **Figure 4.02** shows that air travellers spent more than twice as much per visit as those travelling by sea or via the Channel Tunnel. Those travelling by air spent an average of £69 per day and stayed an average of nine nights compared with £35 per day and seven nights among those travelling by sea. Those travelling to the UK via the Channel Tunnel spent an average of £50 per day, but had the shortest average length of stay of five nights per visit.

Visits and spending by area of residence

The greatest number of visitors to the UK continue to come from EU Europe, 14 million in total. In 2000, EU Europeans accounted for 56 per cent of all visits to the UK but only 36 per cent of total spending. In comparison, those travelling from 'Other Countries' made up only 17 per cent of visits, but accounted for 30 per cent of spending. **Figure 4.03** illustrates the low levels of spending in the UK of EU European visitors compared with other visitors. On average, those from 'Other Countries' spent £905 per visit, nearly three times the average spend per visit by residents of EU Europe. This difference is mainly due to residents of 'Other Countries' staying an average of 15 nights per visit, two and a half times longer than the average stay by residents of EU Europe.

Visits and spending by purpose of visit

Figure 4.04 shows that in 2000 overseas residents made 9.3 million holiday trips to the UK. This accounts for 37 per cent of total visits and 34 per cent of spending. Business trips were the second most popular reason for visit, accounting for 29 per cent of visits and 32 per cent of spending.

Figure 4.05 shows that holidaymakers accounted for only a third of visits by air compared with over a half of visits by sea and almost a half of all visits via the Channel Tunnel. In contrast, those on business trips accounted for a third of visits by air, but less than a fifth of visits by sea and a quarter of visits via the Channel Tunnel.

It was noted above that air travellers spent more than twice as much per visit as those travelling by sea or via the Channel Tunnel. This difference was most marked for business visitors who spent an average of £649 per visit when travelling by air, more than three times the amount spent by business visitors travelling by sea or via the Channel Tunnel.

4.04 Number of visits by purpose and mode of travel

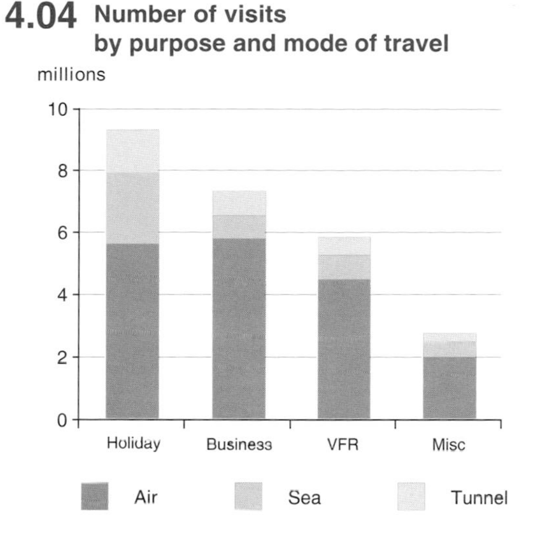

4.05 Proportion of visits by mode of travel and purpose

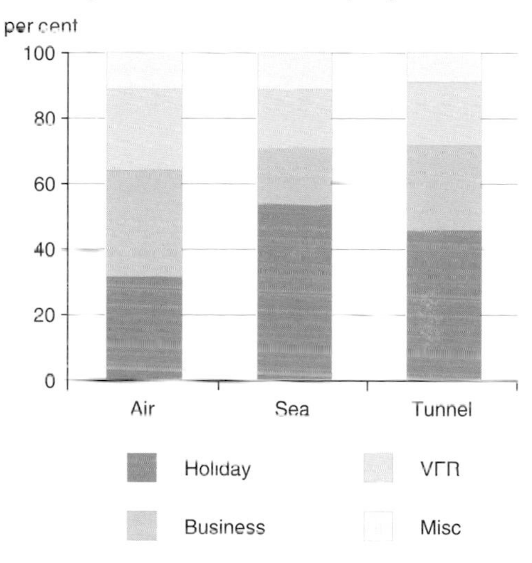

Visits and spending by quarter

Table 4.02 gives the breakdown of visits and spending by overseas residents in the UK by quarter of 2000, area of residence and purpose of visit. Holiday visits were the most seasonal, peaking between July and September. Visits between July and September made up over a third of all visits (37 per cent) and two-fifths of total spending by overseas holidaymakers in 2000. In contrast, business visits showed little seasonality, with a similar number of visits and little variation in spending throughout the year.

Visits and spending by region of stay in the UK

Table 4.03 provides a breakdown of overseas residents' visits and spending during 2000 by their region of stay in the UK, area of residence and reason for visit. As a single visit to the UK may involve an overnight stay in more than one region, the sub totals for London and Other England will not sum to the number of visits shown for Total England. London continues to be the most popular region of stay for overseas residents visiting the UK. Over 13 million overnight visits were made to London in 2000 and nearly £7 billion was spent on these visits, an average of £525 per visit. Overseas visitors to Wales spent the least, an average of £272 per visit (**figure 4.06**). The average

4.06 Average spending per visit by region of stay in the UK

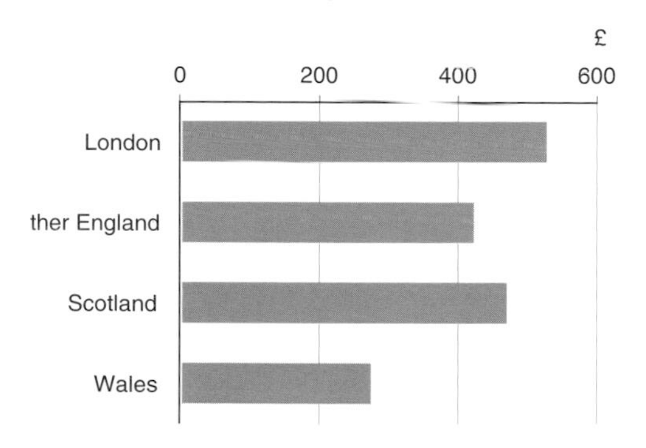

4.07 Proportion of visits by region of stay and purpose

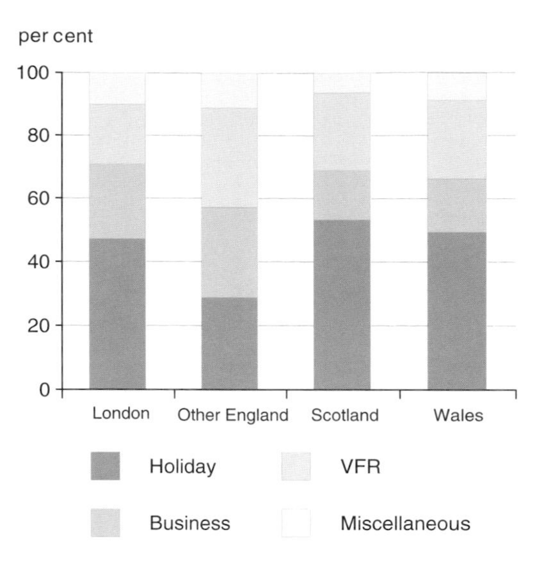

length of stay in London and Wales was similar, at just over six nights per visit. However, visitors to London spent £84 per day, nearly twice as much as the £43 per day spent by visitors to Wales.

Looking at the breakdown by purpose of visit, **figure 4.07** shows that 'holiday' was the single most popular reason for overseas residents visiting London, Scotland and Wales, making up around a half of all visits to these regions. In contrast, similar proportions of overseas residents went to other parts of England to visit friends and family (32 per cent), to have a holiday (29 per cent) or on business (28 per cent). There was some variation in the general pattern by area of residence. For example, among residents of non-EU European countries, the number of business trips to London were almost as high as the number of holiday visits. Looking at visits to 'Other England', residents of North America and 'Other Countries' were most likely to be on holiday or visiting friends or relatives, and those from EU Europe were most likely to be on business or visiting friends or relatives.

4.08 Visits and spending for top 10 countries of residence by main reason for visit

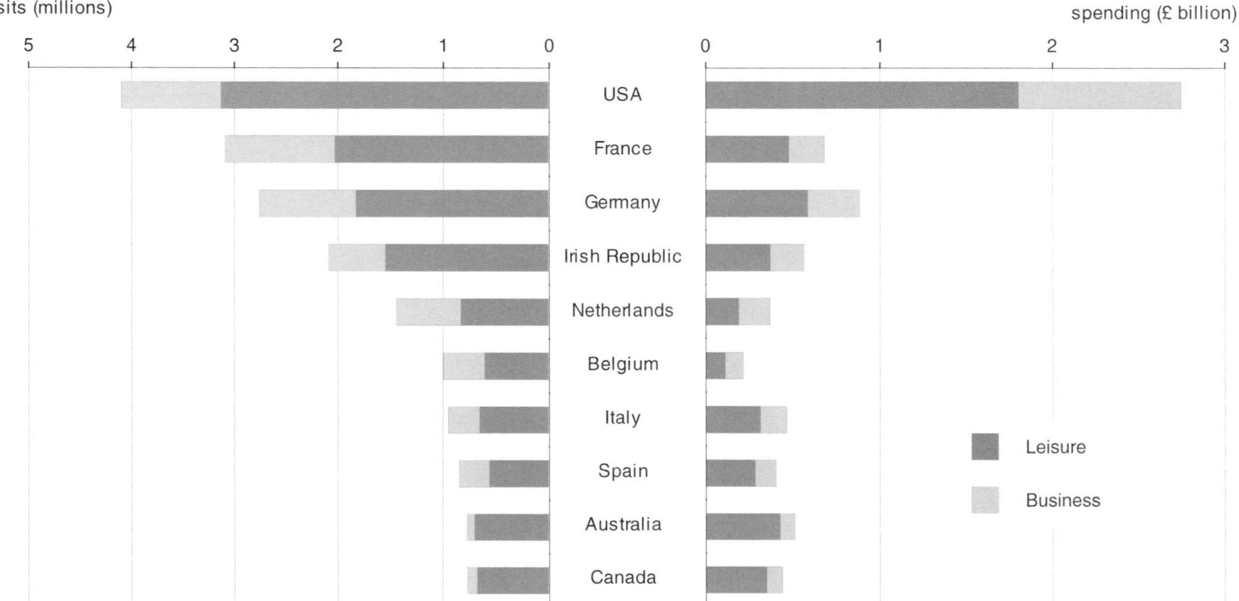

Visits, nights and spending by country of residence

Table 4.04 gives a detailed breakdown of overseas residents' visits, nights and spending by their country of residence and their main reason for visit to the UK. **Figure 4.08** shows the top 10 countries of residence with the greatest number of visits to the UK in 2000 together with the associated spending, split by leisure trips (holiday visits, visits to friends or relatives and miscellaneous reasons for visit) and business trips. Residents of the USA continue to make the greatest number of visits to the UK. In 2000, they made over four million visits, a million more than the number made by residents of France, the next most popular country of residence. Residents of the USA spent the most on their trips to the UK, a total of £2.8 billion. This was three times more than German residents, the next highest spending group of visitors.

Average length of stay and spending

Table 4.05 provides a detailed breakdown of the average length of stay, the average spend per visit and the average spend per day of overseas residents visiting the UK during 2000 by both country of residence and purpose of visit. Residents of 'Other Middle East' are shown to have the highest average spend per visit of £1765. This is largely due to high levels of spending among residents of countries such as Kuwait who, for example, stayed an average of 16 nights and spent an average of £140 per day. Residents of Kuwait made nearly 22.5 thousand independent holiday visits to the UK in 2000, spending a total of £50.7 million on these visits.

Figures 4.09 to **4.11** show the relationship between average spend per visit, average spend per day and average length of stay by purpose of visit. The dotted line on each figure represents the overall average for all overseas residents travelling to the UK. Visits by overseas residents for miscellaneous purposes produced the highest average spending per visit of £752, as a result of them staying on average for 16 nights - the longest for any purpose. Those visiting friends and family stayed an average of 11 nights which is above the average of eight nights stayed by all overseas residents visiting the UK in 2000. However, because they spent an average of only £36 per day, this resulted in the lowest average spend per visit of £389.

4.09 Average spending per visit by purpose of visit

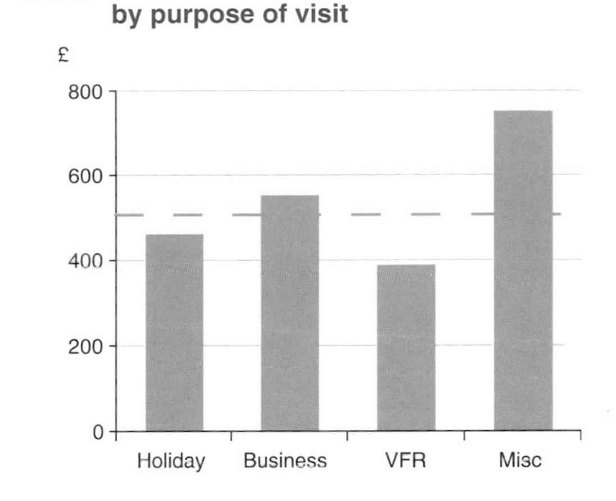

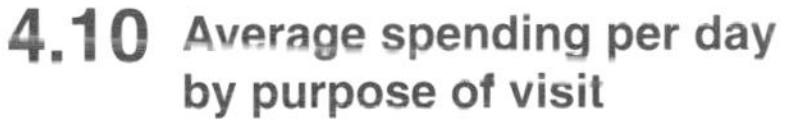

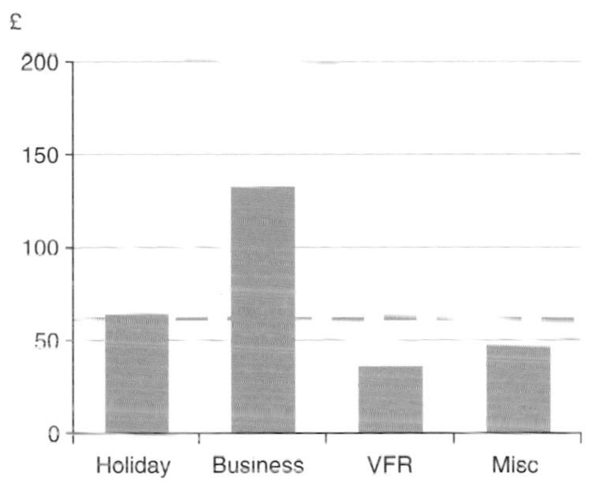

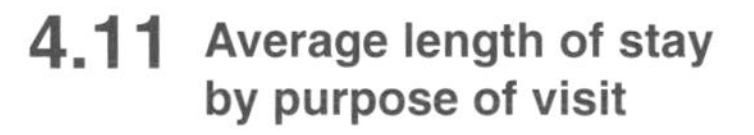

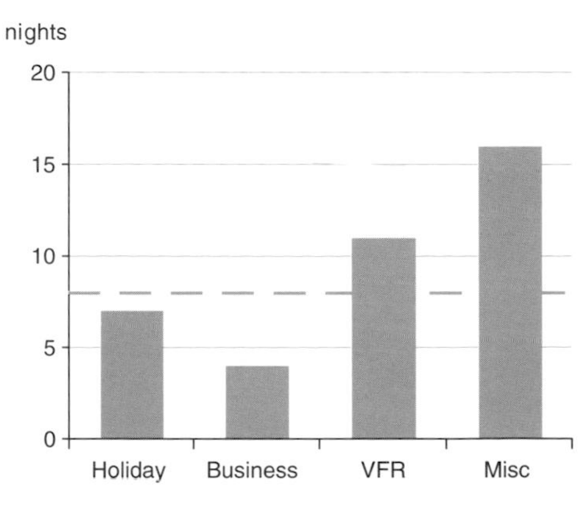

4.12 Visits and spending by length of stay

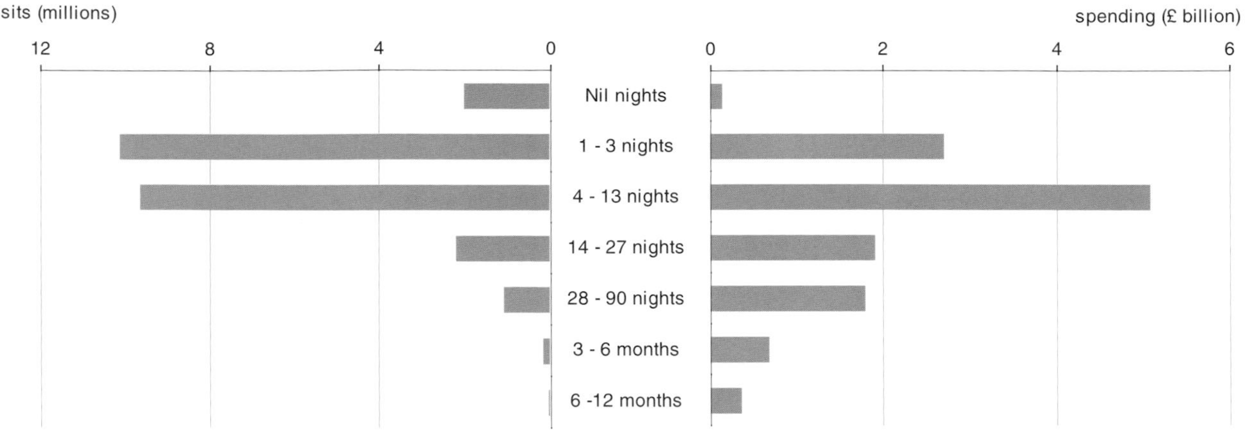

Visits and spending by length of stay

Table 4.06 gives details of overseas residents' visits and spending by their length of stay and country of residence. **Figure 4.12** shows the distribution of visits and spend by length of stay. Short stay visits, lasting one to three nights, were the most popular, accounting for 40 per cent of all visits, but only 21 per cent of spending. In comparison, visits lasting 4-13 nights accounted for 38 per cent of all visits and 40 per cent of spending. Residents of France and the USA made up the greatest proportion of short stay visits to the UK, each making over 1.4 million visits. However, residents of the USA spent nearly half a billion pounds on short stay visits, twice the amount spent by residents of France.

Nearly two million day trips were made to the UK in 2000. A third of these (0.6 million) were made by residents of France, more than twice the number of day trips made by residents of Belgium, the second most popular country of residence for day trips. Residents of France and Belgium, together with residents of Germany, the Irish Republic and Netherlands made 1.6 million day trips to the UK, accounting for 80 per cent of the total.

4.13 Number of visits by UK port

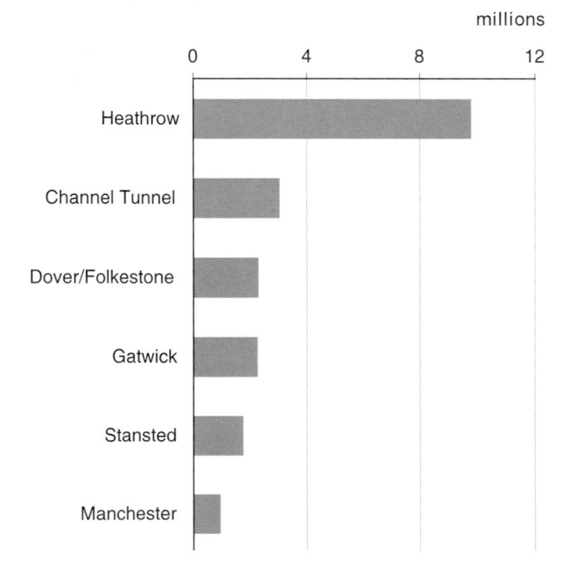

Visits by port

Table 4.07 provides a breakdown of overseas residents' visits by each of the main ports of entry to the UK during 2000 by their country of residence. **Figure 4.13** shows the number of overseas residents' visits via the six most frequently used ports: Heathrow, the Channel Tunnel, Dover, Gatwick, Stansted and Manchester. These ports catered for 20.3 million visits, accounting for 80 per cent of all overseas visits to the UK in 2000. Heathrow was the most popular port for all the main regions of the world, catering for 39 per cent of all visits. Looking at the breakdown by country of residence, a particular exception to this was that more residents of France and Belgium travelled via the Channel Tunnel and Dover than via Heathrow and more residents of Denmark travelled via Stansted than Heathrow.

Visits by vehicle type

Table 4.08 gives a breakdown of the number of overseas residents' visits to the UK by vehicle type and country of residence. Passengers travelling on Eurostar passenger trains are included in the 'foot' category. Looking at sea and tunnel traffic, travelling on 'foot' was the most popular mode of travel among visitors from EU Europe, North America and 'Other Countries'. Coach travel was the most popular among non-EU Europeans. Since 1999, travelling on 'foot' has overtaken private vehicle as the most popular mode of travel among EU Europeans and now accounts for 34 per cent of all non-air visits. The number of visits by EU Europeans using private vehicles fell from 2.2 million in 1999 (not shown in table) to 1.7 million in 2000.

Visits and spending by gender

Table 4.09 gives a breakdown of overseas residents' visits and spending by gender and country of residence for both business and leisure visits to the UK. Males made 14.8 million visits to the UK and spent £7.6 billion in 2000, accounting for approximately 60 per cent of all visits and spending compared with 10.4 million visits and £5.2 billion spend by females.

Figure 4.14 shows that the number of business trips made by males (6.0 million) was nearly five times the number made by females (1.3 million). Females made slightly more leisure visits to the UK than males. The difference was most marked among North Americans, with females making 11 per cent more leisure trips to the UK than males.

Males and females on leisure trips to the UK had a similar average spend per visit. However, among those on business, females spent 12 per cent more per visit on average than males. The difference was most marked among those travelling from European countries; females spent nearly 25 per cent more per visit than males in spite of males having a higher average spend per day. This was due to females staying on average twice as long as males in this group (**figure 4.15**).

4.14 Number of visits by purpose and gender

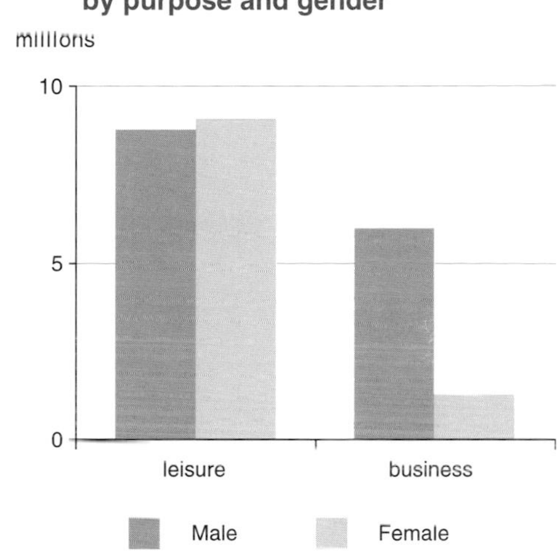

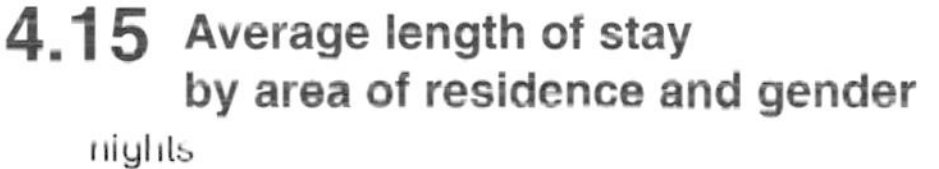

4.15 Average length of stay by area of residence and gender

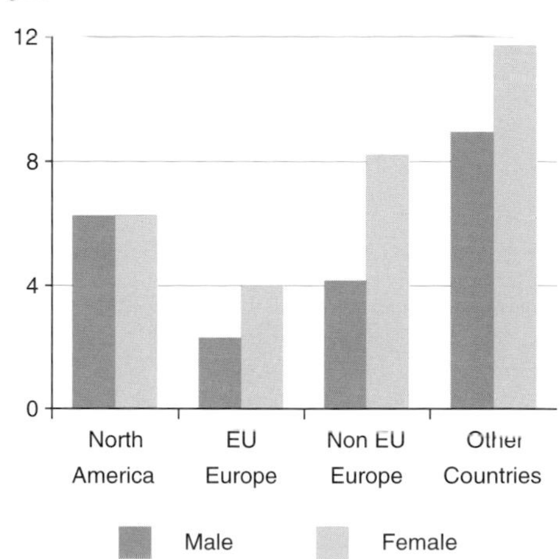

4.16 Number of visits by age group and area of residence

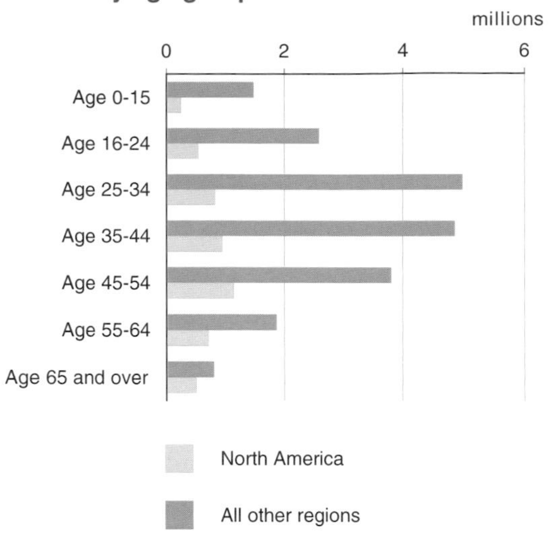

4.17 Top 15 UK towns (excluding London) by number of visits

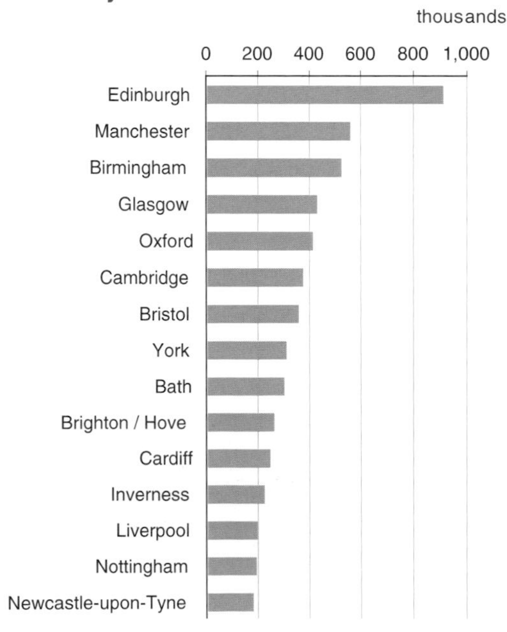

Visits and spending by age group

Table 4.10 shows a breakdown of overseas residents' visits and spending by their age group and country of residence. **Figure 4.16** shows that the largest number of visits to the UK in 2000 from all regions of the world, other than North America, were made by those in the 25-34 year and 35-44 year age groups - each accounting for nearly a quarter of visits and spending from these regions. However, visitors from North America were most likely to be in the 45-54 age group, making up nearly a quarter of all visits and spending from this region of the world.

Visits, nights and spending by UK region of visit

Table 4.11 provides a detailed breakdown of visits, nights and spending by county/region of stay in the UK and purpose of visit. As each visit may include more than one UK area, the number of visits shown in the table will not sum to the country or UK totals. The table shows that the highest levels of spending were recorded in the urban areas in and around London, the West Midlands, Edinburgh, Glasgow and Manchester, as well as the areas near the main sea and tunnel ports along the south coast of England.

Figure 4.17 shows the number of visits by overseas residents' to the 15 most popular towns and cities of visit, after London, in the UK. Over 14 times as many visits were made to London in 2000 than to Edinburgh, the second most popular location.

Figures 4.18 and **4.19** show the number of overseas residents' visits and levels of spending by region of stay in the UK.

4.18 Overseas residents' overnight visits to the UK 2000 by region of stay in the UK

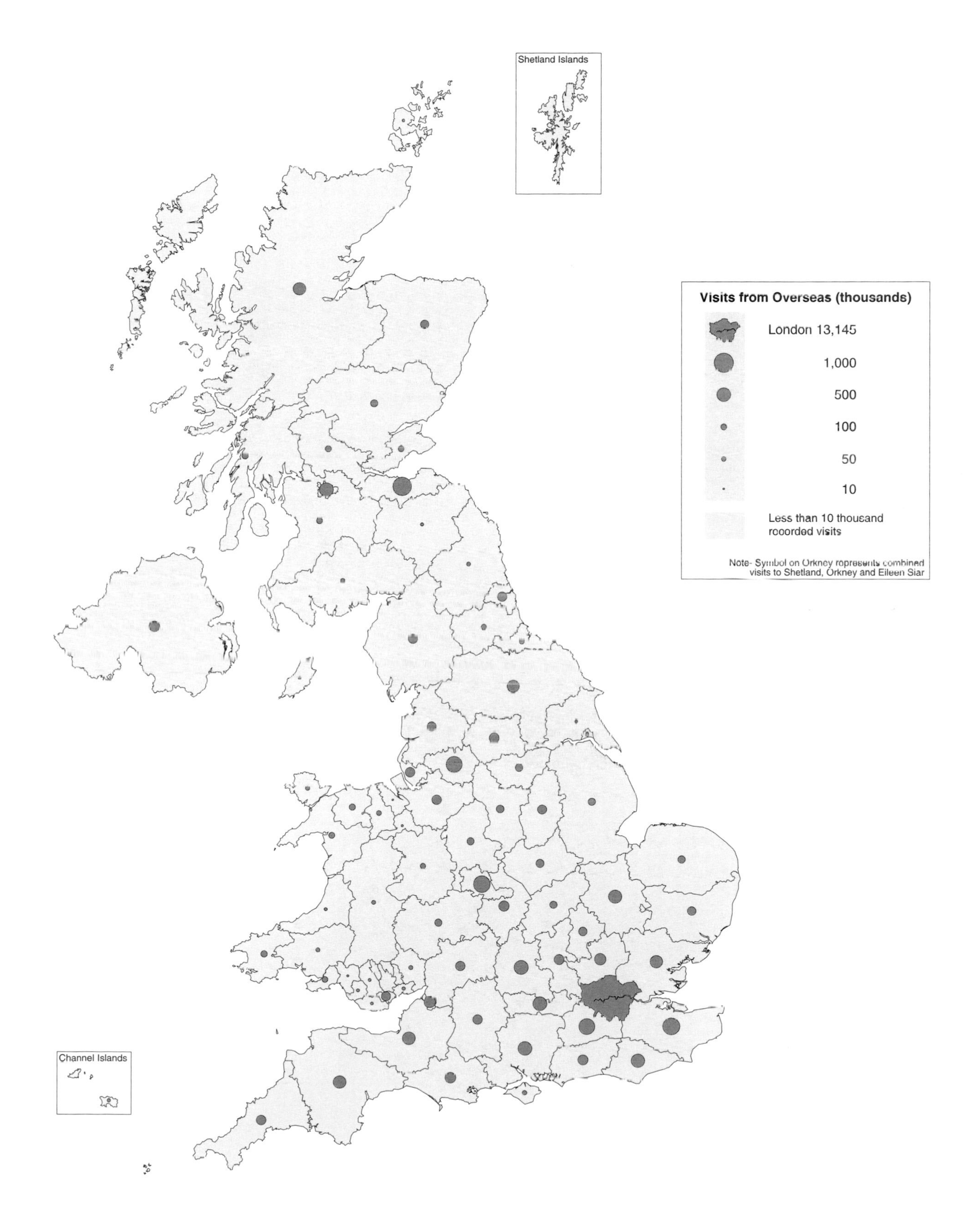

4.19 Overseas residents' spending on overnight visits to the UK 2000 by region of stay in the UK

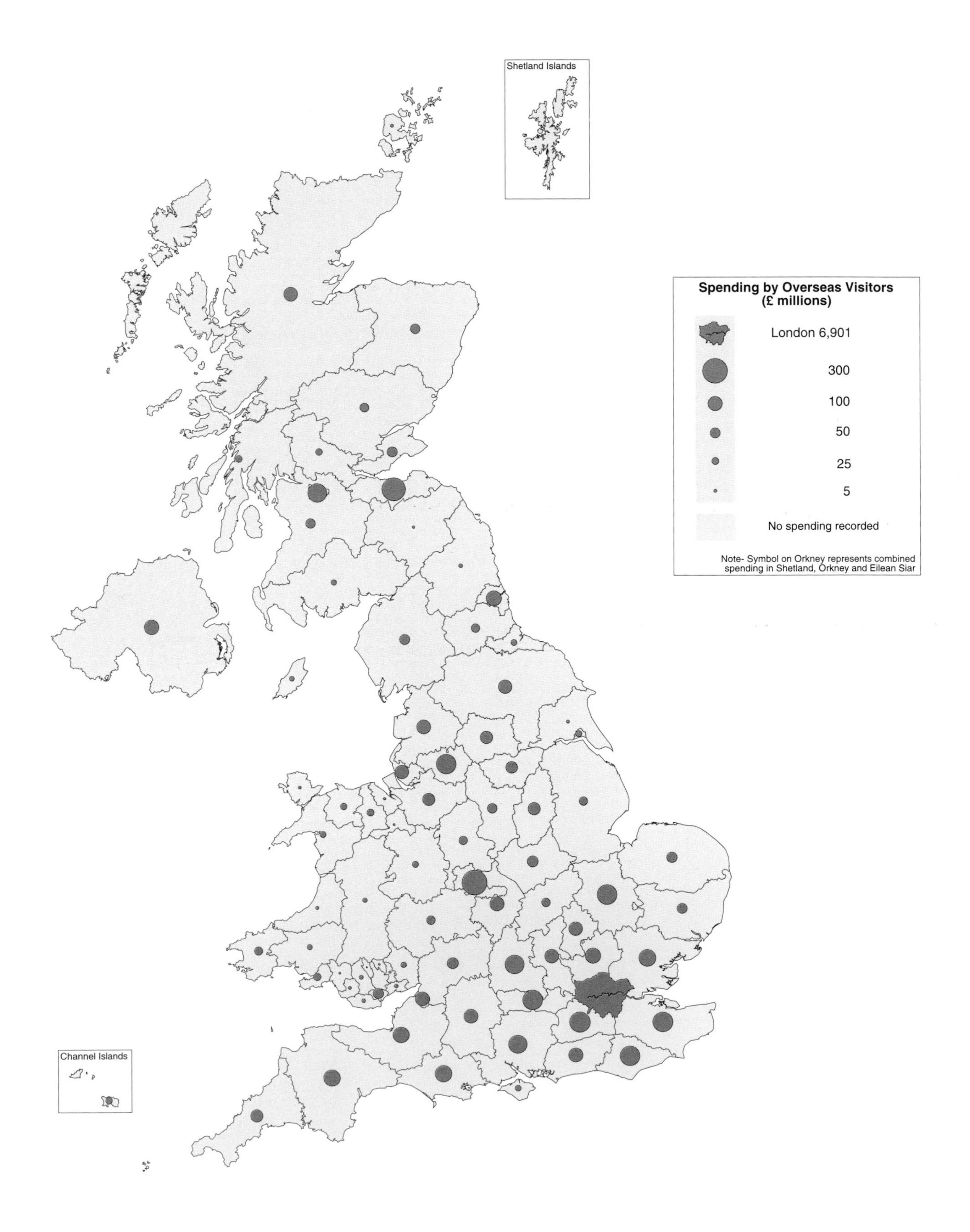

4.01 Number of visits and spending by mode of travel and purpose of visit 2000

	Air		Sea		Channel Tunnel		Total	
	visits (thousands)	spending (£ million)	visits (thousands)	spending (£ million)	visits (thousands)	spending (£ million)	visits (thousands)	spending (£ million)
North America								
Holiday	1,578	1,078	300	91	289	119	2,168	1,288
of which inclusive tour	*312*	*211*	*176*	*26*	*61*	*13*	*549*	*250*
Business	1,007	993	12	11	40	33	1,059	1,037
Visiting friends or relatives	1,032	473	31	7	53	25	1,116	505
Miscellaneous	479	304	23	26	25	27	527	356
All visits	4,096	2,857	366	134	407	205	4,869	3,197
EU Europe								
Holiday	2,180	905	1,609	376	837	162	4,625	1,443
of which inclusive tour	*498*	*179*	*603*	*123*	*213*	*43*	*1,315*	*346*
Business	3,424	1,338	614	110	717	101	4,754	1,549
Visiting friends or relatives	2,065	532	682	126	475	81	3,223	738
Miscellaneous	832	574	370	180	217	73	1,418	827
All visits	8,501	3,359	3,275	794	2,245	416	14,020	4,570
Non EU Europe								
Holiday	450	252	186	42	43	11	679	304
of which inclusive tour	*116*	*52*	*46*	*8*	*20*	*4*	*182*	*63*
Business	573	428	105	11	20	3	698	442
Visiting friends or relatives	350	160	39	19	10	2	399	181
Miscellaneous	234	224	44	23	12	3	290	250
All visits	1,607	1,066	374	94	85	19	2,066	1,180
Other Countries								
Holiday	1,395	1,178	201	71	235	98	1,831	1,347
of which inclusive tour	*299*	*138*	*60*	*12*	*63*	*11*	*421*	*101*
Business	772	988	11	3	27	29	810	1,020
Visiting friends or relatives	1,012	807	28	12	57	29	1,097	847
Miscellaneous	447	572	44	32	24	31	516	635
All visits	3,627	3,554	284	118	343	187	4,253	3,859
Total World								
Holiday	5,604	3,413	2,295	579	1,403	390	9,302	4,383
of which inclusive tour	*1,225*	*580*	*886*	*169*	*356*	*72*	*2,467*	*820*
Business	5,776	3,748	741	134	804	166	7,322	4,048
Visiting friends or relatives	4,459	1,971	780	163	595	137	5,834	2,271
Miscellaneous	1,992	1,673	481	261	278	134	2,750	2,068
All visits	17,831	10,837	4,298	1,140	3,080	828	25,209	12,805

4.02 Number of visits and spending by quarter of the year and purpose of visit 2000

	January - March		April - June		July - September		October - December	
	visits (thousands)	spending (£ million)	visits (thousands)	spending (£ million)	visits (thousands)	spending (£ million)	visits (thousands)	spending (£ million)
North America								
Holiday	374	196	729	403	717	460	348	229
of which inclusive tour	*81*	*34*	*229*	*91*	*176*	*95*	*64*	*30*
Business	231	208	274	256	302	303	252	270
Visiting friends or relatives	243	111	293	136	327	158	253	100
Miscellaneous	82	45	137	104	189	106	119	101
All visits	929	562	1,433	902	1,535	1,030	972	703
EU Europe								
Holiday	838	232	1,345	385	1,634	570	808	257
of which inclusive tour	*281*	*62*	*430*	*102*	*375*	*123*	*229*	*59*
Business	1,160	359	1,213	413	1,113	357	1,268	420
Visiting friends or relatives	719	166	872	202	889	211	742	159
Miscellaneous	222	101	357	196	486	292	353	238
All visits	2,939	861	3,787	1,199	4,122	1,434	3,172	1,076
Non EU Europe								
Holiday	102	49	166	66	270	110	141	80
of which inclusive tour	*20*	*8*	*53*	*18*	*79*	*26*	*30*	*12*
Business	158	96	172	140	180	97	188	110
Visiting friends or relatives	86	37	91	38	118	61	104	44
Miscellaneous	50	38	51	41	109	92	80	80
All visits	395	220	481	285	676	361	513	314
Other Countries								
Holiday	286	218	423	274	781	609	341	246
of which inclusive tour	*72*	*26*	*105*	*50*	*164*	*59*	*80*	*27*
Business	153	183	230	286	216	299	211	252
Visiting friends or relatives	203	166	261	198	410	292	223	190
Miscellaneous	86	102	119	149	203	257	108	127
All visits	729	672	1,032	911	1,609	1,459	883	817
Total World								
Holiday	1,600	694	2,663	1,127	3,401	1,749	1,638	812
of which inclusive tour	*453*	*129*	*816*	*261*	*795*	*303*	*403*	*127*
Business	1,703	846	1,889	1,095	1,811	1,056	1,919	1,052
Visiting friends or relatives	1,251	480	1,517	575	1,744	723	1,323	494
Miscellaneous	439	286	664	490	987	747	660	545
All visits	4,993	2,314	6,733	3,297	7,943	4,284	5,540	2,911

4.03 Number of visits and spending by region of the UK and purpose of visit 2000

	London		Other England		Total England		Scotland		Wales	
	visits (1000s)	spending (£ million)	visits (1000s)	spending (£ million)	visits (1000s)	spending (£ million)	visits (1000s)	spending (£ million)	visits (1000s)	spending (£ million)
North America										
Holiday	1,723	817	752	273	2,043	1,090	298	162	131	30
of which inclusive tour	*496*	*165*	*144*	*42*	*532*	*208*	*81*	*37*	*50*	*5*
Business	666	652	446	325	977	977	76	41	21	8
Visiting friends or relatives	508	205	641	215	981	420	158	64	47	14
Miscellaneous	384	235	168	103	508	338	30	15	7	3
All visits	3,282	1,910	2,007	915	4,509	2,825	561	282	206	54
EU Europe										
Holiday	2,575	746	1,415	357	3,728	1,104	326	149	231	55
of which inclusive tour	*883*	*220*	*339*	*65*	*1,174*	*285*	*85*	*40*	*83*	*18*
Business	1,532	738	2,003	648	3,388	1,386	118	56	110	24
Visiting friends or relatives	1,227	281	1,839	373	2,873	653	149	43	137	21
Miscellaneous	481	301	664	431	1,078	732	51	31	60	18
All visits	5,815	2,066	5,922	1,810	11,066	3,875	644	280	538	119
Non EU Europe										
Holiday	413	166	257	105	602	271	82	26	25	3
of which inclusive tour	*137*	*45*	*60*	*10*	*175*	*55*	*35*	*9*	*8*	*0*
Business	374	280	272	143	606	424	23	12	10	1
Visiting friends or relatives	193	90	223	75	374	166	22	9	13	6
Miscellaneous	131	113	144	125	262	238	8	9	3	1
All visits	1,110	650	897	448	1,844	1,098	135	56	51	11
Other Countries										
Holiday	1,478	916	621	320	1,769	1,236	191	78	97	23
of which inclusive tour	*400*	*128*	*72*	*21*	*417*	*149*	*37*	*10*	*18*	*1*
Business	558	641	300	311	749	953	49	40	25	19
Visiting friends or relatives	570	375	666	405	1,046	780	89	44	46	16
Miscellaneous	332	343	211	248	500	591	20	9	17	24
All visits	2,939	2,275	1,799	1,285	4,064	3,560	348	171	185	83
Total World										
Holiday	6,189	2,646	3,045	1,055	8,142	3,701	898	416	483	111
of which inclusive tour	*1,917*	*558*	*614*	*138*	*2,298*	*696*	*239*	*95*	*160*	*25*
Business	3,129	2,311	3,022	1,428	5,720	3,739	266	148	166	53
Visiting friends or relatives	2,498	951	3,369	1,068	5,274	2,019	418	161	244	57
Miscellaneous	1,329	993	1,188	907	2,348	1,900	108	64	86	46
All visits	13,145	6,901	10,624	4,458	21,484	11,359	1,689	789	980	267

Channel Islands and transit passengers are excluded from spending figures

4.04 Number of visits, nights and spending by purpose of visit 2000

	Holiday visits						Business visits		
	total			*of which inclusive tour*					
	visits (thousands)	nights (thousands)	spending (£ million)	*visits (thousands)*	*nights (thousands)*	*spending (£ million)*	visits (thousands)	nights (thousands)	spending (£ million)
Canada	280	2,731	168	*48*	*326*	*18*	90	619	91
USA	1,888	13,953	1,121	*501*	*2,846*	*232*	969	6,054	946
North America	2,168	16,683	1,288	*549*	*3,171*	*250*	1,059	6,673	1,037
Austria	87	636	33	*24*	*118*	*7*	55	172	19
Belgium	374	1,138	71	*99*	*367*	*20*	385	668	106
Denmark	157	810	55	*43*	*189*	*16*	147	443	63
Finland	41	250	12	*13*	*71*	*4*	82	281	32
France	1,080	4,308	197	*316*	*1,218*	*56*	1,065	2,560	202
Germany	961	6,079	312	*316*	*1,554*	*86*	937	2,509	299
Greece	64	440	35	*11*	*43*	*5*	48	181	29
Irish Republic	562	2,175	143	*111*	*490*	*29*	545	1,161	195
Italy	335	2,428	144	*70*	*408*	*28*	290	1,094	155
Luxembourg	17	73	4	*2*	*7*	*1*	14	22	6
Netherlands	434	2,308	119	*164*	*665*	*43*	608	1,332	181
Portugal	61	376	31	*15*	*66*	*7*	60	247	25
Spain	244	1,947	101	*53*	*279*	*18*	283	1,044	122
Sweden	208	947	88	*78*	*308*	*26*	236	814	117
EU Europe	4,625	23,916	1,443	*1,315*	*5,783*	*346*	4,754	12,530	1,549
Cyprus	12	162	8	.	.	.	8	59	7
Gibraltar	2	17	1	.	.	.	3	16	1
Iceland	27	107	14	*11*	*47*	*7*	9	45	7
Malta	15	123	7	*2*	*14*	*1*	12	53	6
Norway	186	802	59	*45*	*201*	*18*	108	382	55
Switzerland	197	1,040	87	*51*	*247*	*22*	199	620	110
Turkey	19	176	18	*3*	*15*	*1*	34	180	32
Central & Eastern Europe	145	1,356	39	*47*	*228*	*8*	225	1,199	80
Former USSR	60	875	36	*16*	*121*	*4*	75	802	127
Former Yugoslavia	17	389	36	*5*	*29*	*2*	25	141	17
Non EU Europe	679	5,048	304	*182*	*901*	*63*	698	3,497	442
North Africa	26	315	26	*1*	*3*	*1*	29	228	57
South Africa	121	1,758	83	*15*	*77*	*5*	58	307	59
Rest of Africa	96	1,853	98	*1*	*12*	*0*	65	693	98
Israel	100	593	49	*32*	*144*	*11*	54	243	44
Other Middle East	156	2,603	269	*8*	*52*	*4*	70	953	141
Hong Kong	72	806	45	*17*	*54*	*6*	41	208	43
India	69	1,003	53	*15*	*68*	*4*	64	726	54
Japan	326	1,878	169	*160*	*697*	*71*	114	793	120
Rest of Asia	245	2,030	159	*71*	*248*	*25*	162	1,748	198
Australia	367	5,136	215	*64*	*452*	*21*	72	700	84
New Zealand	71	1,546	60	*6*	*58*	*3*	17	411	27
Caribbean	21	293	20	.	.	.	20	136	19
Central & South America	157	1,044	96	*32*	*124*	*11*	42	466	76
Rest of the World	5	46	5	.	.	.	2	13	1
Other Countries	1,831	20,905	1,347	*421*	*1,990*	*161*	810	7,628	1,020
Total World	9,302	66,552	4,383	*2,467*	*11,846*	*820*	7,322	30,327	4,048

4.04 Number of visits, nights and spending by purpose of visit 2000

	Visiting friends or relatives			Miscellaneous			Total visits		
	visits (thousands)	nights (thousands)	spending (£ million)	visits (thousands)	nights (thousands)	spending (£ million)	visits (thousands)	nights (thousands)	spending (£ million)
Canada	325	4,570	132	78	964	52	772	8,885	445
USA	791	8,430	373	448	4,787	304	4,097	33,223	2,752
North America	1,116	13,001	505	527	5,751	356	4,869	42,108	3,197
Austria	42	262	11	44	742	26	227	1,812	89
Belgium	143	581	24	94	307	18	997	2,695	219
Denmark	89	505	17	29	736	35	421	2,494	170
Finland	16	158	4	15	461	18	154	1,150	65
France	626	4,570	110	316	4,759	173	3,087	16,196	684
Germany	617	4,782	146	244	3,749	128	2,758	17,120	887
Greece	61	835	32	51	1,366	71	224	2,823	167
Irish Republic	743	3,609	160	237	901	67	2,087	7,847	570
Italy	170	1,450	53	154	3,100	120	949	8,073	472
Luxembourg	16	72	3	4	39	2	51	206	15
Netherlands	316	1,935	58	81	356	16	1,440	5,931	374
Portugal	39	364	12	14	118	5	174	1,105	73
Spain	234	2,674	82	88	2,960	103	849	8,624	409
Sweden	109	792	28	49	1,275	44	602	3,829	276
EU Europe	3,223	22,590	738	1,418	20,869	827	14,020	79,904	4,570
Cyprus	32	805	41	15	377	23	66	1,403	79
Gibraltar	10	90	6	10	48	4	24	172	12
Iceland	8	48	2	3	18	4	47	219	27
Malta	15	350	7	6	51	3	49	577	23
Norway	86	400	25	76	850	43	455	2,542	103
Switzerland	127	745	42	57	1,082	50	579	3,488	289
Turkey	10	145	5	16	861	36	78	1,363	91
Central & Eastern Europe	72	1,209	20	62	1,550	55	504	5,317	180
Former USSR	30	439	22	40	848	46	204	2,965	232
Former Yugoslavia	11	138	6	7	243	4	60	912	63
Non EU Europe	399	4,470	181	290	5,942	250	2,066	18,956	1,180
North Africa	18	524	12	14	120	14	87	1,186	108
South Africa	90	1,009	52	28	620	21	304	4,381	215
Rest of Africa	83	2,095	103	33	399	45	277	5,041	345
Israel	47	638	25	20	230	14	220	1,704	132
Other Middle East	108	2,056	137	60	931	148	394	6,543	696
Hong Kong	46	590	45	24	380	21	183	1,984	154
India	51	2,024	14	22	365	11	206	4,118	134
Japan	50	627	30	67	2,786	136	557	6,084	456
Rest of Asia	140	3,569	104	98	2,397	112	645	9,745	574
Australia	288	5,786	191	49	548	26	777	12,170	517
New Zealand	74	1,342	39	12	196	3	174	3,496	129
Caribbean	45	1,425	53	15	151	8	101	2,005	100
Central & South America	46	763	40	72	1,852	71	317	4,125	283
Rest of the World	3	86	2	2	64	6	11	209	14
Other Countries	1,097	23,214	847	516	11,044	635	4,253	62,791	3,859
Total World	5,834	63,274	2,271	2,750	43,605	2,068	25,209	203,759	12,805

4.05 Average length of stay, spending per visit and spending per day by purpose of visit 2000

	Holiday visits						Business visits		
	total			*of which inclusive tour*					
	average			*average*			average		
	stay (nights)	spend per visit (£s)	spend per day (£s)	*stay (nights)*	*spend per visit (£s)*	*spend per day (£s)*	stay (nights)	spend per visit (£s)	spend per day (£s)
Canada	10	599	61	*7*	*373*	*55*	7	1,021	148
USA	7	594	80	*6*	*462*	*81*	6	976	156
North America	8	594	77	*6*	*455*	*79*	6	980	155
Austria	7	378	52	*5*	*293*	*61*	3	351	112
Belgium	3	189	62	*4*	*206*	*56*	2	274	158
Denmark	5	348	67	*4*	*384*	*87*	3	429	142
Finland	6	286	47	*5*	*333*	*61*	3	384	112
France	4	183	46	*4*	*177*	*46*	2	189	79
Germany	6	325	51	*5*	*272*	*55*	3	319	119
Greece	7	538	78	*4*	*420*	*104*	4	607	159
Irish Republic	4	255	66	*4*	*260*	*59*	2	358	168
Italy	7	430	59	*6*	*400*	*68*	4	534	141
Luxembourg	4	260	61	*4*	*329*	*84*	2	441	268
Netherlands	5	274	52	*4*	*260*	*64*	2	298	136
Portugal	6	509	83	*4*	*445*	*102*	4	418	102
Spain	8	416	52	*5*	*352*	*66*	4	429	116
Sweden	5	421	93	*4*	*329*	*83*	3	496	144
EU Europe	5	291	56	*4*	*263*	*60*	3	326	124
Cyprus	13	691	52	.	.	.	8	863	112
Gibraltar	7	495	67	.	.	.	6	202	36
Iceland	4	523	130	*4*	*613*	*143*	5	793	167
Malta	8	451	55	*6*	*444*	*81*	4	469	108
Norway	4	315	73	*4*	*396*	*89*	4	512	145
Switzerland	5	441	83	*5*	*424*	*88*	3	554	178
Turkey	9	978	103	*5*	*479*	*98*	5	945	178
Central & Eastern Europe	9	266	28	*5*	*175*	*36*	5	355	67
Former USSR	15	602	41	*8*	*264*	*35*	11	1,705	159
Former Yugoslavia	23	2,160	92	*6*	*371*	*67*	6	682	122
Non EU Europe	7	448	60	*5*	*349*	*70*	5	634	126
North Africa	12	1,004	82	*6*	*964*	*171*	8	1,935	248
South Africa	15	685	47	*5*	*333*	*65*	5	1,014	191
Rest of Africa	19	1,014	53	*17*	*469*	*28*	11	1,515	141
Israel	6	489	82	*4*	*343*	*76*	4	801	179
Other Middle East	17	1,729	103	*6*	*461*	*71*	14	2,021	148
Hong Kong	11	623	56	*3*	*344*	*106*	5	1,037	204
India	14	769	53	*5*	*263*	*58*	11	845	74
Japan	6	519	90	*4*	*446*	*102*	7	1,049	151
Rest of Asia	8	648	78	*3*	*345*	*99*	11	1,228	113
Australia	14	586	42	*7*	*324*	*46*	10	1,155	119
New Zealand	22	851	39	*10*	*564*	*56*	25	1,639	66
Caribbean	14	975	69	.	.	.	7	916	138
Central & South America	7	610	92	*4*	*341*	*89*	11	1,807	164
Rest of the World	10	1,092	113	.	.	.	7	682	96
Other Countries	11	736	64	*5*	*382*	*81*	9	1,258	134
Total World	7	461	64	*5*	*332*	*69*	4	553	133

4.05 Average length of stay, spending per visit and spending per day by purpose of visit 2000

	Visiting friends or relatives			Miscellaneous			Total visits		
	average			average			average		
	stay (nights)	spend per visit (£s)	spend per day (£s)	stay (nights)	spend per visit (£s)	spend per day (£s)	stay (nights)	spend per visit (£s)	spend per day (£s)
Canada	14	405	29	12	669	54	12	574	50
USA	11	471	44	11	678	63	8	670	83
North America	12	452	39	11	676	62	9	654	76
Austria	6	267	42	17	587	35	8	392	49
Belgium	4	167	41	3	190	58	3	219	81
Denmark	6	193	34	26	1,233	48	6	403	68
Finland	10	219	23	31	1,244	40	7	422	57
France	7	176	24	15	549	36	5	221	42
Germany	8	237	31	15	527	34	6	321	52
Greece	14	527	39	27	1,394	52	13	745	59
Irish Republic	5	215	44	4	282	74	4	270	72
Italy	9	308	36	20	781	39	9	497	58
Luxembourg	4	157	36	10	605	60	4	301	75
Netherlands	6	182	30	4	203	46	4	260	63
Portugal	9	301	32	8	368	43	6	420	66
Spain	11	352	31	34	1,162	35	10	480	47
Sweden	7	254	35	26	889	34	6	459	72
EU Europe	7	229	33	15	583	40	6	318	56
Cyprus	25	1,281	50	26	1,584	62	21	1,192	56
Gibraltar	9	613	65	5	425	84	7	480	68
Iceland	6	212	35	7	1,427	209	5	577	123
Malta	23	481	20	8	511	64	12	472	40
Norway	6	296	51	11	572	50	6	401	72
Switzerland	[illegible]	[illegible]	[illegible]	10	886	46	6	499	83
Turkey	15	510	34	55	2,318	42	18	1,174	67
Central & Eastern Europe	17	357	21	25	574	23	11	357	34
Former USSR	15	724	49	21	1,170	55	15	1,133	78
Former Yugoslavia	13	540	43	34	573	17	15	1,053	69
Non EU Europe	11	454	40	21	863	42	9	570	62
North Africa	29	668	23	9	978	115	14	1,244	91
South Africa	17	535	31	22	733	33	14	704	49
Rest of Africa	25	1,242	49	12	1,344	111	18	1,239	68
Israel	14	544	40	12	724	62	8	598	77
Other Middle East	19	1,266	67	16	2,463	158	17	1,765	106
Hong Kong	13	978	76	16	899	56	11	841	77
India	40	283	7	17	510	31	20	645	32
Japan	13	605	48	42	2,031	49	11	817	75
Rest of Asia	26	740	29	24	1,149	47	15	890	59
Australia	20	664	33	11	523	47	16	664	42
New Zealand	18	519	29	16	215	13	20	740	37
Caribbean	32	1,172	37	10	558	54	20	991	50
Central & South America	17	869	52	26	977	38	13	890	68
Rest of the World	30	749	25	33	2,878	88	18	1,246	68
Other Countries	21	773	37	21	1,231	57	15	905	61
Total World	11	389	36	16	752	47	8	503	62

4.06 Number of visits and spending by duration of stay 2000

	Nil nights		1 to 3 nights		4 to 13 nights		14 to 27 nights	
	visits (thousands)	spending (£ million)	visits (thousands)	spending (£ million)	visits (thousands)	spending (£ million)	visits (thousands)	spending (£ million)
Canada	6	2	210	47	325	170	177	143
USA	53	17	1,413	469	2,080	1,461	392	443
North America	59	19	1,623	516	2,405	1,630	569	586
Austria	13	1	86	24	95	34	24	13
Belgium	270	18	499	103	203	73	22	14
Denmark	36	1	165	56	197	76	17	14
Finland	7	0	74	22	59	23	7	5
France	603	24	1,464	225	795	222	130	63
Germany	244	12	1,122	249	1,103	387	227	138
Greece	4	1	76	23	103	64	22	16
Irish Republic	265	26	1,093	297	661	201	54	29
Italy	41	3	350	96	386	176	133	106
Luxembourg	9	0	22	7	18	8	2	0
Netherlands	213	10	757	162	400	134	49	26
Portugal	4	1	72	18	79	43	13	8
Spain	28	2	316	70	352	160	76	40
Sweden	26	2	316	101	224	114	17	10
EU Europe	1,764	99	6,412	1,453	4,675	1,714	794	483
Cyprus	0	0	15	6	23	15	10	8
Gibraltar	.	0	12	2	7	4	6	6
Iceland	2	1	21	11	21	13	1	2
Malta	1	0	11	4	24	10	9	6
Norway	48	3	215	74	162	70	18	7
Switzerland	50	3	285	101	197	116	33	28
Turkey	1	0	20	22	38	36	10	13
Central & Eastern Europe	15	1	196	34	207	83	45	28
Former USSR	3	0	55	25	101	71	23	21
Former Yugoslavia	0	0	20	8	25	16	8	7
Non EU Europe	121	9	850	287	805	434	162	125
North Africa	2	1	20	11	39	58	15	19
South Africa	5	1	88	41	122	77	56	42
Rest of Africa	5	2	58	31	98	105	62	85
Israel	4	1	77	26	111	63	18	16
Other Middle East	2	2	96	72	149	173	82	138
Hong Kong	2	1	61	28	82	70	26	25
India	1	1	60	20	86	56	20	12
Japan	4	1	217	64	242	177	54	69
Rest of Asia	11	4	212	72	255	202	82	94
Australia	3	1	178	40	324	167	152	131
New Zealand	0	0	33	8	62	33	38	24
Caribbean	3	0	21	17	40	27	19	19
Central & South America	10	2	99	30	123	89	49	47
Rest of the World	.	0	2	1	7	6	1	1
Other Countries	53	18	1,221	460	1,740	1,303	672	721
Total World	1,997	145	10,106	2,715	9,625	5,083	2,198	1,916

4.06 Number of visits and spending by duration of stay 2000

	28 to 90 nights		3 to 6 months		6 months to 1 year		All visits	
	visits (thousands)	spending (£ million)	visits (thousands)	spending (£ million)	visits (thousands)	spending (£ million)	visits (thousands)	spending (£ million)
Canada	49	55	3	5	2	24	772	445
USA	141	283	15	72	4	7	4,097	2,752
North America	190	338	17	77	5	31	4,869	3,197
Austria	9	10	1	6	0	2	227	89
Belgium	2	1	0	9	.	.	997	219
Denmark	4	2	3	21	.	.	421	170
Finland	5	7	2	8	.	.	154	65
France	76	118	14	30	4	2	3,087	684
Germany	52	79	7	17	3	5	2,758	887
Greece	15	43	3	9	1	11	224	167
Irish Republic	12	15	1	2	.	.	2,087	570
Italy	33	66	4	15	2	10	949	472
Luxembourg	0	1	.	.	.	.	51	15
Netherlands	19	43	1	0	.	.	1,440	374
Portugal	5	3	.	.	.	.	174	73
Spain	69	92	6	33	2	12	849	409
Sweden	14	30	3	18	1	2	602	276
EU Europe	317	509	46	168	13	44	14,020	4,570
Cyprus	16	44	3	7	.	.	66	79
Gibraltar	.	.	.	.	.	.	24	12
Iceland	1	1	.	.	.	.	47	27
Malta	3	2	1	0	.	.	49	23
Norway	9	11	2	12	1	5	455	183
Switzerland	9	23	3	11	1	7	579	289
Turkey	0	12	1	4	1	4	78	91
Central & Eastern Europe	33	24	5	3	3	8	504	180
Former USSR	18	30	4	38	1	47	204	232
Former Yugoslavia	4	3	2	29	.	.	60	63
Non EU Europe	98	149	21	105	7	71	2,066	1,180
North Africa	11	19	1	1	.	.	87	108
South Africa	26	28	5	10	2	16	304	215
Rest of Africa	48	64	7	58	.	.	277	345
Israel	9	20	1	6	.	.	220	132
Other Middle East	56	175	7	66	2	71	394	696
Hong Kong	11	22	1	2	0	6	183	154
India	27	22	12	22	0	1	206	134
Japan	28	76	7	29	4	39	557	456
Rest of Asia	70	112	12	37	3	53	645	574
Australia	102	137	17	37	1	5	777	517
New Zealand	37	55	4	6	1	3	174	129
Caribbean	12	8	3	10	2	19	101	100
Central & South America	31	69	5	42	1	5	317	283
Rest of the World	1	1	1	5	.	.	11	14
Other Countries	467	807	83	331	17	218	4,253	3,859
Total World	1,073	1,803	168	682	42	363	25,209	12,805

4.07 Number of visits by UK port 2000

	Airports							thousands
	Heathrow	Gatwick	Manchester	Birmingham	Stansted	Other England	Scotland	Wales
Canada	419	87	45	17	8	17	81	6
USA	2,146	864	117	64	61	58	107	1
North America	2,565	950	163	81	69	74	188	7
Austria	143	10	7	8	20	9	.	.
Belgium	103	10	39	35	8	80	14	7
Denmark	118	55	19	22	146	3	7	.
Finland	71	27	18	4	19	9	3	.
France	374	112	81	81	91	189	24	6
Germany	723	82	117	225	395	153	51	5
Greece	116	36	7	6	.	35	2	2
Irish Republic	366	113	153	.	263	472	39	39
Italy	355	138	24	32	269	14	22	1
Luxembourg	9	5	3	2	4	12	1	.
Netherlands	339	46	81	61	52	189	38	13
Portugal	105	27	6	1	5	3	1	2
Spain	322	119	38	25	56	111	16	1
Sweden	245	58	30	19	195	25	7	2
EU Europe	3,389	840	622	521	1,524	1,304	226	76
Cyprus	46	1	3	3	4	.	1	.
Gibraltar	1	13	.	.	.	11	.	.
Iceland	21	1	.	.	16	1	8	.
Malta	25	9	8	2	.	1	2	.
Norway	178	34	28	3	59	40	1	2
Switzerland	256	37	19	14	8	200	13	.
Turkey	71	2	3	.	0	1	.	.
Central & Eastern Europe	165	24	15	7	17	8	4	.
Former USSR	114	53	3	2	3	.	.	.
Former Yugoslavia	37	12	.	.	1	.	.	.
Non EU Europe	913	187	78	31	108	259	29	2
North Africa	64	6	2	.	3	4	.	.
South Africa	248	13	4	.	2	4	3	2
Rest of Africa	184	61	4	.	6	5	2	2
Israel	136	38	5	.	16	5	.	2
Other Middle East	318	17	9	3	2	12	2	1
Hong Kong	147	5	10	2	2	1	2	.
India	174	4	5	5	1	6	.	.
Japan	436	6	8	4	2	4	2	2
Rest of Asia	473	11	29	8	9	8	10	3
Australia	487	47	28	6	23	18	2	3
New Zealand	106	12	3	1	7	5	.	1
Caribbean	52	30	1	1	5	5	.	.
Central & South America	138	57	3	1	9	1	.	.
Rest of the World	7	2	.	.	.	.	.	.
Other Countries	2,972	309	112	30	88	77	24	16
Total World	9,838	2,286	974	663	1,788	1,714	466	100

4.07 Number of visits by UK port 2000

thousands

	Sea and Channel Tunnel						
	Dover and Folkestone	Other channel ports	East coast ports	Long haul sea routes	Irish Sea & land routes	Channel Tunnel	All air and sea ports
Canada	26	4	3	0	21	39	772
USA	155	31	9	5	111	369	4,097
North America	181	36	12	5	132	407	4,869
Austria	21	.	4	.	.	6	227
Belgium	236	2	70	0	6	386	997
Denmark	5	2	42	.	.	3	421
Finland	.	.	1	.	.	4	154
France	552	247	20	.	15	1,296	3,087
Germany	522	8	196	0	29	252	2,758
Greece	10	.	.	.	.	10	224
Irish Republic	18	3	4	.	598	20	2,087
Italy	51	3	3	0	3	33	949
Luxembourg	8	.	2	.	.	4	51
Netherlands	201	1	266	0	7	147	1,440
Portugal	18	.	.	.	.	5	174
Spain	76	9	.	0	3	74	849
Sweden	6	.	7	.	2	6	602
EU Europe	1,723	275	614	1	663	2,245	14,020
Cyprus	1	.	1	.	5	1	66
Gibraltar	.	.	.	.	.	.	24
Iceland	.	.	.	.		0	47
Malta	.	.	.	.	.	1	49
Norway	2	.	108	.	.	1	455
Switzerland	14	1	5	.	4	10	579
Turkey	.	.	.	.	.	1	78
Central & Eastern Europe	191	.	2	.	6	65	504
Former USSR	26	.	2	.	.	2	204
Former Yugoslavia	7	.	.		1	1	60
Non EU Europe	240	1	117	.	15	85	2,066
North Africa	2	.	.	.	.	7	87
South Africa	10	2	3	0	.	13	304
Rest of Africa	1	1	.	0	2	8	277
Israel	6	.	.	0	1	10	220
Other Middle East	3	1	.	.	5	19	394
Hong Kong	2	.	1	.	4	6	183
India	4	.	1	.	.	6	206
Japan	12	2	.	.	.	79	557
Rest of Asia	35	.	3	.	1	53	645
Australia	51	2	.	0	54	56	777
New Zealand	11	4	.	.	9	15	174
Caribbean	.	2	.	.	.	5	101
Central & South America	34	5	4	.	1	65	317
Rest of the World	3	.	.	.	.	.	11
Other Countries	175	18	12	0	79	343	4,253
Total World	2,320	329	754	6	889	3,080	25,209

4.08 Number of visits by type of vehicle used 2000

thousands

	Air	Sea and Channel Tunnel					
	All travellers	Foot	Private vehicle	Coach	Goods vehicle	Vehicle type unknown	All sea and Channel Tunnel
Canada	679	70	9	12	2	.	93
USA	3,417	547	54	79	.	.	680
North America	4,096	617	63	91	2	.	773
Austria	196	5	8	8	10	.	31
Belgium	296	344	199	93	61	4	700
Denmark	370	37	11	1	1	1	51
Finland	150	2	2	.	.	.	4
France	957	1,051	419	440	210	10	2,130
Germany	1,751	105	444	331	113	14	1,007
Greece	204	3	6	.	9	1	20
Irish Republic	1,444	153	225	37	20	208	642
Italy	856	8	42	2	41	.	93
Luxembourg	37	5	5	2	1	.	14
Netherlands	818	121	309	107	76	8	622
Portugal	150	2	3	.	18	.	24
Spain	688	18	22	16	101	5	161
Sweden	581	9	5	5	1	.	21
EU Europe	8,501	1,863	1,701	1,043	663	250	5,520
Cyprus	58	1	7	.	.	.	8
Gibraltar	24	.	.	.	.	.	.
Iceland	46	0	.	.	.	.	0
Malta	47	1	.	.	.	.	1
Norway	345	84	21	2	.	3	110
Switzerland	546	8	22	4	.	.	33
Turkey	76	1	.	.	.	.	1
Central & Eastern Europe	240	10	19	134	98	5	264
Former USSR	175	2	5	18	3	2	30
Former Yugoslavia	51	0	2	.	6	.	9
Non EU Europe	1,607	109	75	157	107	10	458
North Africa	78	9	.	.	.	.	9
South Africa	276	22	2	4	.	.	28
Rest of Africa	264	9	3	1	.	.	13
Israel	202	14	.	3	.	1	18
Other Middle East	365	17	9	3	.	.	29
Hong Kong	170	9	4	.	.	.	13
India	195	10	.	2	.	.	11
Japan	464	75	6	12	.	.	93
Rest of Asia	551	59	6	28	.	.	94
Australia	615	87	47	28	.	.	162
New Zealand	136	24	9	5	.	.	39
Caribbean	94	4	3	.	.	.	7
Central & South America	209	68	8	33	.	.	109
Rest of the World	9	3	.	.	.	.	3
Other Countries	3,627	408	97	120	.	1	627
Total World	17,831	2,997	1,936	1,411	772	261	7,378

4.09 Number of visits and spending by gender and purpose of visit 2000

	Male				Female			
	Leisure		Business		Leisure		Business	
	visits (thousands)	spending (£ million)	visits (thousands)	spending (£ million)	visits (thousands)	spending (£ million)	visits (thousands)	spending (£ million)
Canada	319	166	75	78	364	187	15	14
USA	1,485	876	759	728	1,643	930	210	218
North America	1,803	1,043	834	806	2,007	1,117	225	231
Austria	73	29	44	15	100	41	11	4
Belgium	342	58	322	84	270	55	63	21
Denmark	143	48	120	52	131	59	27	11
Finland	30	10	56	21	42	24	26	11
France	987	244	878	155	1,034	239	188	47
Germany	943	309	810	251	878	279	126	48
Greece	77	60	37	24	100	78	11	5
Irish Republic	745	201	397	150	797	175	140	45
Italy	324	138	243	121	335	180	47	33
Luxembourg	22	7	12	4	16	2	2	2
Netherlands	434	105	535	157	398	88	73	24
Portugal	52	25	48	18	62	23	12	7
Spain	289	160	251	101	278	127	32	20
Sweden	158	71	182	79	208	89	54	38
EU Europe	4,617	1,512	3,934	1,232	4,648	1,509	821	317
Cyprus	22	14	6	6	36	58	2	1
Gibraltar	14	8	2	0	7	3	1	0
Iceland	18	9	8	6	20	11	1	1
Malta	20	9	11	5	17	9	1	1
Norway	169	57	90	46	178	71	18	9
Switzerland	180	92	170	89	195	87	29	21
Turkey	22	31	22	22	22	29	12	10
Central & Eastern Europe	134	55	180	52	144	46	45	28
Former USSR	63	56	53	107	67	49	21	21
Former Yugoslavia	17	11	19	11	18	35	6	6
Non EU Europe	665	340	560	343	703	397	138	99
North Africa	37	31	23	46	21	20	6	10
South Africa	114	74	48	51	133	82	10	8
Rest of Africa	108	130	54	86	105	117	11	11
Israel	73	40	50	41	92	48	5	3
Other Middle East	197	346	66	136	127	210	4	5
Hong Kong	68	58	31	33	74	53	10	9
India	78	44	57	50	64	36	7	4
Japan	195	144	96	100	247	192	19	20
Rest of Asia	261	204	138	163	222	172	24	35
Australia	333	218	57	63	372	215	15	21
New Zealand	75	39	14	26	83	63	2	1
Caribbean	44	52	18	17	36	29	3	2
Central & South America	121	97	34	61	151	110	9	15
Rest of the World	5	9	2	1	4	4	0	0
Other Countries	1,712	1,487	688	875	1,731	1,352	122	145
Total World	8,798	4,382	6,016	3,256	9,089	4,375	1,306	792

4.10 Number of visits and spending by age group 2000

	Age 0-15		Age 16-24		Age 25-34		Age 35-44	
	visits (thousands)	spending (£ million)	visits (thousands)	spending (£ million)	visits (thousands)	spending (£ million)	visits (thousands)	spending (£ million)
Canada	38	11	72	33	118	82	118	62
USA	199	77	465	321	698	459	826	609
North America	237	89	538	354	816	541	944	671
Austria	31	9	40	22	49	19	46	15
Belgium	80	9	125	26	224	63	273	58
Denmark	25	5	44	34	114	42	104	35
Finland	6	3	23	10	52	23	35	12
France	387	54	450	156	711	170	721	141
Germany	210	60	379	149	676	196	737	218
Greece	8	2	44	41	59	38	44	24
Irish Republic	117	17	210	57	568	152	445	147
Italy	89	43	132	79	253	131	221	90
Luxembourg	8	1	4	1	8	3	16	5
Netherlands	68	10	132	34	385	116	415	113
Portugal	10	3	24	9	45	19	42	14
Spain	41	16	119	104	234	105	204	81
Sweden	29	10	69	51	149	66	135	52
EU Europe	1,111	243	1,793	773	3,529	1,145	3,440	1,005
Cyprus	3	1	9	17	15	15	12	9
Gibraltar	1	0	2	1	6	2	6	3
Iceland	0	0	6	2	15	10	10	5
Malta	2	1	4	2	8	3	9	6
Norway	26	7	71	39	95	38	90	33
Switzerland	17	5	65	54	145	74	163	77
Turkey	8	9	9	26	20	19	20	17
Central & Eastern Europe	31	14	88	31	136	53	148	47
Former USSR	23	9	24	25	50	118	51	43
Former Yugoslavia	3	1	10	34	13	7	13	8
Non EU Europe	114	48	288	229	503	339	522	246
North Africa	8	5	6	5	20	36	18	25
South Africa	14	8	35	34	51	31	60	39
Rest of Africa	17	9	20	16	47	53	76	107
Israel	19	9	25	13	42	27	42	24
Other Middle East	39	46	32	52	85	151	99	167
Hong Kong	14	8	10	11	57	52	49	34
India	12	12	17	10	37	22	50	37
Japan	23	25	123	107	142	115	109	89
Rest of Asia	41	27	63	77	161	158	158	151
Australia	33	13	83	54	160	93	119	80
New Zealand	5	1	20	7	34	27	27	35
Caribbean	2	1	5	11	24	13	22	17
Central & South America	17	13	65	56	84	92	58	57
Rest of the World	.	0	1	0	2	2	3	3
Other Countries	244	176	504	453	946	871	891	864
Total World	1,706	555	3,123	1,809	5,793	2,897	5,797	2,786

4.10 Number of visits and spending by age group 2000

	Age 45-54		Age 55-64		Age 65 and over		All visits	
	visits (thousands)	spending (£ million)	visits (thousands)	spending (£ million)	visits (thousands)	spending (£ million)	visits (thousands)	spending (£ million)
Canada	174	114	143	85	109	57	772	445
USA	958	656	563	398	387	231	4,097	2,752
North America	1,131	771	706	484	497	289	4,869	3,197
Austria	42	18	14	6	4	1	227	89
Belgium	189	39	80	19	26	5	997	219
Denmark	75	30	46	21	12	3	421	170
Finland	29	13	9	3	1	1	154	65
France	537	91	213	62	68	11	3,087	684
Germany	440	135	236	96	80	31	2,758	887
Greece	40	30	19	23	9	8	224	167
Irish Republic	368	96	227	68	152	32	2,087	570
Italy	149	88	84	31	22	9	949	472
Luxembourg	10	3	4	1	1	0	51	15
Netherlands	272	60	120	29	48	12	1,440	374
Portugal	28	15	18	10	7	3	174	73
Spain	144	57	71	29	37	17	849	409
Sweden	120	47	72	44	21	7	602	276
EU Europe	2,449	724	1,212	442	487	140	14,020	4,570
Cyprus	10	10	9	5	7	21	66	79
Gibraltar	3	3	5	3	1	0	24	12
Iceland	9	7	6	4	1	0	47	27
Malta	13	6	6	3	7	2	49	23
Norway	108	45	36	15	29	7	455	183
Switzerland	114	44	53	25	21	10	579	289
Turkey	13	14	6	6	1	1	78	91
Central & Eastern Europe	87	29	10	4	4	3	504	180
Former USSR	40	32	9	3	7	2	204	232
Former Yugoslavia	16	11	3	2	1	0	60	83
Non EU Europe	415	202	145	69	79	47	2,066	1,180
North Africa	20	22	12	14	2	2	87	108
South Africa	72	48	42	27	30	27	304	215
Rest of Africa	67	97	36	38	13	25	277	345
Israel	41	20	31	18	20	23	220	132
Other Middle East	100	188	32	82	8	11	394	696
Hong Kong	41	32	11	11	1	7	183	154
India	50	30	27	18	12	4	206	134
Japan	99	91	48	23	14	7	557	456
Rest of Asia	145	104	58	43	18	14	645	574
Australia	179	131	130	86	72	60	777	517
New Zealand	40	29	29	19	20	12	174	129
Caribbean	24	35	17	9	6	15	101	100
Central & South America	56	38	25	16	12	11	317	283
Rest of the World	4	9	1	1	.	.	11	14
Other Countries	939	871	501	405	229	219	4,253	3,859
Total World	4,934	2,567	2,565	1,400	1,291	694	25,209	12,805

4.11 Number of visits, nights and spending by UK region of visit 2000

	Total Purposes			Holiday	*of which inclusive tour*	Business	Visiting friends or relatives	Other
	Visits (000s)	Nights (000s)	Spending (£million)	Visits (000s)	*Visits (000s)*	Visits (000s)	Visits (000s)	Visits (000s)
Bedfordshire	199	1,660	91	33	*2*	57	92	17
Berkshire	547	3,768	198	123	*37*	236	153	35
Bristol UA	358	1,981	99	95	*17*	126	115	22
Buckinghamshire	266	1,814	95	61	*1*	94	93	18
Cambridgeshire	466	3,987	197	154	*14*	133	111	69
Cheshire	237	1,431	75	74	*22*	68	76	18
Cornwall	256	2,042	77	168	*27*	11	65	12
Cumbria	220	1,021	52	137	*31*	23	53	7
Derbyshire	154	923	45	34	*0*	51	56	13
Devon	450	3,779	135	230	*62*	37	129	54
Dorset	317	3,340	139	116	*26*	37	109	55
Durham	84	832	36	27	*5*	16	34	6
East Sussex	518	4,527	198	218	*51*	81	146	73
East Yorkshire	18	163	4	4	*.*	2	12	.
Essex	417	2,959	144	105	*16*	114	156	42
Gloucestershire	255	1,348	61	115	*14*	50	84	7
Hampshire	503	3,819	169	176	*33*	125	164	38
Hereford/Worcs	150	1,040	37	51	*8*	31	59	9
Hertfordshire	356	2,909	119	81	*7*	102	139	33
Hull UA	44	539	18	8	*1*	7	19	10
Isle of Wight	58	412	17	21	*2*	10	14	13
Kent	760	5,171	195	299	*80*	158	221	82
Lancashire	224	1,998	95	68	*6*	49	83	23
Leicestershire	186	1,631	61	34	*0*	56	80	16
Lincolnshire	138	1,065	34	33	*2*	33	67	4
London	13,145	82,040	6,901	6,189	*1,917*	3,129	2,498	1,329
Manchester	678	4,636	190	156	*25*	253	183	85
Merseyside	247	1,629	87	81	*19*	64	80	21
Norfolk	142	1,244	53	38	*6*	25	64	15
Northamptonshire	150	853	36	33	*1*	59	53	5
Northumberland	41	232	7	15	*2*	7	19	.
North Yorkshire	427	1,865	89	245	*82*	66	95	22
Nottinghamshire	219	1,910	74	51	*6*	72	80	17
Oxfordshire	533	3,658	175	200	*40*	103	153	77
Shropshire	84	656	19	20	*2*	30	30	5
Somerset	459	2,837	125	256	*44*	52	121	28
South Yorkshire	165	1,415	66	32	*3*	62	56	15
Staffordshire	134	1,068	34	35	*3*	37	53	9
Surrey	676	3,954	212	156	*8*	164	199	158
Suffolk	192	1,304	50	55	*4*	45	71	21
Tees Valley	64	479	17	17	*2*	15	32	1
Tyne & Wear	256	2,543	109	73	*6*	72	81	31
Warwickshire	306	1,722	99	156	*54*	57	66	27
West Midlands	783	6,255	306	134	*33*	391	211	46
West Sussex	276	1,967	100	88	*18*	60	98	29
West Yorkshire	263	2,042	78	63	*6*	84	90	26
Wiltshire	254	2,049	98	82	*11*	69	87	17
England unspecified	86	541	43	41	*5*	18	18	10
Total England	21,484	181,060	11,359	8,142	*2,298*	5,720	5,274	2,348

4.11 Number of visits, nights and spending by UK region of visit 2000

	Total Purposes			Holiday	*of which inclusive tour*	Business	Visiting friends or relatives	Other
	Visits (000s)	Nights (000s)	Spending £million	Visits (000s)	*Visits (000s)*	Visits (000s)	Visits (000s)	Visits (000s)
Argyle	88	394	23	59	*9*	4	24	1
Borders	26	75	3	18	*2*	0	7	.
Central	100	468	21	69	*20*	7	20	4
Dumfries & Galloway	50	329	15	16	*3*	8	24	2
Fife	88	504	49	49	*14*	8	27	5
Grampian	172	1,132	45	104	*26*	22	37	8
Greater Glasgow	502	3,326	170	223	*67*	100	152	26
Highlands	407	1,618	96	335	*84*	14	50	8
Islands	18	118	5	14	*2*	1	2	.
Lothian	939	4,412	265	614	*190*	116	140	69
Strathclyde	99	724	44	57	*10*	14	26	1
Tayside	149	887	37	96	*19*	13	35	5
Scotland unspecified	51	405	16	44	*12*	2	4	1
Total Scotland	1,689	14,394	789	898	*239*	266	418	108
Aberconway/Colwyn	105	404	20	64	*36*	13	19	8
Anglesey	41	95	4	24	*1*	4	12	1
Blaenau Gwent	9	47	2	2	*0*	6	1	0
Bridgend	24	157	5	7	*0*	9	8	0
Caernarfonshire/Merionethshire	94	479	18	61	*20*	1	22	11
Caerphilly	5	34	0	3	*.*	.	1	1
Cardiff	243	974	52	118	*48*	57	47	20
Cardiganshire	30	141	5	21	*2*	1	6	2
Carmarthenshire	48	385	13	24	*3*	1	15	7
Denbighshire	66	406	22	44	*15*	3	15	4
Flintshire	10	124	3	2	*1*	2	6	0
Merthyr Tydfil	7	21	1	2	*2*	3	.	2
Monmouthshire	49	300	14	23	*1*	13	13	1
Neath/Port Talbot	11	43	2	5	*1*	1	5	1
Newport	39	212	7	15	*7*	12	10	1
Pembrokeshire	105	541	34	64	*14*	11	24	7
Powys	41	292	10	26	*4*	3	11	2
Rhondda	25	244	8	4	*0*	1	19	1
Swansea	88	750	30	41	*14*	20	18	10
Torfaen	8	115	3	0	*0*	2	6	.
Vale of Glamorgan	29	373	7	10	*1*	3	4	12
Wrexham	13	35	2	5	*3*	3	4	1
Wales unspecified	15	79	3	8	*1*	2	5	1
Total Wales	980	6,261	267	483	*160*	166	244	86
Northern Ireland	296	1,409	107	53	*29*	76	110	57
Nights spent Travelling	164	190	6	37	*2*	68	7	51
Isle of Man	21	127	12	11	*4*	3	5	1
Channel Islands	37	317	23	21	*5*	4	8	4
UK area unknown	1	2	0	0	*0*	1	.	0
All staying Visits	23,211	203,759	12,562	8,770	*2,493*	6,099	5,776	2,567
Nil Nights	1,997	0	110	530	*.*	1,227	61	179
All visits to the UK	25,209	203,759	12,672	9,300	*2,493*	7,325	5,837	2,746

Spending by residents of the Channel Islands and transit passengers is excluded from this table.

Chapter 5

UK residents' visits abroad 2000

- *Nearly 57 million visits in 2000 with spending of £24.3 billion*

- *Over 41 million visits within EU Europe accounting for 72 per cent of all visits abroad but only 55 per cent of total spending*

- *Over 36 million holiday visits accounting for 65 per cent of all visits abroad and the same proportion of total spending*

- *France and Spain by far the most popular destinations with over 11 million visits each and spending of over £3 billion and £4 billion respectively*

- *Over 4 million visits to the USA, making it the third most popular destination, taking over this position from the Irish Republic*

UK residents' visits abroad in 2000 by country or region visited

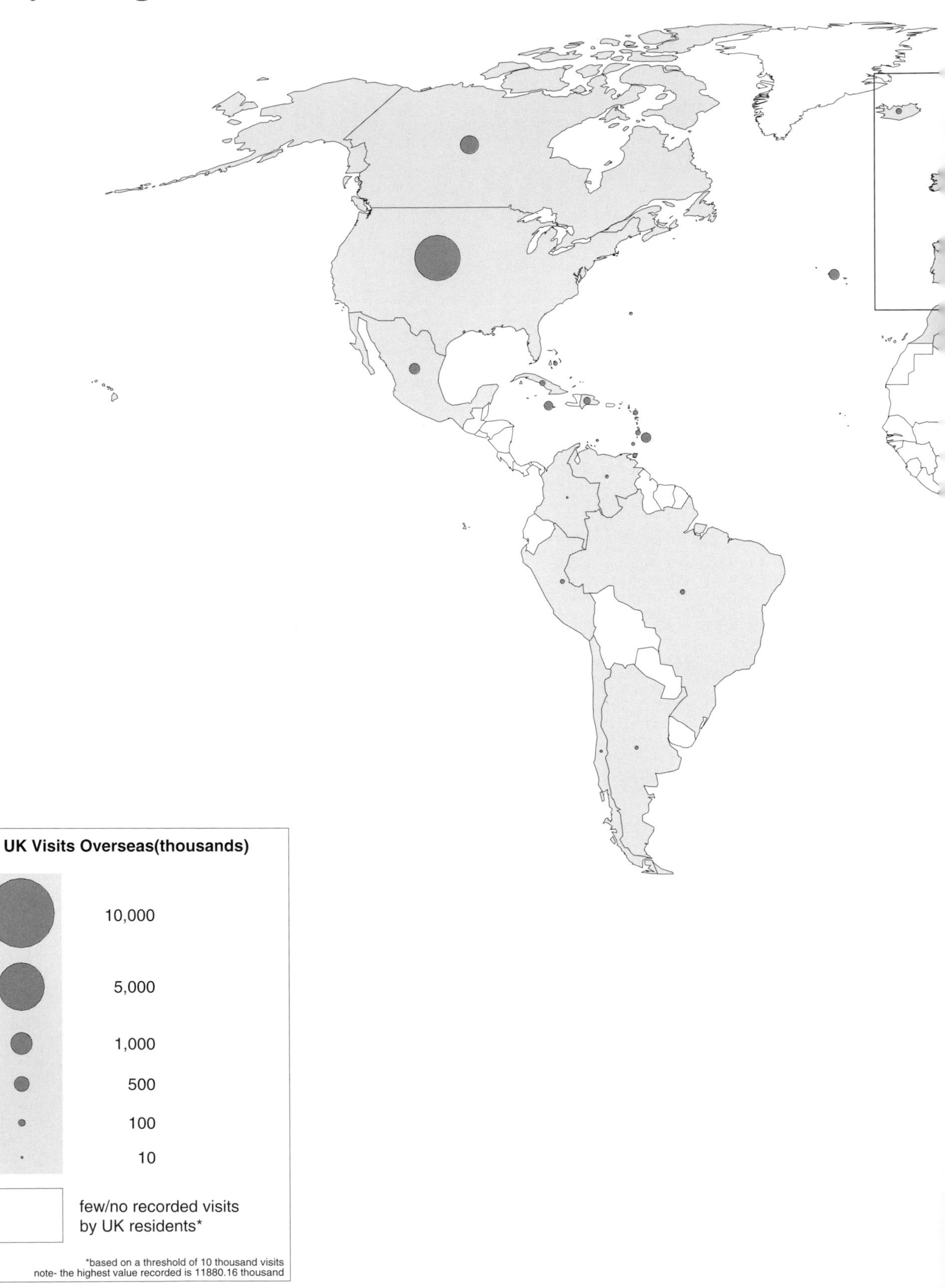

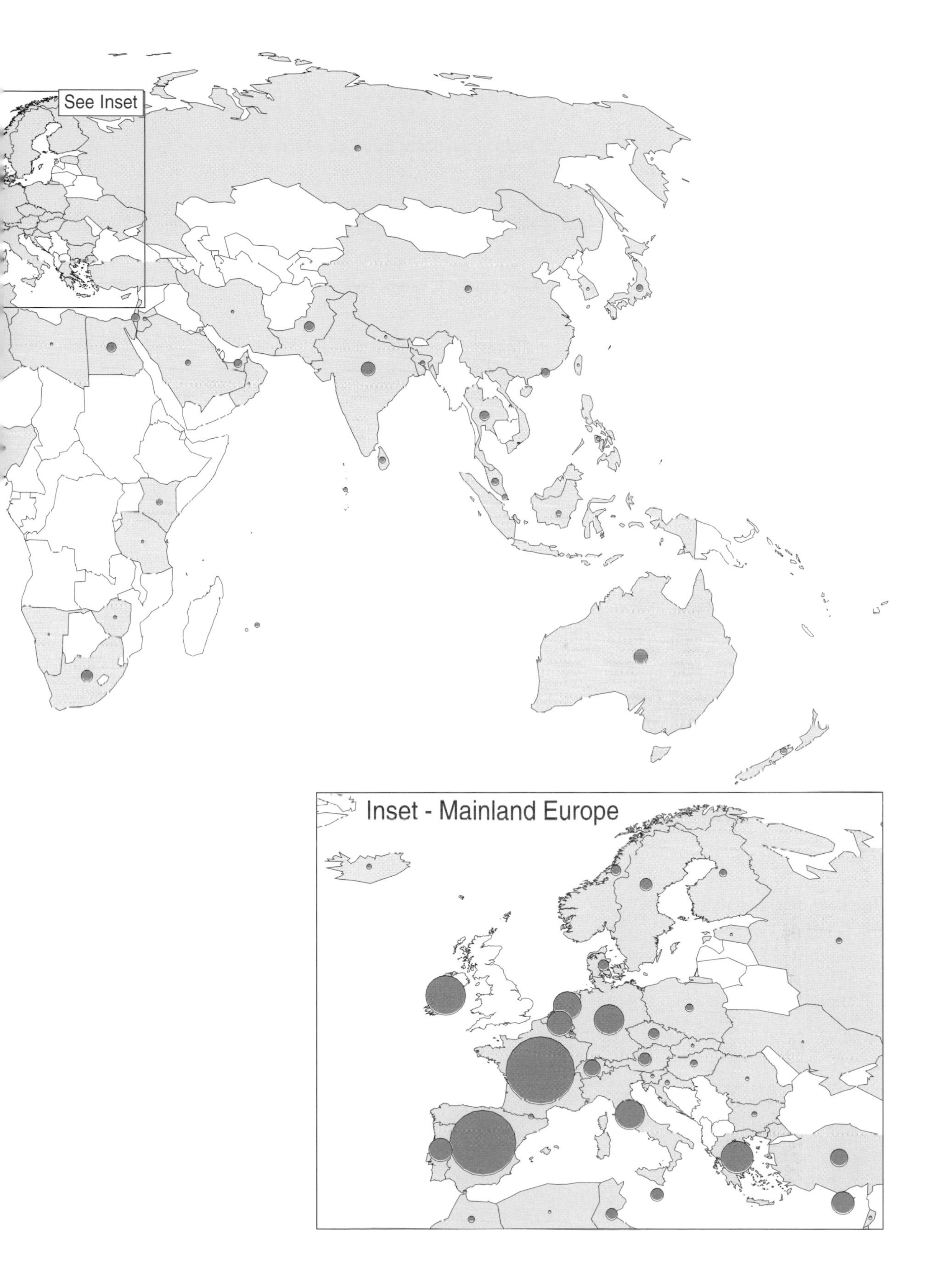
See Inset
Inset - Mainland Europe

Chapter 5

UK residents' visits abroad 2000

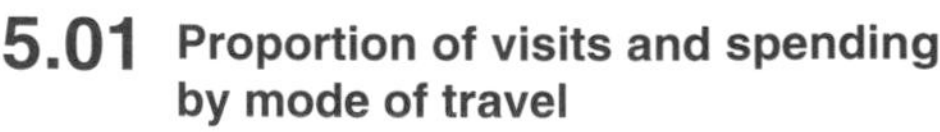

5.01 Proportion of visits and spending by mode of travel

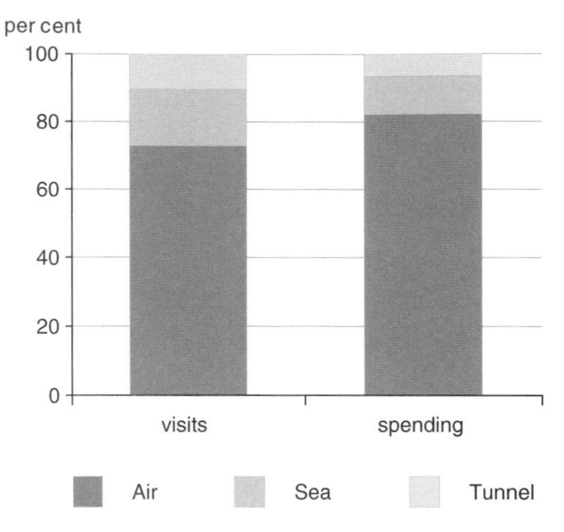

5.02 Proportion of visits and spending by area of visit

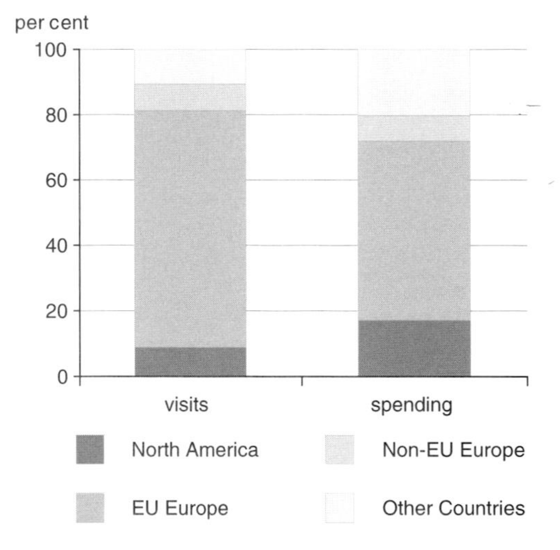

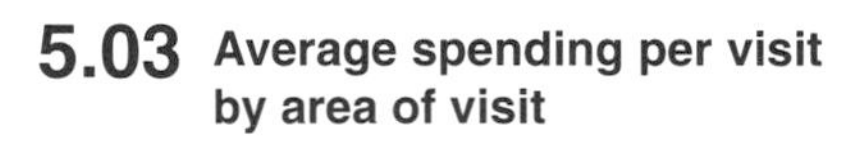

5.03 Average spending per visit by area of visit

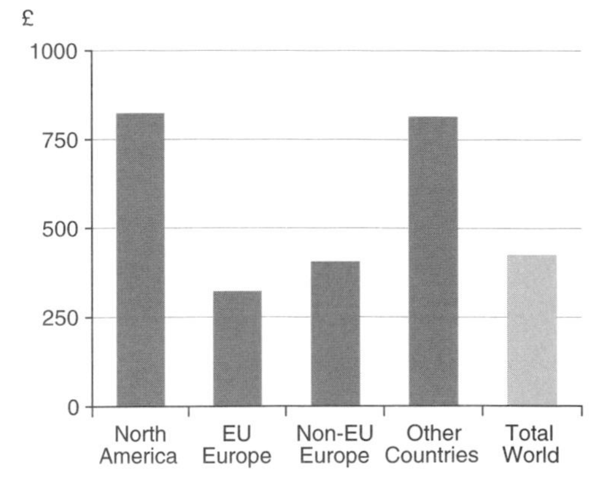

In 2000, UK residents made 56.8 million visits abroad and spent £24.3 billion, an average of £426 per visit. This chapter examines some of the characteristics exhibited by these travellers.

Visits and spending by mode of travel

Table 5.01 provides a breakdown of visits and spending by UK residents by mode of travel, area of the world visited and reason for visit. Air travel was the most popular mode of transport, accounting for 73 per cent of all visits and 82 per cent of spending (**figure 5.01**), with an average spend per visit of £481. By comparison, the average spend per visit for trips made by sea was only £286 and for trips made via the Channel Tunnel £272. These differences are due to a combination of factors, including the area of the world visited, the reason for the visit and the longer average duration of visits made by air (12 nights) compared with sea visits (7 nights) and visits made via the Channel Tunnel (4 nights) (not shown in table).

Visits and spending by area of visit

Figure 5.02 shows that EU Europe was the most popular area of visit for UK residents. Although this region accounted for 72 per cent of all visits abroad, it only accounted for 55 per cent of spending. In comparison, UK residents travelling to North America accounted for only 9 per cent of visits but 17 per cent of spending. This region accounted for the highest average spend per visit at £824, while visits to EU Europe had the lowest spend per visit at £323 (**figure 5.03**). The high spend per visit to North America was due to a high average spend per day, which at £58 was the highest of any region of the world. Spend per visit to 'Other Countries' was also high at £816, however this was a result of travellers to this region staying for longer periods, on average 23 nights, rather than a high spend per day. Visits to EU Europe were the shortest at only 7 nights per visit on average and spend per day was £43 resulting in the lowest spend per visit.

Visits by spending and purpose of visit

Holidays continue to account for the largest proportion of visits by UK residents (**figure 5.04**). In 2000, 65 per cent of all visits abroad were holidays. Around two-thirds of all air and sea visits made were for a holiday compared with less than half of visits made via the tunnel. Business was the next most popular reason for visits abroad accounting for 16 per cent of visits. Business accounted for 17 per cent of visits by air and tunnel but only 10 per cent of sea visits. Twenty eight per cent of all visits made via the tunnel were for miscellaneous reasons,which is explained by the large number of shopping trips made to France and Belgium.

While holidays accounted for around the same proportion of visits as spending (65 per cent), business visits accounted for 20 per cent of spending but only 16 per cent of visits. The average spend per visit for business trips was £533 while that for holiday visits was only £430. As expected, visits to friends or relatives resulted in the lowest spend per visit at only £315, three-fifths of average spending for those on business trips.

5.04 Number of visits by purpose and mode of travel

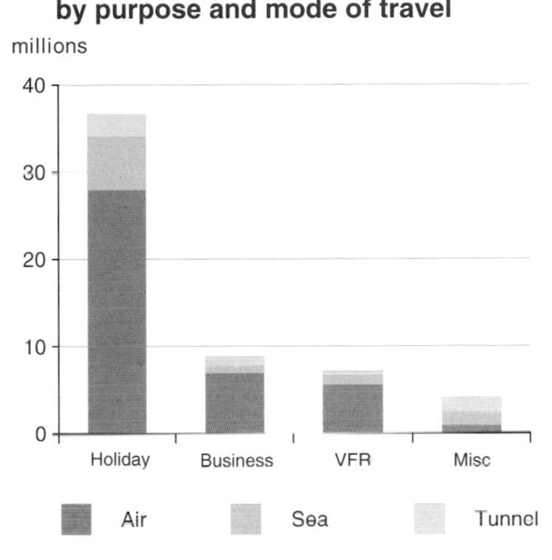

Visits and spending by quarter

Table 5.02 gives a breakdown of visits and spending by UK residents abroad for each quarter in 2000, by region and purpose of visit. There were almost twice as many visits in quarter three (July to September) as there were in quarter one (January to March). Holiday visits showed the greatest seasonality with 13.9 million holiday visits in quarter three and only 5.8 million visits in quarter one (**figure 5.05**). Visits to friends or family were most common in quarter three with 2.3 million visits, while business visits showed little seasonality. Spending by UK residents abroad showed the same seasonal pattern as visits, peaking at £8.5 billion in quarter three. This represented just over a third of spending for the year, a similar proportion as visits occurring in quarter three.

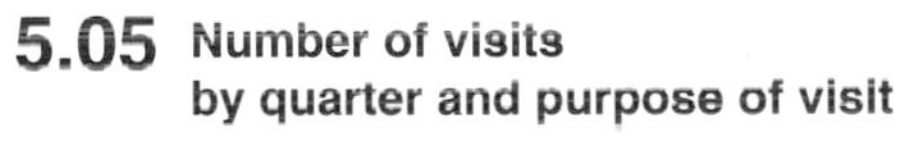

5.05 Number of visits by quarter and purpose of visit

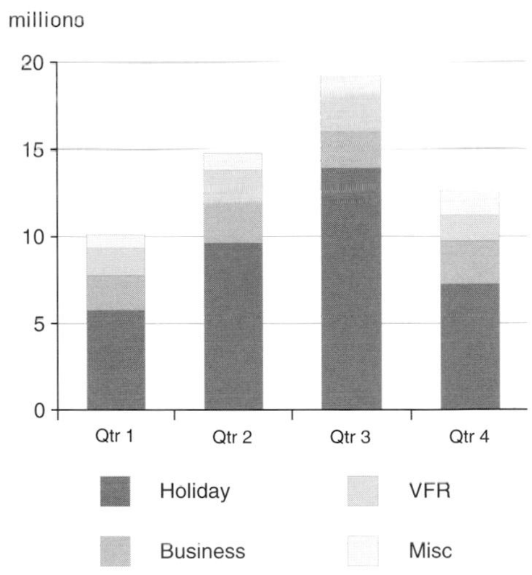

Visits, nights and spending by country of visit

Table 5.04 provides a breakdown of UK residents' visits abroad by country and purpose of visit. **Figure 5.06** overleaf shows the top ten countries visited by UK residents in 2000 and the resulting spend. France and Spain were by far the most popular destinations with 11.9 million and 11.2 million visits respectively. Together these two countries accounted for over 40 per cent of visits. Nine out of the top ten countries visited were in EU Europe, the exception was the USA which with 4.3 million visits was the third most popular destination taking over this position in 2000 from the Irish Republic. Within non-EU Europe, Cyprus was the most popular destination with 1.3 million visits, while the Caribbean was the most popular destination among 'Other Countries' accounting for 0.8 million visits.

5.06 Visits and spending for top 10 counties visited

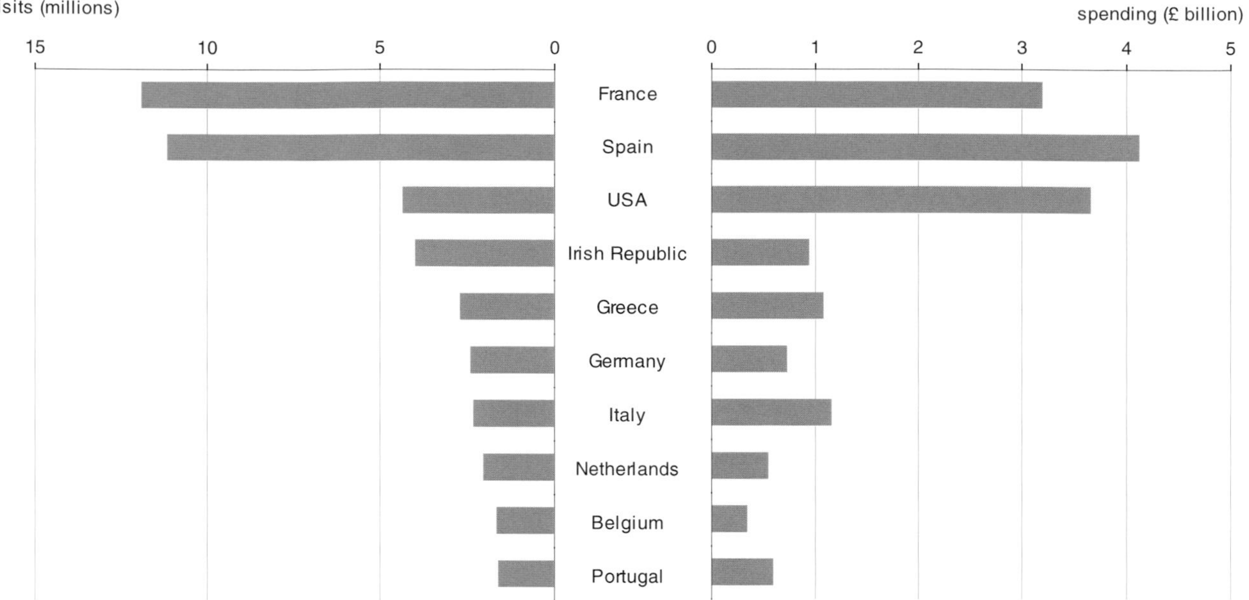

5.07 Proportion of visits by country and purpose of visit

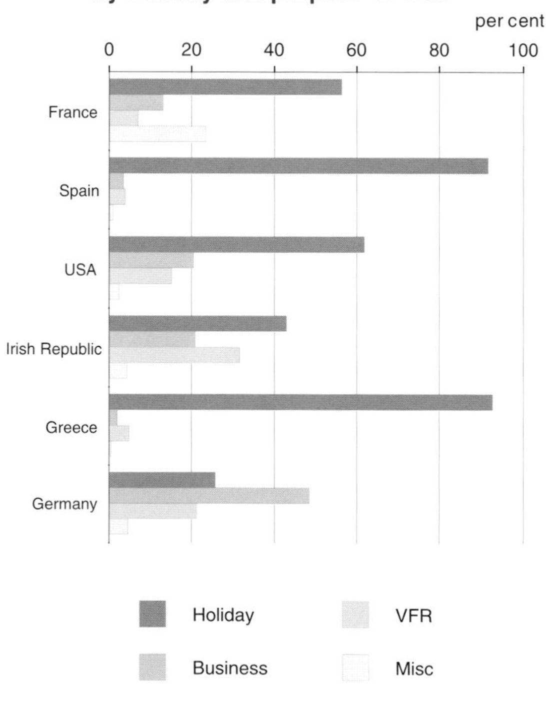

Although the highest number of visits was made to France, it was visitors to Spain who spent the greatest amount of money. A total of £4.1 billion was spent in Spain in 2000, followed by £3.7 billion in the USA and £3.2 billion in France. Italy was the seventh most popular country visited but accounted for the fourth highest spending with £1.2 billion. Australia, Cyprus and the Caribbean were not in the top ten countries visited but were among the top ten countries with the highest levels of spending. These differences are due to a number of factors, including the purpose of the visit and the length of stay. A total of 122 million nights were spent in Spain, twice as many as were spent in either the USA or France, which resulted in the highest total spend, even though the USA saw the highest spend per day (£60) and the longest average length of visit (14 nights) of these three most popular countries.

Figure 5.07 shows the proportion of visits by purpose of visit made to the most popular destinations. Over 90 per cent of visits to Spain were for holiday purposes, the equivalent of 10.2 million visits, making it the most popular holiday destination for UK residents travelling abroad. France was the second most popular holiday destination with 6.7 million visits, accounting for over half of all visits to this country. Over 90 per cent of visits to Greece were holidays accounting for 2.5 million visits, while the USA had 2.7 million holiday visits accounting for 62 per cent of visits to this country.

A quarter of visits to France were for miscellaneous reasons. This includes personal shopping which was the reason why France in particular had such a high proportion of visits in this category. Just over 2.4 million visits were made for personal shopping to France out of a total of 2.8 million miscellaneous visits.

UK residents made a total of 1.3 million visits to friends and family in the Irish Republic during 2000, accounting for a third of all visits to the Irish Republic, making it the most common destination for this purpose of visit. A fifth of all visits made to Germany were visits to friends or family, a total of 0.5 million making it the fourth most popular destination for visiting friends or family after the Irish Republic, France and the USA.

Overall, 1.6 million visits were made to France for business reasons. Germany was the second most frequently visited country for business reasons with 1.2 million visits, making business the most popular reason for visiting this country. Business trips accounted for only 13 per cent of all visits to France compared with almost half of all visits to Germany.

Average length of stay and spending

Table 5.05 provides a detailed breakdown of the average length of stay, spending per visit and spending per day, by country visited and purpose of visit for UK residents travelling abroad.

Figures 5.08 to **5.10** show the relationship between average length of stay, average spend per visit and average spend per day by purpose of visit. The dotted line on each figure represents the overall average for all UK residents travelling abroad in 2000. UK residents visiting friends or relatives stayed the longest on average (15 nights) while those travelling on holiday averaged 11 nights per stay. Both business and miscellaneous trips were much shorter at 5 nights on average. Those on business visits spent the most on average per trip at £533, the equivalent of £97 per day. By comparison, those visiting friends or relatives stayed the longest, on average, but had the lowest average spend per day at only £20.

Table 5.05 shows that visits to New Zealand and Australia were the longest at 47 and 43 nights respectively, mainly due to long holidays being taken in this part of the world. Visits to Bangladesh and Pakistan, included in the table in 'Rest of Asia', were also long, averaging 67 and 47 nights respectively. This was mainly due to long visits to friends

5.08 Average length of stay by purpose of visit

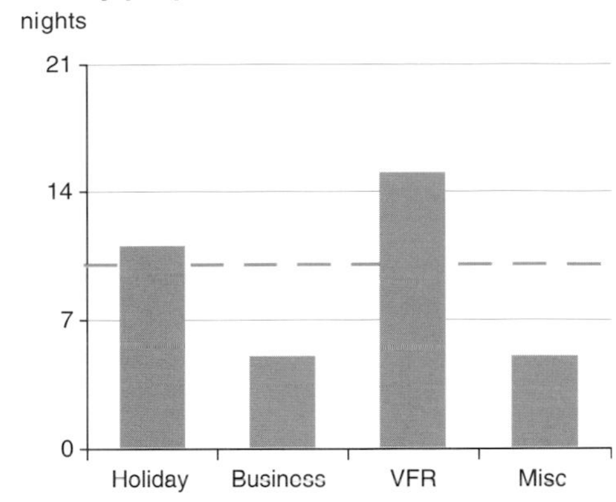

5.09 Average spending per visit by purpose of visit

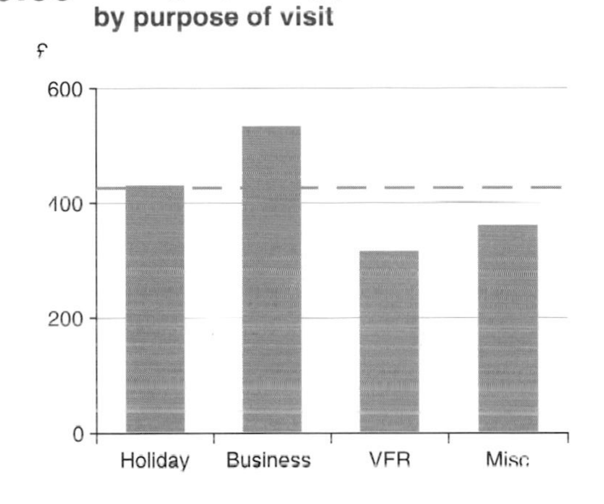

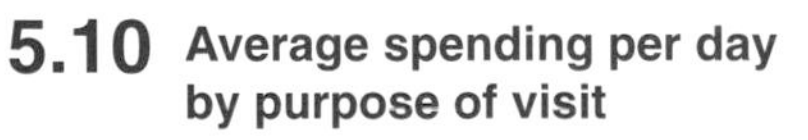

5.10 Average spending per day by purpose of visit

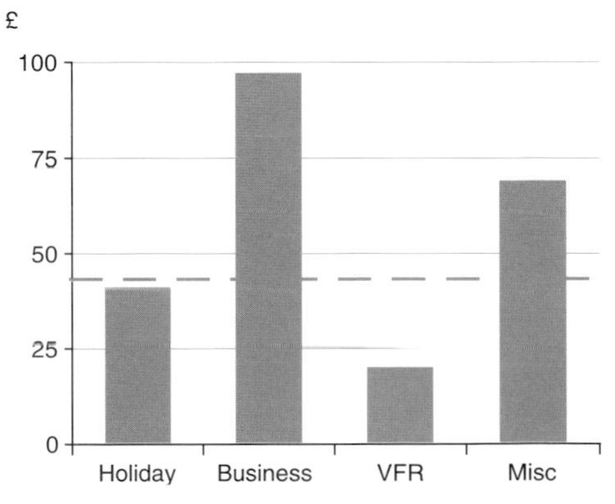

5.11 Visits and spending by length of stay

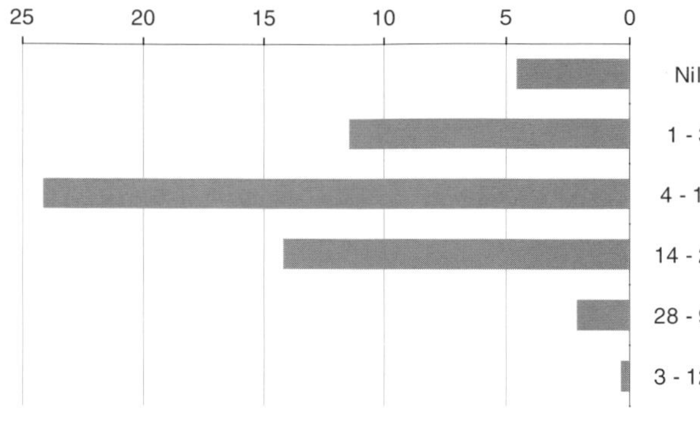

5.12 Proportion of visits to France and Spain by length of stay

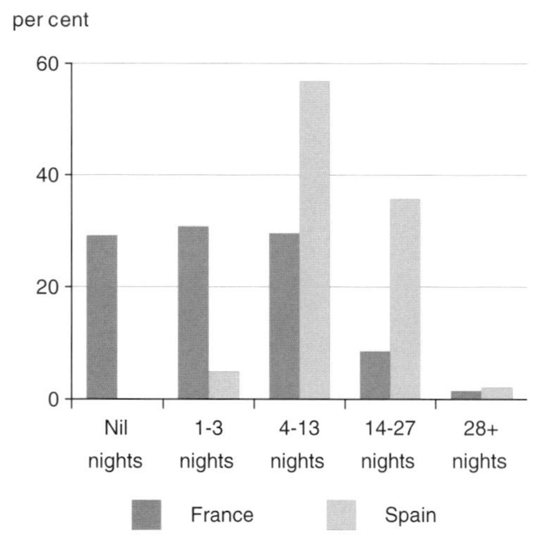

or relatives rather than long holidays. Countries with the highest levels of spending per visit included Australia (£1,472), New Zealand (£1,383) and Japan (£1,002). The high cost of trips to New Zealand and Australia were due to long holidays and visits to friends or family being taken there, whereas 55 thousand business trips to Japan, with an average cost per visit of £1,577, contributed towards the high average cost per visit there. Visitors to Singapore and Thailand, included under 'Rest of Asia', also had high spends per visit (£1,136 and £1,021 respectively).

Visits and spending by length of stay

Table 5.06 gives the breakdown of UK residents' visits and spending abroad by country of visit and length of stay. The distribution of visits and spending by length of stay is shown in **figure 5.11**. Over 24 million visits during 2000 lasted between 4 and 13 nights, accounting for 42 per cent of all visits. A total of £9.3 billion was spent on these visits. Longer trips, between 14 and 27 nights, accounted for 14.2 million visits, 25 per cent of all visits and a total of £8.5 billion, 35 per cent of all spending. Eight per cent of all visits abroad in 2000 were day trips (4.6 million), accounting for just two per cent of spending.

Figure 5.12 shows the proportion of visits made by UK residents to France and Spain, the most popular destinations in 2000, by length of stay. There is a striking difference in length of stay. Overall, trips to France tend to be shorter than trips to Spain with 90 per cent of all visits to France being 13 nights or less while only 62 per cent of trips to Spain fall into this category. The two main differences seem to be the relatively high number of day trips made to France (3.5 million to France in 2000 compared with seven thousand to Spain) and the large number of visits to Spain lasting between 14 and 27 nights (4.0 million compared with 1.0 million to France).

Visits by port

Table 5.07 provides a detailed breakdown of the number of UK residents' visits by each of the main ports of entry into the UK by country of visit in 2000. **Figure 5.13** shows the ports with the greatest number of visits. Together, these ports accounted for three-quarters of all visits by UK residents travelling abroad in 2000; Heathrow and Gatwick alone accounting for over a third of visits. Overall, airports accounted for 73 per cent of all visits, sea routes a further 17 per cent and the Channel Tunnel 10 per cent. For the first time in 2000, Stansted accounted for more visits than Birmingham, 3.3 million compared with 2.7 million.

5.13 Number of visits by UK port

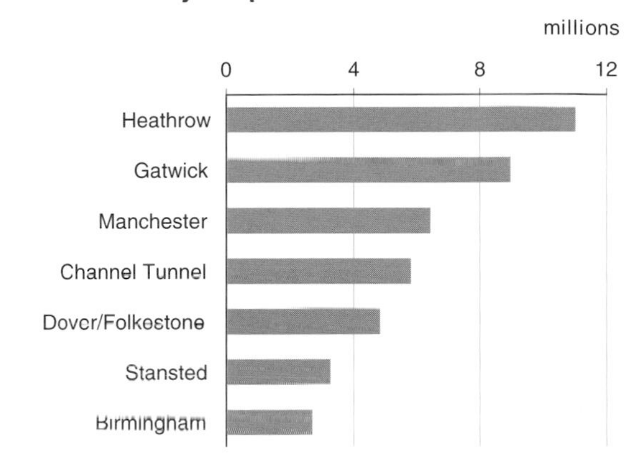

The Channel Tunnel saw more visits by UK residents to EU Europe than any other port in 2000. Visits to France, our most popular destination, were most likely to be made by sea or the Channel Tunnel whereas visits to Spain, our second most popular destination, were most likely to be made from either Manchester or Gatwick airport

Visits by vehicle type

Table 5.08 gives the breakdown of UK residents' visits abroad by type of vehicle used and country of visit. Of the 15.4 million visits made by sea or via the tunnel in 2000, 55 per cent were made by private vehicles, 20 per cent were made by 'foot' and 17 per cent by coach. The most popular destination for foot passengers was France with 1.9 million visits. Belgium also had a substantial number of foot passengers with 0.4 million visits. There were more than four times as many visits to France by private vehicle as there were by coach but only slightly more visits to Spain were made by private vehicle than by coach. This perhaps indicates that the length of journey has a large effect on the mode of travel used. The Irish Republic was the second most popular destination for those travelling with private vehicles, with 0.8 million visits in 2000.

5.14 Number of visits by gender and purpose

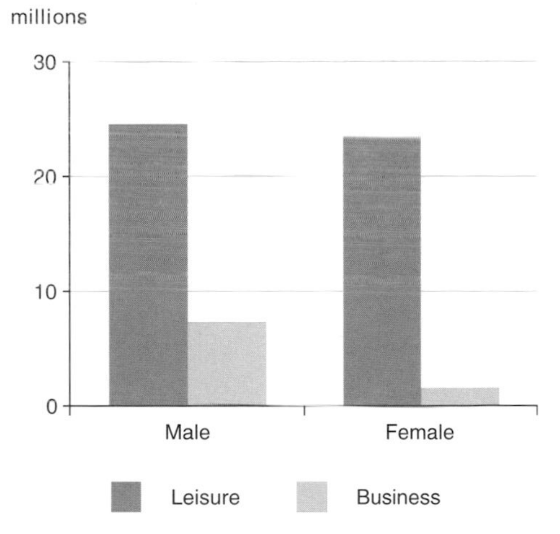

Visits and spending by gender

Table 5.09 provides a breakdown of UK residents' visits and spending abroad by gender and country of visit for both business and leisure purposes. Males made a total of 31.8 million visits abroad in 2000, while females made 25.0 million visits, 21 per cent less than males. Males spent a total of £14.4 billion, £4.5 billion more than females. **Figure 5.14** shows that males and females made a similar number of

5.15 Proportion of visits and spending by age group

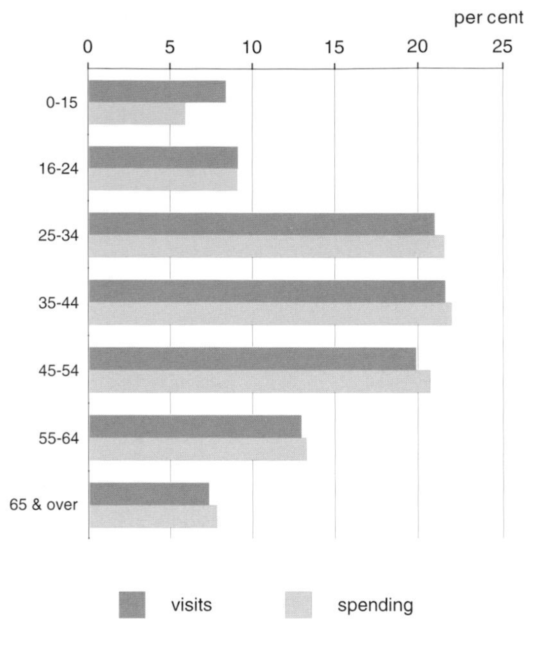

5.16 Proportion of visits by area of residence and purpose

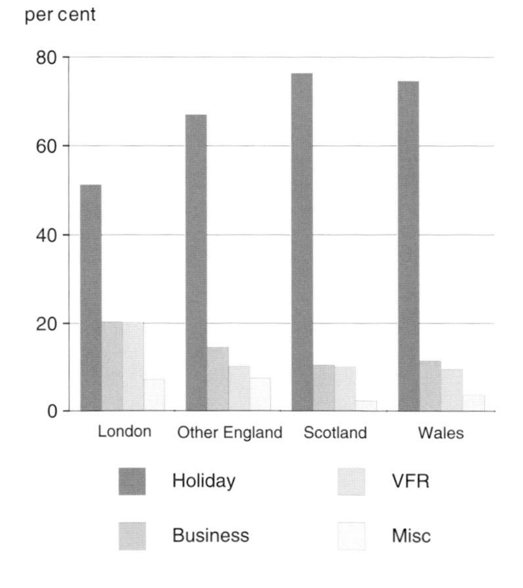

leisure visits but that males made over four times as many business visits as females.

Even though females stayed longer on average than males on business trips (7 days compared to 5 days), males spent more than females per day (on average £102 compared to £81 - not shown in table). This resulted in males and females on business trips spending on average about the same per visit.

Visits and spending by age group

Table 5.10 gives a detailed breakdown of UK residents' visits and spending abroad by age group and country of visit. A similar proportion of visits abroad were made by those in the 25-34, 35-44 and 45-54 age groups, together accounting for three-fifths of all visits (**figure 5.15**). Of trips made by children (0-15 age group), a higher proportion were made to EU Europe and a lower proportion to 'Other countries' than all other age groups. This youngest age group also spent the least amount of money in total (£1.4 billion), less than those in the oldest group (£1.9 billion) even though they made more visits (4.7 million compared with 4.1 million).

Visits and spending by region of residence

Tables 5.03 and **5.11** provide breakdowns of UK residents' visits and spending abroad by region of residence. **Figure 5.16** shows that the proportion of trips by purpose made by UK residents abroad varies depending on where they live in the UK. Around three quarters of all visits abroad made by those living in Scotland or Wales were holidays compared with only half of the trips abroad made by those living in London. A fifth of all trips made abroad by those living in London were for business reasons.

5.01 Number of visits and spending by mode of travel and purpose of visit 2000

	Air		Sea		Channel Tunnel		Total	
	visits (thousands)	spending (£ million)	visits (thousands)	spending (£ million)	visits (thousands)	spending (£ million)	visits (thousands)	spending (£ million)
North America								
Holiday	3,051	2,511	2	1	.	.	3,052	2,512
of which inclusive tour	*1,131*	*1,013*	*0*	*0*	.	.	*1,131*	*1,013*
Business	963	1,015	.	.	1	1	965	1,017
Visiting friends or relatives	922	457	0	0	1	2	924	459
Miscellaneous	120	182	.	.	.	.	120	182
All visits	5,056	4,166	2	1	2	4	5,060	4,170
EU Europe								
Holiday	18,505	6,805	5,625	1,509	2,637	753	26,768	9,067
of which inclusive tour	*11,278*	*4,217*	*2,197*	*649*	*1,069*	*326*	*14,544*	*5,192*
Business	4,529	1,647	906	358	985	384	6,420	2,390
Visiting friends or relatives	2,774	579	1,008	176	479	87	4,262	842
Miscellaneous	499	409	1,561	276	1,630	309	3,691	995
All visits	26,307	9,440	9,101	2,320	5,732	1,533	41,140	13,294
Non EU Europe								
Holiday	2,990	1,222	168	49	36	19	3,193	1,290
of which inclusive tour	*2,153*	*877*	*61*	*23*	*12*	*7*	*2,226*	*907*
Business	749	383	23	7	6	14	778	404
Visiting friends or relatives	523	126	32	11	12	1	567	138
Miscellaneous	77	43	3	2	4	1	84	46
All visits	4,339	1,773	226	69	58	35	4,623	1,878
Other Countries								
Holiday	3,356	2,541	311	368	4	6	3,671	2,915
of which inclusive tour	*1,848*	*1,146*	*303*	*360*	*2*	*5*	*2,154*	*1,511*
Business	705	914	3	7	1	0	709	922
Visiting friends or relatives	1,420	817	1	0	2	1	1,426	819
Miscellaneous	205	254	1	0	1	0	207	254
All visits	5,689	4,526	317	376	8	8	6,014	4,909
Total World								
Holiday	27,901	13,079	6,106	1,927	2,677	778	36,685	15,784
of which inclusive tour	*10,411*	*7,252*	*2,561*	*1,032*	*1,083*	*338*	*20,055*	*8,623*
Business	6,946	3,960	933	373	993	399	8,872	4,732
Visiting friends or relatives	5,643	1,979	1,042	188	494	92	7,178	2,258
Miscellaneous	902	888	1,565	278	1,635	311	4,102	1,477
All visits	41,392	19,905	9,646	2,766	5,799	1,580	56,837	24,251

Number of visits and spending by quarter of the year and purpose of visit 2000

	January - March		April - June		July - September		October - December	
	visits (thousands)	spending (£ million)	visits (thousands)	spending (£ million)	visits (thousands)	spending (£ million)	visits (thousands)	spending (£ million)
North America								
Holiday	615	424	739	602	975	878	724	608
of which inclusive tour	*214*	*149*	*322*	*289*	*335*	*357*	*260*	*218*
Business	209	207	262	283	200	221	293	306
Visiting friends or relatives	179	74	215	109	310	160	220	117
Miscellaneous	21	23	28	86	30	34	41	40
All visits	1,023	728	1,245	1,079	1,515	1,291	1,278	1,072
EU Europe								
Holiday	3,907	1,182	7,096	2,213	10,694	4,175	5,071	1,497
of which inclusive tour	*2,019*	*641*	*3,834*	*1,267*	*5,951*	*2,455*	*2,740*	*829*
Business	1,458	509	1,674	627	1,522	568	1,765	686
Visiting friends or relatives	897	156	1,121	230	1,355	284	889	172
Miscellaneous	656	207	880	324	827	173	1,328	290
All visits	6,918	2,054	10,772	3,395	14,398	5,200	9,052	2,645
Non EU Europe								
Holiday	397	139	911	348	1,305	592	580	212
of which inclusive tour	*212*	*66*	*654*	*253*	*947*	*449*	*413*	*140*
Business	161	70	198	90	215	136	205	107
Visiting friends or relatives	127	37	140	33	197	46	103	22
Miscellaneous	20	14	13	8	31	11	21	14
All visits	704	260	1,262	478	1,747	786	909	355
Other Countries								
Holiday	874	790	913	708	954	739	930	677
of which inclusive tour	*446*	*344*	*564*	*380*	*546*	*379*	*597*	*409*
Business	160	219	178	201	169	184	202	318
Visiting friends or relatives	397	224	373	212	397	232	259	152
Miscellaneous	66	65	49	75	57	71	35	44
All visits	1,497	1,297	1,513	1,195	1,577	1,226	1,427	1,191
Total World								
Holiday	5,793	2,535	9,659	3,871	13,928	6,384	7,305	2,994
of which inclusive tour	*2,891*	*1,200*	*5,375*	*2,188*	*7,779*	*3,640*	*4,010*	*1,595*
Business	1,988	1,005	2,313	1,200	2,106	1,110	2,465	1,418
Visiting friends or relatives	1,599	491	1,850	583	2,259	722	1,470	463
Miscellaneous	762	309	970	493	944	288	1,425	388
All visits	10,142	4,339	14,792	6,146	19,236	8,503	12,666	5,263

5.03 Visits and spending by UK region of residence and by area and purpose of visit 2000

	London		Other England		Total England		Scotland		Wales	
	visits (1000s)	spending (£ million)	visits (1000s)	spending (£ million)	visits (1000s)	spending (£ million)	visits (1000s)	spending (£ million)	visits (1000s)	spending (£ million)
North America										
Total Holiday	534	419	2,062	1,714	2,595	2,133	272	228	138	106
of which inclusive tour	*139*	*130*	*840*	*745*	*978*	*875*	*73*	*68*	*69*	*57*
Business	279	354	595	572	874	926	60	59	12	15
Visiting friends or relatives	220	115	544	264	764	380	124	61	27	14
Shopping	0	6	15	10	24	16	1	2	4	2
Miscellanous	22	19	58	99	80	118	6	29	3	4
All visits										
EU Europe	0	0	0	0	0	0	0	0	0	0
Total Holiday	*3,809*	*1,342*	*19,293*	*6,407*	*23,102*	*7,750*	*1,970*	*740*	*1,222*	*413*
of which inclusive tour	1,296	488	11,034	3,876	12,330	4,364	1,398	541	760	261
Business	1,534	611	4,246	1,506	5,780	2,117	231	103	194	114
Visiting friends or relatives	1,335	258	2,361	488	3,696	746	142	29	130	26
Shopping	475	89	2,101	434	2,576	523	12	2	39	5
Miscellanous										
All visits	7,372	2,377	28,659	9,179	36,032	11,557	2,404	896	1,614	566
Non EU Europe	*0*	*0*	*0*	*0*	*0*	*0*	*0*	*0*	*0*	*0*
Total Holiday	519	239	2,240	881	2,759	1,120	271	110	130	47
of which inclusive tour	226	105	1,673	672	1,899	777	221	93	101	36
Business	269	161	446	188	715	349	32	33	20	11
Visiting friends or relatives	197	49	311	76	509	125	33	8	15	4
Shopping										
Miscellanous	31	14	41	27	72	41	5	2	2	1
All visits	*1,018*	*464*	*3,040*	*1,172*	*4,058*	*1,636*	*341*	*154*	*187*	*80*
Other Countries	0	0	0	0	0	0	0	0	0	0
Total Holiday	875	676	2,443	1,906	3,317	2,502	144	119	101	81
of which inclusive tour	327	217	1,595	1,108	1,923	1,325	80	52	72	49
Business	208	247	421	572	630	819	47	66	21	16
Visiting friends or relatives										
Shopping	1	1	5	1	5	2	0	0	.	.
Miscellanous	*66*	*79*	*109*	*117*	*174*	*196*	*16*	*27*	*6*	*11*
All visits	1,673	1,286	3,762	3,067	5,435	4,354	264	242	164	131
Total World	0	0	0	0	0	0	0	0	0	0
Total Holiday	5,736	2,677	26,038	10,909	31,774	13,585	2,658	1,197	1,591	647
of which inclusive tour	1,987	940	15,142	6,401	17,130	7,341	1,772	755	1,003	403

5.04 Number of visits, nights and spending by purpose of visit 2000

	Holiday visits						Business visits		
	total			*of which inclusive tour*					
	visits (thousands)	nights (thousands)	spending (£ million)	*visits (thousands)*	*nights (thousands)*	*spending (£ million)*	visits (thousands)	nights (thousands)	spending (£ million)
Canada	372	5,301	303	*180*	*2,099*	*165*	78	612	55
USA	2,681	38,889	2,209	*951*	*12,489*	*849*	887	7,714	962
North America	3,052	44,189	2,512	*1,131*	*14,589*	*1,013*	965	8,326	1,017
Austria	351	2,859	164	*262*	*2,123*	*120*	63	281	25
Belgium	674	1,567	111	*253*	*765*	*55*	594	1,451	171
Denmark	92	505	31	*11*	*47*	*4*	133	391	38
Finland	28	175	10	*9*	*37*	*5*	89	353	39
France	6,713	45,385	1,946	*2,522*	*17,437*	*811*	1,557	5,483	556
Germany	621	3,757	184	*242*	*1,342*	*81*	1,169	4,305	423
Greece	2,508	29,776	1,006	*2,182*	*24,884*	*867*	54	477	41
Irish Republic	1,702	9,492	438	*348*	*1,766*	*92*	827	2,864	230
Italy	1,526	13,875	777	*777*	*6,690*	*390*	446	2,541	269
Luxembourg	8	18	1	*3*	*10*	*1*	42	89	10
Netherlands	811	3,360	201	*241*	*916*	*70*	791	2,447	273
Portugal	1,444	14,726	533	*863*	*8,314*	*304*	68	357	30
Spain	10,212	109,835	3,614	*6,830*	*70,494*	*2,393*	390	4,303	213
Sweden	77	556	26	.	.	.	197	586	73
EU Europe	26,768	235,886	9,067	*14,544*	*134,825*	*5,192*	6,420	25,928	2,390
Cyprus	1,195	14,374	546	*946*	*10,592*	*439*	19	152	11
Gibraltar	15	93	5	*10*	*49*	*3*	2	34	0
Iceland	54	357	24	*23*	*170*	*12*	18	243	25
Malta	394	4,474	117	*319*	*3,318*	*87*	11	48	4
Norway	125	822	35	*32*	*243*	*18*	77	415	35
Switzerland	324	2,692	153	*107*	*856*	*57*	279	872	132
Turkey	675	8,891	266	*572*	*7,063*	*216*	50	425	31
Central & Eastern Europe	305	2,708	97	*157*	*1,266*	*49*	237	1,426	112
Former USSR	42	449	30	*14*	*124*	*15*	64	495	42
Former Yugoslavia	65	738	18	*47*	*464*	*11*	22	187	12
Non EU Europe	3,193	35,599	1,290	*2,226*	*24,144*	*907*	778	4,298	404
North Africa	625	7,387	253	*526*	*5,203*	*200*	66	1,019	50
South Africa	176	3,439	139	*40*	*632*	*39*	44	477	45
Rest of Africa	190	3,684	159	*106*	*1,819*	*89*	63	1,206	46
Israel	75	962	41	*22*	*202*	*12*	27	169	18
Other Middle East	132	1,594	84	*50*	*439*	*27*	86	850	89
Hong Kong	52	990	40	*14*	*171*	*14*	35	366	59
India	242	6,442	157	*101*	*1,579*	*49*	48	844	70
Japan	17	268	10	*3*	*21*	*1*	55	707	86
Rest of Asia	566	13,581	452	*269*	*4,077*	*201*	144	2,287	284
Australia	211	10,496	394	*29*	*783*	*55*	37	797	63
New Zealand	51	2,092	88	*6*	*189*	*13*	4	177	9
Caribbean	664	9,910	464	*441*	*5,773*	*272*	32	322	31
Central & South America	320	5,465	232	*208*	*3,142*	*146*	68	869	70
Rest of the World	350	4,273	404	*339*	*4,131*	*393*	1	7	1
Other Countries	3,671	70,585	2,915	*2,154*	*28,162*	*1,511*	709	10,097	922
Total World	36,685	386,258	15,784	*20,055*	*201,720*	*8,623*	8,872	48,648	4,732

5.04 Number of visits, nights and spending by purpose of visit 2000

	Visiting friends or relatives			Miscellaneous			Total visits		
	visits (thousands)	nights (thousands)	spending (£ million)	visits (thousands)	nights (thousands)	spending (£ million)	visits (thousands)	nights (thousands)	spending (£ million)
Canada	264	4,927	116	15	566	36	729	11,406	510
USA	659	12,508	343	105	1,899	146	4,331	61,010	3,660
North America	924	17,435	459	120	2,465	182	5,060	72,415	4,170
Austria	41	731	10	13	66	5	467	3,937	205
Belgium	174	858	23	215	272	43	1,657	4,148	347
Denmark	62	447	11	12	83	3	299	1,426	82
Finland	26	237	7	9	37	3	152	802	59
France	835	6,680	165	2,798	2,758	531	11,903	60,306	3,198
Germany	511	4,755	89	110	712	31	2,411	13,529	728
Greece	132	2,583	26	14	324	6	2,709	33,160	1,080
Irish Republic	1,257	8,287	235	175	644	38	3,961	21,287	941
Italy	275	3,231	68	79	723	45	2,327	20,370	1,159
Luxembourg	8	127	1	11	67	3	69	302	14
Netherlands	329	2,285	55	113	369	21	2,044	8,461	550
Portugal	75	869	18	24	413	15	1,612	16,366	597
Spain	439	5,828	114	113	2,019	186	11,154	121,985	4,127
Sweden	98	979	20	5	22	63	377	2,143	182
EU Europe	4,262	37,897	842	3,691	8,511	995	41,140	308,221	13,294
Cyprus	91	1,376	26	6	81	2	1,310	15,983	585
Gibraltar	13	100	2	4	118	2	35	346	9
Iceland	4	30	1	.	.	.	76	630	50
Malta	22	354	6	2	5	0	428	4,882	128
Norway	64	1,374	20	5	168	1	271	2,780	91
Switzerland	144	1,025	31	21	180	3	768	4,769	318
Turkey	44	985	16	6	113	6	775	10,413	319
Central & Eastern Europe	127	1,651	24	31	297	12	700	6,082	246
Former USSR	30	499	6	6	217	17	142	1,660	95
Former Yugoslavia	27	551	7	3	24	1	117	1,501	38
Non EU Europe	567	7,946	138	84	1,203	46	4,623	49,046	1,878
North Africa	64	1,962	15	3	27	1	758	10,396	319
South Africa	95	2,400	48	9	446	13	325	6,762	245
Rest of Africa	86	3,046	55	16	979	15	356	8,915	276
Israel	53	731	19	13	277	12	168	2,140	90
Other Middle East	100	2,577	38	48	1,203	33	366	6,223	244
Hong Kong	84	2,421	45	4	31	3	175	3,808	147
India	162	5,934	87	22	716	17	474	13,936	331
Japan	35	825	13	4	240	2	111	2,041	111
Rest of Asia	385	15,900	224	34	1,351	47	1,129	33,119	1,007
Australia	197	6,724	166	24	2,392	69	470	20,410	692
New Zealand	48	1,962	47	3	828	4	107	5,058	148
Caribbean	79	1,923	44	19	466	25	794	12,622	563
Central & South America	33	773	17	6	287	12	427	7,394	331
Rest of the World	3	88	1	0	9	0	355	4,378	406
Other Countries	1,426	47,266	819	207	9,254	254	6,014	137,202	4,909
Total World	7,178	110,544	2,258	4,102	21,433	1,477	56,837	566,884	24,251

5.05 Average length of stay, spending per visit and spending per day by purpose of visit 2000

	Holiday visits						Business visits		
	total			*of which inclusive tour*					
	average			*average*			average		
	stay (nights)	spend per visit (£s)	spend per day (£s)	*stay (nights)*	*spend per visit (£s)*	*spend per day (£s)*	stay (nights)	spend per visit (£s)	spend per day (£s)
Canada	14	816	57	*12*	*912*	*78*	8	705	90
USA	15	824	57	*13*	*893*	*68*	9	1,085	125
North America	14	823	57	*13*	*896*	*69*	9	1,054	122
Austria	8	468	57	*8*	*458*	*56*	4	399	89
Belgium	2	164	71	*3*	*216*	*71*	2	287	118
Denmark	5	338	62	*4*	*363*	*86*	3	282	96
Finland	6	363	59	*4*	*529*	*125*	4	439	110
France	7	290	43	*7*	*322*	*47*	4	357	101
Germany	6	297	49	*6*	*336*	*60*	4	362	98
Greece	12	401	34	*11*	*398*	*35*	9	757	86
Irish Republic	6	257	46	*5*	*265*	*52*	3	278	80
Italy	9	509	56	*9*	*501*	*58*	6	602	106
Luxembourg	2	133	55	*3*	*149*	*50*	2	228	109
Netherlands	4	248	60	*4*	*289*	*76*	3	345	111
Portugal	10	369	36	*10*	*352*	*37*	5	448	85
Spain	11	354	33	*10*	*350*	*34*	11	546	49
Sweden	7	338	47	.	.	.	3	373	125
EU Europe	9	338	38	*9*	*357*	*39*	4	372	92
Cyprus	12	457	38	*11*	*464*	*41*	8	599	73
Gibraltar	6	307	49	*5*	*347*	*70*	15	57	4
Iceland	7	453	68	*7*	*525*	*71*	14	1,404	101
Malta	11	296	26	*10*	*273*	*26*	5	424	92
Norway	7	278	42	*8*	*570*	*75*	5	445	83
Switzerland	8	471	57	*8*	*530*	*66*	3	472	151
Turkey	13	394	30	*12*	*378*	*31*	9	619	72
Central & Eastern Europe	9	319	36	*8*	*313*	*39*	6	473	78
Former USSR	11	713	66	*9*	*1,068*	*121*	8	657	85
Former Yugoslavia	11	276	24	*10*	*229*	*23*	9	551	64
Non EU Europe	11	404	36	*11*	*408*	*38*	6	519	94
North Africa	12	405	34	*10*	*381*	*38*	16	760	49
South Africa	20	789	40	*16*	*968*	*62*	11	1,023	95
Rest of Africa	19	834	43	*17*	*845*	*49*	19	739	39
Israel	13	547	42	*9*	*562*	*61*	6	671	108
Other Middle East	12	634	53	*9*	*532*	*61*	10	1,033	104
Hong Kong	19	761	40	*12*	*1,043*	*84*	11	1,687	160
India	27	648	24	*16*	*487*	*31*	18	1,457	83
Japan	16	596	37	*8*	*479*	*64*	13	1,577	122
Rest of Asia	24	800	33	*15*	*746*	*49*	16	1,972	124
Australia	50	1,861	37	*27*	*1,870*	*70*	21	1,710	80
New Zealand	41	1,719	42	*29*	*1,987*	*68*	43	2,108	50
Caribbean	15	698	47	*13*	*617*	*47*	10	986	97
Central & South America	17	723	42	*15*	*704*	*47*	13	1,034	81
Rest of the World	12	1,154	94	*12*	*1,157*	*95*	6	500	90
Other Countries	19	794	41	*13*	*702*	*54*	14	1,299	91
Total World	11	430	41	*10*	*430*	*43*	5	533	97

5.05 Average length of stay, spending per visit and spending per day by purpose of visit 2000

	Visiting friends or relatives			Miscellaneous			Total visits		
	average			average			average		
	stay (nights)	spend per visit (£s)	spend per day (£s)	stay (nights)	spend per visit (£s)	spend per day (£s)	stay (nights)	spend per visit (£s)	spend per day (£s)
Canada	19	440	24	37	2,362	63	16	700	45
USA	19	521	27	18	1,396	77	14	845	60
North America	19	408	26	21	1,518	74	14	824	58
Austria	18	254	14	5	429	82	8	439	52
Belgium	5	130	26	1	201	159	3	209	84
Denmark	7	177	25	7	237	34	5	276	58
Finland	9	283	31	4	301	74	5	390	74
France	8	197	25	1	190	193	5	269	53
Germany	9	175	19	6	285	44	6	302	54
Greece	20	200	10	22	441	20	12	399	33
Irish Republic	7	187	28	4	220	60	5	238	44
Italy	12	246	21	9	574	63	9	498	57
Luxembourg	16	70	4	6	243	40	4	201	46
Netherlands	7	168	24	3	184	56	4	269	65
Portugal	12	242	21	17	630	37	10	371	37
Spain	13	261	20	18	1,638	92	11	370	34
Sweden	10	199	20	4	12,901	2,870	6	484	85
EU Europe	9	197	22	2	270	117	7	323	43
Cyprus	15	286	19	13	363	27	12	447	37
Gibraltar	8	167	22	27	428	16	10	252	26
Iceland	7	149	22	.	.	.	8	655	79
Malta	16	282	18	3	257	86	11	299	26
Norway	22	316	15	34	295	9	10	335	33
Switzerland	7	213	30	9	156	18	6	414	67
Turkey	22	361	16	19	1,068	55	13	412	31
Central & Eastern Europe	13	188	14	9	396	42	9	351	40
Former USSR	17	200	12	36	2,819	79	12	670	57
Former Yugoslavia	20	244	12	7	309	44	13	321	25
Non EU Europe	14	244	17	14	546	38	11	406	38
North Africa	31	239	8	8	160	19	14	421	31
South Africa	25	505	20	49	1,417	29	21	755	36
Rest of Africa	35	640	18	60	928	16	25	775	31
Israel	14	356	26	22	920	43	13	536	42
Other Middle East	26	378	15	25	687	28	17	665	39
Hong Kong	29	542	19	7	738	101	22	839	39
India	37	538	15	32	781	24	29	698	24
Japan	23	368	16	62	411	7	18	1,002	54
Rest of Asia	41	581	14	39	1,377	35	29	892	30
Australia	34	841	25	98	2,848	29	43	1,472	34
New Zealand	40	964	24	287	1,405	5	47	1,383	29
Caribbean	24	550	23	25	1,348	54	16	710	45
Central & South America	23	508	22	47	1,988	43	17	774	45
Rest of the World	27	279	10	23	625	27	12	1,143	93
Other Countries	33	574	17	45	1,227	27	23	816	36
Total World	15	315	20	5	360	69	10	426	43

5.06 Number of visits and spending by duration of stay 2000

	Nil nights		1 to 3 nights		4 to 13 nights		14 to 27 nights	
	visits (thousands)	spending (£ million)	visits (thousands)	spending (£ million)	visits (thousands)	spending (£ million)	visits (thousands)	spending (£ million)
Canada	.	.	15	4	335	181	317	241
USA	1	3	207	87	2,045	1,494	1,815	1,660
North America	1	3	223	91	2,381	1,675	2,133	1,901
Austria	5	0	65	16	333	149	49	30
Belgium	423	43	929	190	267	88	28	15
Denmark	17	1	168	37	94	32	14	4
Finland	3	0	72	18	64	28	11	12
France	3,482	443	3,671	802	3,534	1,214	1,026	530
Germany	135	6	1,160	277	919	307	149	88
Greece	.	.	44	15	1,195	356	1,411	669
Irish Republic	214	8	1,632	351	1,833	450	232	97
Italy	27	2	553	160	1,293	604	386	251
Luxembourg	12	1	42	7	10	4	3	1
Netherlands	169	10	1,204	286	583	185	66	38
Portugal	2	0	90	19	961	307	526	230
Spain	7	0	560	138	6,344	1,860	3,993	1,765
Sweden	19	64	182	53	132	44	34	10
EU Europe	4,515	578	10,373	2,368	17,563	5,628	7,927	3,740
Cyprus	.	.	14	3	661	219	594	325
Gibraltar	1	0	3	1	25	7	5	1
Iceland	1	0	26	6	39	27	7	11
Malta	.	.	7	1	241	60	164	58
Norway	6	0	115	20	104	39	30	15
Switzerland	41	3	284	96	366	165	67	39
Turkey	.	.	29	9	244	79	466	198
Central & Eastern Europe	4	0	198	51	334	108	135	55
Former USSR	1	1	28	10	72	53	24	16
Former Yugoslavia	.	.	13	2	64	17	30	12
Non EU Europe	54	4	718	198	2,150	775	1,522	731
North Africa	0	0	26	10	443	154	232	114
South Africa	.	.	6	3	109	50	153	116
Rest of Africa	1	0	10	2	78	54	186	143
Israel	.	.	22	8	94	45	40	19
Other Middle East	0	0	24	10	186	113	94	70
Hong Kong	.	.	1	1	83	76	44	38
India	.	.	5	3	88	55	218	133
Japan	.	.	4	3	56	50	36	46
Rest of Asia	1	1	14	19	281	203	475	417
Australia	.	.	.	.	41	31	214	213
New Zealand	0	0	1	1	7	4	44	49
Caribbean	.	.	9	3	268	176	459	309
Central & South America	1	0	8	2	102	58	279	214
Rest of the World	1	0	2	1	209	199	140	199
Other Countries	5	2	129	65	2,043	1,269	2,615	2,082
Total World	4,576	587	11,443	2,722	24,137	9,347	14,197	8,453

5.06 Number of visits and spending by duration of stay 2000

	28 to 90 nights		3 to 6 months		6 months to 1 year		All visits	
	visits (thousands)	spending (£ million)	visits (thousands)	spending (£ million)	visits (thousands)	spending (£ million)	visits (thousands)	spending (£ million)
Canada	57	57	3	1	1	26	729	510
USA	235	352	24	49	3	16	4,331	3,660
North America	292	409	26	51	4	41	5,060	4,170
Austria	13	7	1	3	.	.	467	205
Belgium	10	11	.	.	.	.	1,657	347
Denmark	6	9	.	.	.	.	299	82
Finland	1	0	.	.	.	.	152	59
France	161	141	21	45	7	24	11,903	3,198
Germany	39	30	7	21	2	0	2,411	728
Greece	49	36	9	4	.	.	2,709	1,080
Irish Republic	43	25	5	9	1	1	3,961	941
Italy	59	56	6	67	2	19	2,327	1,159
Luxembourg	2	0	.	.	.	.	69	14
Netherlands	19	20	2	11	1	0	2,044	550
Portugal	32	40	1	1	.	.	1,612	597
Spain	207	276	32	65	11	23	11,154	4,127
Sweden	9	12	.	.	.	.	377	182
EU Europe	652	661	84	227	25	66	41,140	13,294
Cyprus	34	24	6	13	2	2	1,310	585
Gibraltar	.	.	1	0	.	.	35	9
Iceland	3	6	.	.	.	.	76	50
Malta	16	7	0	2	.	.	428	128
Norway	14	15	2	2	1	0	271	91
Switzerland	10	16	1	0	.	.	768	318
Turkey	32	27	4	5	.	.	775	310
Central & Eastern Europe	28	29	1	2	.	.	700	246
Former USSR	17	16			.	.	142	95
Former Yugoslavia	9	6	.	.	.		117	38
Non EU Europe	162	144	14	23	3	2	4,623	1,878
North Africa	50	37	1	0	5	3	758	319
South Africa	52	62	3	6	2	9	325	245
Rest of Africa	70	58	8	10	3	9	356	276
Israel	9	6	3	11	.	.	168	90
Other Middle East	59	44	3	2	1	4	366	244
Hong Kong	45	30	2	1	.	.	175	147
India	138	101	22	31	3	7	474	331
Japan	13	11	1	0	1	1	111	111
Rest of Asia	301	258	45	57	12	52	1,129	1,007
Australia	164	218	35	111	17	119	470	692
New Zealand	42	57	9	24	5	12	107	148
Caribbean	52	58	5	11	1	7	794	563
Central & South America	34	54	4	3	.	.	427	331
Rest of the World	3	6	0	1	.	.	355	406
Other Countries	1,030	1,000	140	270	50	223	6,014	4,909
Total World	2,136	2,215	265	571	82	332	56,837	24,251

5.07 Number of visits by UK port 2000

	Airports							thousands
	Heathrow	Gatwick	Manchester	Birmingham	Stansted	Other England	Scotland	Wales
Canada	315	144	108	37	8	10	99	9
USA	1,913	1,388	544	148	6	80	216	34
North America	2,227	1,532	652	184	14	90	314	42
Austria	117	105	35	31	55	53	6	1
Belgium	165	17	38	59	21	98	35	18
Denmark	97	19	31	20	72	10	20	1
Finland	84	13	12	6	32	2	1	.
France	592	427	253	200	321	498	125	17
Germany	692	102	132	206	398	95	40	8
Greece	184	868	689	276	46	431	183	20
Irish Republic	466	190	179	.	414	787	.	61
Italy	536	500	149	119	566	122	66	4
Luxembourg	9	17	2	3	10	8	3	.
Netherlands	420	92	117	112	107	393	91	23
Portugal	210	453	234	145	151	214	134	45
Spain	579	2,318	2,406	939	666	2,573	820	406
Sweden	168	41	28	17	84	20	6	1
EU Europe	4,321	5,161	4,307	2,133	2,944	5,304	1,531	606
Cyprus	195	334	292	76	54	187	113	58
Gibraltar	.	21	.	.	.	14	.	.
Iceland	38	1	1	2	20	.	13	.
Malta	49	119	78	34	10	76	61	.
Norway	104	14	16	5	27	22	4	1
Switzerland	299	52	44	37	28	200	9	1
Turkey	136	186	228	23	36	105	46	16
Central & Eastern Europe	353	59	59	15	78	11	25	2
Former USSR	77	37	14	2	4	3	1	.
Former Yugoslavia	47	35	10	13	1	5	2	.
Non EU Europe	1,298	858	741	207	258	622	275	79
North Africa	195	354	119	36	9	31	7	.
South Africa	273	1	16	10	2	15	7	1
Rest of Africa	190	103	39	4	3	4	9	1
Israel	82	50	15	.	11	8	.	1
Other Middle East	282	15	37	9	1	11	8	3
Hong Kong	147	1	12	3	0	6	6	.
India	293	81	40	48	2	4	4	2
Japan	95	.	2	7	2	1	1	3
Rest of Asia	877	30	167	23	2	18	10	.
Australia	393	18	49	2	1	1	.	2
New Zealand	88	7	7	1	1	1	.	.
Caribbean	122	548	106	1	0	10	3	.
Central & South America	114	182	106	12	3	6	2	1
Rest of the World	24	25	4	.	.	.	.	.
Other Countries	3,174	1,416	718	155	38	116	57	15
Total World	11,020	8,967	6,419	2,681	3,254	6,132	2,178	742

5.07 Number of visits by UK port 2000

	Sea and Channel Tunnel						thousands
	Dover and Folkestone	Other channel ports	East coast ports	Long haul sea routes	Irish Sea & land routes	Channel Tunnel	All air and sea ports
Canada	.	.	.	.	.	1	729
USA	.	.	.	2	.	1	4,331
North America	.	.	.	2	.	2	5,060
Austria	40	.	6	.	.	17	467
Belgium	483	2	106	.	.	613	1,657
Denmark	3	.	24	.	.	1	200
Finland	.	.	.	.	.	1	152
France	3,132	1,796	34	.	.	4,508	11,904
Germany	375	2	104	.	.	257	2,411
Greece	5	3	.	.	.	3	2,709
Irish Republic	.	.	.	.	1,862	.	3,959
Italy	161	3	13	.	.	88	2,327
Luxembourg	7	.	3	.	.	8	69
Netherlands	217	.	312	.	.	162	2,044
Portugal	7	12	.	.	.	8	1,612
Spain	242	142	1	.	.	63	11,154
Sweden	2	.	2	.	.	4	377
EU Europe	4,674	1,960	605	.	1,862	5,732	41,140
Cyprus	.	.	.	.	.	.	1,310
Gibraltar	.	.	.	.	.		35
Iceland	.	.	.	.	.	.	76
Malta	.	.	.	.	.	.	428
Norway	1	.	76		.	.	271
Switzerland	47	2	6		.	41	768
Turkey	.	.		.	.	.	775
Central & Eastern Europe	81	.	8	.	.	11	700
Former USSR	2	.	.		.	2	142
Former Yugoslavia	2	.	.	.	.	3	117
Non EU Europe	133	2	90	.	.	58	4,623
North Africa	3	2	.	.	1	.	750
South Africa	.		.	.	.	.	325
Rest of Africa	1	.	.	.	.	2	356
Israel	.	.	.	.	.	1	168
Other Middle East	2	.	.	.	.	.	366
Hong Kong	.	.	.	.	.	1	175
India	.	.	.	.	.	.	474
Japan	.	.	.	.	.	.	111
Rest of Asia	.	.	1	.	.	1	1,129
Australia	3	.	.	.	.	0	470
New Zealand	.	.	1	.	.	.	107
Caribbean	.	.	.	.	.	3	794
Central & South America	1	.	.	.	.	.	427
Rest of the World	.	.	.	302	.	.	355
Other Countries	11	2	1	302	1	8	6,014
Total World	4,818	1,964	697	304	1,863	5,799	56,836

5.08 Number of visits by type of vehicle used 2000

	Air	Sea and Channel Tunnel					thousands
	All travellers	Foot	Private vehicle	Coach	Goods vehicle	Vehicle type unknown	All sea and Channel Tunnel
Canada	728	1	.	.	.	.	1
USA	4,328	3	.	.	.	.	3
North America	5,056	4	.	.	.	.	4
Austria	404	1	17	40	5	.	63
Belgium	451	388	482	259	72	5	1,205
Denmark	272	13	12	.	2	.	27
Finland	151	1	.	.	.	.	1
France	2,432	1,869	6,086	1,336	168	12	9,471
Germany	1,673	48	312	277	93	7	737
Greece	2,698	3	7	.	1	.	11
Irish Republic	2,099	164	807	184	1	705	1,862
Italy	2,062	15	105	91	53	.	265
Luxembourg	52	3	11	2	2	.	17
Netherlands	1,354	178	312	152	44	5	690
Portugal	1,585	1	21	3	1	.	26
Spain	10,706	34	204	182	28	.	448
Sweden	368	1	8	.	.	.	9
EU Europe	26,307	2,717	8,383	2,528	471	734	14,833
Cyprus	1,310	.	.	.	.	.	.
Gibraltar	35	.	.	.	.	.	.
Iceland	76	.	.	.	.	.	.
Malta	428	.	.	.	.	.	.
Norway	194	55	14	6	.	2	77
Switzerland	671	8	57	29	2	.	97
Turkey	775	.	.	.	.	.	.
Central & Eastern Europe	601	2	36	59	3	.	100
Former USSR	137	1	.	4	.	.	5
Former Yugoslavia	112	.	4	.	1	.	5
Non EU Europe	4,339	66	111	98	7	2	283
North Africa	752	.	6	.	.	.	6
South Africa	325	.	.	.	.	.	.
Rest of Africa	353	2	1	.	.	.	3
Israel	167	1	.	.	.	.	1
Other Middle East	364	.	.	.	2	.	2
Hong Kong	174	1	.	.	.	.	1
India	474	.	.	.	.	.	.
Japan	111	.	.	.	.	.	.
Rest of Asia	1,127	2	.	.	.	.	2
Australia	467	.	3	1	.	.	4
New Zealand	106	1	.	.	.	.	1
Caribbean	790	2	1	.	.	.	3
Central & South America	426	.	.	.	1	.	1
Rest of the World	53	302	.	.	.	.	302
Other Countries	5,689	309	11	1	3	.	325
Total World	41,392	3,097	8,505	2,627	481	736	15,445

5.09 Number of visits and spending by gender and purpose of visit 2000

	Male				Female			
	Leisure		Business		Leisure		Business	
	visits (thousands)	spending (£ million)	visits (thousands)	spending (£ million)	visits (thousands)	spending (£ million)	visits (thousands)	spending (£ million)
Canada	283	228	58	43	369	227	20	12
USA	1,753	1,461	728	783	1,692	1,237	159	179
North America	2,035	1,689	786	825	2,060	1,465	179	191
Austria	195	87	52	22	209	93	11	3
Belgium	603	112	500	141	459	64	94	29
Denmark	86	28	109	33	80	17	24	4
Finland	31	9	72	35	32	11	17	4
France	5,935	1,585	1,232	438	4,411	1,057	325	118
Germany	595	157	1,005	370	647	148	164	54
Greece	1,233	500	38	18	1,421	539	16	24
Irish Republic	1,644	402	700	193	1,489	309	127	37
Italy	905	438	362	202	976	451	85	67
Luxembourg	15	3	39	9	12	1	3	0
Netherlands	682	167	669	234	571	111	122	38
Portugal	773	311	51	25	771	256	17	6
Spain	5,196	2,008	202	165	5,569	1,906	98	48
Sweden	93	27	160	62	86	82	37	11
EU Europe	17,987	5,846	5,281	1,946	16,734	5,058	1,139	444
Cyprus	591	278	14	9	700	296	4	2
Gibraltar	17	4	2	0	10	4	.	.
Iceland	31	14	15	24	27	11	2	1
Malta	196	58	9	3	222	65	2	1
Norway	102	33	75	34	92	24	2	1
Switzerland	230	100	224	114	258	87	55	18
Turkey	342	134	37	21	383	154	12	10
Central & Eastern Europe	225	69	179	90	239	64	57	22
Former USSR	43	42	55	35	34	10	9	7
Former Yugoslavia	48	13	17	11	47	13	4	1
Non EU Europe	1,825	746	630	340	2,010	728	148	63
North Africa	302	127	60	48	390	142	5	2
South Africa	144	114	40	44	136	86	4	1
Rest of Africa	146	130	55	35	147	100	8	12
Israel	66	32	24	17	74	40	3	2
Other Middle East	146	81	76	84	134	74	10	5
Hong Kong	79	55	31	50	62	33	4	8
India	206	140	43	54	220	122	4	16
Japan	26	15	47	76	30	10	8	10
Rest of Asia	544	452	124	240	440	271	20	44
Australia	211	386	29	50	222	243	9	13
New Zealand	47	63	3	7	56	76	1	2
Caribbean	404	307	20	20	358	225	12	11
Central & South America	188	124	54	59	172	136	14	11
Rest of the World	173	192	1	1	181	213	.	.
Other Countries	2,682	2,218	607	785	2,623	1,770	102	136
Total World	24,529	10,499	7,304	3,897	23,436	9,020	1,568	835

5.10 Number of visits and spending by age group 2000

	Age 0-15		Age 16-24		Age 25-34		Age 35-44	
	visits (thousands)	spending (£ million)	visits (thousands)	spending (£ million)	visits (thousands)	spending (£ million)	visits (thousands)	spending (£ million)
Canada	47	23	52	58	122	74	147	86
USA	349	222	377	269	970	874	1,056	944
North America	396	244	429	328	1,091	948	1,203	1,030
Austria	23	8	30	8	89	32	98	41
Belgium	87	7	114	18	341	85	398	89
Denmark	19	5	25	3	101	29	66	26
Finland	2	1	7	2	51	18	48	20
France	1,236	274	874	237	2,312	633	2,766	750
Germany	127	21	146	38	595	190	579	176
Greece	221	73	464	175	544	226	491	193
Irish Republic	222	29	343	71	1,036	270	845	199
Italy	123	37	178	106	513	215	510	264
Luxembourg	1	0	8	3	29	7	13	1
Netherlands	78	11	225	55	623	160	497	127
Portugal	144	40	111	42	241	84	276	95
Spain	1,306	364	1,038	392	1,882	659	2,250	921
Sweden	16	6	35	6	132	41	87	36
EU Europe	3,606	875	3,598	1,154	8,489	2,649	8,923	2,937
Cyprus	119	36	162	88	199	99	245	106
Gibraltar	2	0	7	1	2	1	7	1
Iceland	7	2	6	2	17	10	17	20
Malta	35	9	17	5	46	15	70	20
Norway	16	2	30	8	57	19	53	21
Switzerland	51	21	54	19	199	75	190	102
Turkey	89	28	89	33	137	64	210	85
Central & Eastern Europe	29	5	67	14	185	79	137	54
Former USSR	4	1	15	6	36	21	42	33
Former Yugoslavia	5	2	7	2	24	6	24	12
Non EU Europe	358	107	454	179	901	389	997	455
North Africa	51	16	70	26	155	69	185	73
South Africa	16	7	32	18	80	69	54	43
Rest of Africa	26	12	34	33	79	61	78	59
Israel	14	6	17	14	41	24	29	15
Other Middle East	27	12	40	14	88	60	70	49
Hong Kong	12	3	39	18	31	32	34	38
India	38	11	50	40	97	63	89	59
Japan	1	0	14	6	38	49	25	26
Rest of Asia	92	51	163	121	275	237	210	238
Australia	14	15	60	111	116	231	68	68
New Zealand	6	5	14	16	32	38	11	12
Caribbean	61	31	80	48	217	135	166	124
Central & South America	19	10	47	46	118	96	82	54
Rest of the World	11	11	22	18	56	58	30	30
Other Countries	389	191	684	531	1,422	1,222	1,130	890
Total World	4,748	1,418	5,165	2,192	11,903	5,208	12,253	5,312

5.10 Number of visits and spending by age group 2000

	Age 45-54		Age 55-64		Age 65 and over		All visits	
	visits (thousands)	spending (£ million)	visits (thousands)	spending (£ million)	visits (thousands)	spending (£ million)	visits (thousands)	spending (£ million)
Canada	157	122	116	84	89	63	729	510
USA	850	733	471	404	258	214	4,331	3,660
North America	1,007	855	588	488	347	277	5,060	4,170
Austria	93	45	76	40	57	32	467	205
Belgium	388	87	217	43	112	18	1,657	347
Denmark	52	9	28	8	9	2	299	82
Finland	26	14	15	4	2	0	152	59
France	2,344	687	1,582	429	790	189	11,903	3,198
Germany	519	168	263	79	181	55	2,411	728
Greece	576	246	294	117	119	51	2,709	1,080
Irish Republic	788	186	462	117	265	68	3,961	941
Italy	484	254	305	147	213	136	2,327	1,159
Luxembourg	10	2	8	1	1	0	69	14
Netherlands	401	124	153	56	66	17	2,044	550
Portugal	363	150	307	128	170	59	1,612	597
Spain	2,036	761	1,589	609	1,052	421	11,154	4,127
Sweden	76	84	26	7	5	1	377	182
EU Europe	8,156	2,818	5,325	1,786	3,043	1,051	41,140	13,294
Cyprus	266	124	217	88	101	44	1,310	585
Gibraltar	8	3	9	3	1	0	35	9
Iceland	15	10	8	3	6	2	76	50
Malta	86	25	86	27	89	26	428	128
Norway	53	19	43	15	19	6	271	91
Switzerland	141	48	80	27	53	27	768	318
Turkey	150	68	68	26	31	15	775	319
Central & Eastern Europe	157	53	84	25	41	15	700	246
Former USSR	25	14	17	11	4	9	142	95
Former Yugoslavia	27	7	19	4	10	5	117	38
Non EU Europe	927	370	632	228	354	150	4,623	1,878
North Africa	169	78	79	34	49	23	758	610
South Africa	57	37	51	39	34	32	325	245
Rest of Africa	72	51	55	44	12	14	356	276
Israel	32	14	18	9	16	8	168	90
Other Middle East	80	63	44	29	18	17	366	244
Hong Kong	34	33	14	13	11	9	175	147
India	105	89	72	53	23	16	474	331
Japan	25	24	6	5	2	1	111	111
Rest of Asia	196	193	147	128	47	40	1,129	1,007
Australia	79	92	82	102	51	72	470	692
New Zealand	14	22	17	27	14	26	107	148
Caribbean	162	121	76	72	33	31	794	563
Central & South America	86	60	57	50	18	14	427	331
Rest of the World	82	88	81	100	74	100	355	406
Other Countries	1,191	966	798	705	401	403	6,014	4,909
Total World	11,281	5,010	7,342	3,207	4,145	1,881	56,837	24,251

5.11 Number of visits and spending by UK region of residence and country visited 2000

	London		Other England		Total England		Scotland		Wales	
	visits (1000s)	spending (£ million)	visits (1000s)	spending (£ million)	visits (1000s)	spending (£ million)	visits (1000s)	spending (£ million)	visits (1000s)	spending (£ million)
Canada	109	69	456	299	565	368	117	104	35	26
USA	954	844	2,817	2,361	3,771	3,204	347	275	149	114
North America	1,063	913	3,274	2,660	4,336	3,572	463	380	184	140
Austria	98	42	316	141	415	183	25	11	19	6
Belgium	353	74	1,194	246	1,547	320	51	17	44	7
Denmark	82	21	180	50	262	72	25	9	7	1
Finland	49	19	91	36	140	55	3	1	4	3
France	2,508	682	8,543	2,225	11,051	2,907	398	145	314	108
Germany	557	162	1,648	500	2,205	662	103	32	75	24
Greece	312	133	2,080	811	2,392	944	242	104	59	27
Irish Republic	772	226	2,173	524	2,945	750	29	6	255	56
Italy	580	288	1,514	726	2,094	1,014	153	74	55	57
Luxembourg	21	4	42	8	63	13	5	1	1	0
Netherlands	468	125	1,364	370	1,832	495	143	39	50	9
Portugal	229	92	1,118	408	1,346	501	176	65	70	25
Spain	1,210	469	8,174	3,000	9,384	3,469	1,039	390	654	239
Sweden	135	41	221	133	355	174	12	3	7	3
EU Europe	7,372	2,377	28,659	9,179	36,032	11,557	2,404	896	1,614	566
Cyprus	217	104	891	394	1,108	498	121	59	72	26
Gibraltar	8	2	21	5	30	7	1	0	3	1
Iceland	17	9	51	20	68	29	6	20	1	0
Malta	36	13	314	92	350	105	64	19	9	2
Norway	48	16	191	68	239	84	24	4	4	3
Switzerland	266	133	444	165	710	297	28	8	11	4
Turkey	133	66	552	214	685	280	49	21	36	14
Central & Eastern Europe	207	80	422	137	628	216	40	15	24	10
Former USSR	47	30	83	54	130	84	5	7	6	4
Former Yugoslavia	38	12	71	23	109	35	4	1	2	0
Non EU Europe	1,018	464	3,040	1,172	4,058	1,636	341	154	167	63
North Africa	202	93	504	201	706	294	24	13	24	8
South Africa	83	60	207	150	290	210	14	21	12	9
Rest of Africa	146	125	183	132	329	257	13	8	9	6
Israel	90	37	66	44	156	82	6	5	1	1
Other Middle East	108	71	218	149	327	221	24	13	7	2
Hong Kong	48	41	109	90	158	132	11	11	3	4
India	168	119	277	190	444	309	15	11	8	3
Japan	40	39	59	64	100	102	5	4	4	1
Rest of Asia	323	255	702	657	1,025	913	55	48	26	19
Australia	92	127	325	465	417	591	24	48	20	27
New Zealand	16	18	77	112	93	131	8	9	3	4
Caribbean	209	159	516	346	725	505	32	22	21	22
Central & South America	116	104	272	193	388	297	20	12	12	9
Rest of the World	34	37	244	273	278	310	13	16	14	16
Other Countries	1,673	1,286	3,762	3,067	5,435	4,354	264	242	164	131
Total World	11,126	5,041	38,735	16,078	49,861	21,119	3,472	1,671	2,128	900

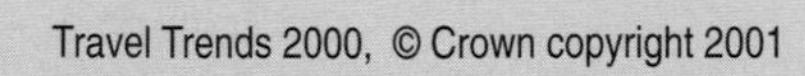

Appendices

Appendix A

Information available from the International Passenger Survey

For most types of analysis of IPS data, and for all analyses within this report, the information is presented separately for two distinct groups of travellers:

a) Overseas residents visiting the UK;
b) UK residents travelling abroad.

For each of these groups of traveller, the results are shown according to one or more of the following observations:

a) the number of visits made;
b) their spending in £ sterling;
c) their length of stay in nights.

For some analyses, additional observations are made, these being:

a) the average length of visit measured in nights;
b) the average spending per visit in £ sterling;
c) the average spending per day in £ sterling.

Within Travel Trends, the IPS data are further analysed by a variety of other characteristics based on variables from the IPS database, for example:

a) mode of travel (air, sea or tunnel);
b) country of visit (for UK residents);
c) country of residence (for overseas residents);
d) main purpose of the visit;
e) year and quarter of travel;
f) age group;
g) gender;
h) duration of stay;
i) type of vehicle used when travelling by sea or Channel Tunnel;
j) the regions of the UK stayed in by overseas residents;
k) the UK airport or seaport used or if via the Channel Tunnel.

All the information published in this report relates to the group of travellers normally termed 'visitors'. A visitor is described as someone on a trip abroad which lasts less than a year. For the purposes of this publication, visitors include day visitors, those on holiday, business travellers, people visiting friends or relatives, those on study trips or travelling to receive medical attention. Those not included are migrants and crews of ships, trains and aircraft who are travelling as part of their work or those on sea trips who do not actually disembark at a foreign port. A fuller definition of a visitor can be found in Appendix C.

Getting further information from the IPS

The full IPS database contains over a 110 variables and therefore the opportunity exists for more detailed analyses than can be replicated here. However, the structure of the IPS database is complex making it rather difficult to analyse.

To enable examination of the IPS data to be made more easily, Travel*pac* (a CD-ROM containing a simplified version of the IPS database using twelve of the most widely used variables) is now available. The information is supplied in several common PC formats and is available for each year from 1993 to 2000. Details of how to obtain a copy are given in Appendix F.

Further analyses of IPS data can be commissioned from either of two companies who act as marketing agents for the IPS. The marketing agents are able to undertake the more specific and specialised forms of analysis not covered in this publication and which would not be possible from the Travel*pac* CD-ROM. Appendix F gives details of how to contact the marketing agents.

The key variables

Visits are described as the number of journeys made in one direction only. Those who came to the UK or went abroad on more than one occasion are counted on each visit they made.

Spending in Travel Trends is normally shown as £ sterling at 'current prices', i.e. the value of money at the time the visit was made, taking no account of inflation. The information on spending is in some cases also shown at 1995 'constant prices'. This gives an indication of spending over time but with the effects of inflation removed.

Using regional tables

The IPS collects information regarding the towns stayed in by overseas residents when they visit the UK. However, due to the very large number of towns in the UK it would not be meaningful to replicate an analysis of visits by the full range of towns possible. In this publication, visits information for overseas residents is therefore shown at "County" or "Unitary Authority", and main UK region levels.

Care must be taken when using the regional information, as the numbers of visits to separate UK areas cannot simply be added together to form larger areas. This is because it is possible for a person to visit more than one area of the UK during a single visit. As a result, the numbers of visits to smaller regions do not sum to the figures given for larger regions in the regional tables in this publication.

For example, a person visiting London, Windsor and Aberdeen in a single visit to the UK would appear as one visit to London, one to Berkshire and one to Grampian. However, the same visitor would be recorded as a single visit in the England total and a visit in the Scotland total, and as just one visit in the UK total. Although visits cannot be summed across UK regions, the spending and nights information can.

Main analysis variables

The full IPS dataset contains a total of over 110 variables, some of which are derived. Some variables are indicators to help identify the quality of data or to show where data have been imputed, and to what degree. **Figure A.1** shows the most widely used variables.

A.1 The main analysis variables from the full 2000 IPS database

Year[1]	:	of the interview.
Quarter[1]	:	" "
Month	:	" "
Date	:	" "
Flow[1]	:	Eight flows with four for each of air and sea; (sea includes Channel Tunnel): - arrivals by UK residents; - departures by UK residents; - arrivals by overseas residents; - departures by overseas residents.
Weight[1]	:	The number of trips the record represents (i.e. the sum of the weights gives total traffic).
Nationality	:	Recorded for all respondents.
Country visited[1]	:	The main country of visit (or country stayed in the longest) by UK residents abroad.
Residence[1]	:	The main country of residence of visitors to the UK.
States of residence	:	States within countries for overseas residents. Limited to four countries a year. In 2000 Australia, France, Netherlands & the USA.
Purpose of visit[1]	:	The main purpose of the visit. Recorded for all respondents.
Stay[1]	:	Length of stay in nights (overseas departures & UK arrivals).
Expenditure[1]	:	Expenditure (excluding fares) in £ sterling (overseas departures & UK arrivals).
UK port	:	Airport, sea route or tunnel route at which interview was recorded.
Second UK port	:	Any UK airport from which a person has just arrived, or is flying to.
First port	:	The overseas port travelling directly to or from.
Second Port	:	The final (or starting) overseas air or sea port.
Flight	:	Origin (or final destination) of flight being taken (air travellers only).
Mileage travelled	:	Computed distance travelled in miles for first, second and direct legs from/to UK port.
Carrier	:	Air or shipping line for first leg of journey.
Class of travel	:	On all air flows.
Type of flight	:	On all air flows - scheduled or charter.
Fares	:	In £ sterling (UK residents only).
Vehicle type	:	Type of vehicle taken on visit (sea and tunnel passengers only).
Number in vehicle	:	The number of people travelling in the vehicle (sea and tunnel passengers only).
Age[1]	:	Age group.
Gender[1]	:	Male or female.
Towns 1-5	:	Up to 5 towns stayed in overnight in the UK (overseas residents only).
Stay 1-5	:	Number of nights spent in towns 1-5.
Spend 1-5	:	Expenditure whilst in towns 1-5 (not collected by IPS but imputed based on length of stay).
Package	:	Package tour or independent.
Money spent	:	by UK residents having visited the EU - on spirits - on beer - on wine - on other alcohol - on tobacco.

[1] data item included in *Travelpac Compact Data Set.*

Appendix B

Methodology

Background

The International Passenger Survey (IPS) is a large multi-purpose survey which collects information from passengers as they enter or leave the United Kingdom. It is carried out by the Office for National Statistics for a range of public and private sector organisations. In particular, the survey provides figures used for the travel account of the balance of payments, international migration statistics, and for informing decisions on tourism policy. The survey's use, however, is also widespread across and outside of Government in providing detailed information on the numbers and types of people travelling to and from the UK. Results are published regularly on a monthly, quarterly and annual basis. More detailed analyses are possible by purchasing the *Travelpac Compact Dataset* or through marketing agents appointed by ONS.

Overview of the survey design

The IPS is based on face to face interviews with a sample of passengers travelling via the principal airports, sea routes and the Channel Tunnel. The number of interviews in 2000 was 261,000 which represented about 0.2 per cent of all travellers. This sample size is large and allows reliable estimates to be produced for various groups of passengers despite the low proportion of travellers interviewed.

The IPS sample is stratified to ensure it is representative by mode of travel (air, sea or tunnel), port or route, and time of day. Interviews are conducted throughout the year. The frequency of sampling within each stratum is varied according to the variability of tourist expenditure, the volume of migrants and the cost of interviewing. For example, where the expenditure quoted on a particular route varies greatly across respondents, a higher sampling frequency is used to enable a more satisfactory estimate to be produced. (For further details on the sample design, see the *Sampling* section below.)

Some questions on the survey are asked of all of the passengers interviewed, whilst others are restricted to certain specific sub-groups. Information on the spending and length of stay of UK residents abroad and overseas residents in the UK is only collected on the return leg of a visit. This is because actual spending and length of stay are required, and these may differ from the respondents' intentions when they start their visit. In 2000, 57,000 interviews were carried out with overseas residents departing from the UK and 57,000 with UK residents arriving back from abroad.

The details collected on the survey are used by ONS, along with other sources of information, to produce overall national estimates of the number and expenditure of different types of travellers. A complex weighting procedure is used to do this which takes into account various factors in order to improve the estimates. (For further details of the weighting procedure, see *Producing national estimates* below.)

Sampling

The sampling scheme used for the IPS is a multi-stage one which is carried out separately for air, sea and tunnel travel. The underlying principle for each mode of travel is broadly similar: in the absence of a sampling frame of travellers, time shifts or sea crossings are selected at the first stage, and travellers are then systematically chosen at fixed intervals from a random start first stage, and travellers are then systematically chosen at fixed intervals from a random start within these shifts or crossings at the second stage. The details of the sampling scheme for each individual mode of travel are as follows:

- Air routes

For air routes, shifts are selected for the first stage at the nine 'main' air sites (i.e. the four terminals at Heathrow airport, the two terminals at Gatwick, and the three terminals at Manchester International Airport) in such a way that the number of shifts are balanced between mornings/ afternoons and days of the week within any quarter. At the second stage, passengers are counted as they cross a predetermined line and every n^{th} one is interviewed. The sampling interval, *n,* differs between sites but is never more than 67. In general, departing passengers are sampled at a higher rate than arriving ones because the expenditure information for overseas residents visiting the UK is more variable than that for UK residents returning from visits abroad.

A small number of shifts every quarter are also conducted at other smaller international airports (termed residual airports), but the coverage is insufficient to provide accurate estimates for each individual airport. Those airports with less than about 50,000 passenger movements per quarter are usually excluded from the survey altogether on the grounds of cost effectiveness, but traffic at these sites is taken into account when producing national figures.

- Sea routes

Sea routes carrying 50,000 passengers a year or more are generally included in the IPS sample. At some seaports, passengers are sampled and interviewed on the quayside as they embark or disembark, whilst at others, IPS interviewers travel on the boat itself with interviewing being carried out on board. The choice between interviewing on the quayside or on crossings is made on practical grounds such as cost, safety and permission.

Where interviewing is conducted on the quayside, the sample is designed to select shifts which are balanced across different days of the week and times of day within a quarter, with each individual shift covering several sailings. Where interviews are conducted on crossings, a predetermined number of return crossings are selected for each route, spread across time of day and day of week each quarter. Similarly to air sampling, sea passengers are selected at fixed sampling intervals from a random start within each shift or crossing.

The IPS also samples long haul ships capable of carrying more than 200 passengers at the port of Southampton; one outward and one inward sailing are randomly selected per quarter.

- Tunnel routes

The method used for the tunnel routes is different for Eurostar passenger trains and for Eurotunnel vehicle shuttles.

Passenger trains are treated in a similar way to air travel, with time shifts being selected and then a sampling interval being used within the time shift. Passengers are interviewed crossing a predetermined line at Waterloo and Ashford International stations on arrival or departure.

In contrast, for vehicle shuttles, crossings are randomly selected and interviewing takes place on board the shuttles themselves. Because of time constraints, only a certain number of interviews can be carried out on any vehicle shuttle crossing and the sampling interval used is therefore dependent on traffic volumes.

Producing national estimates

Once the information has been collected from respondents, ONS produces national estimates based on the sample results which are published on a monthly, quarterly and annual basis. These estimates take account of a variety of factors. The method of producing national estimates varies depending on the mode of travel and type of port:

- Main airports

Each person interviewed at one of the main airports is assigned a value which indicates the number of people they represent in the traffic flow. This initial weight is the inverse of the sampling interval used for the shift adjusted to take account of time slots which were not selected in the sample design. For example, if the sampling interval is 1 in 25, and one 8 hour period in six is sampled, then the initial weight will be 25x6=150.

The initial weight for each respondent is then built upon to take account of a range of other factors. The series of procedures is as follows:

(a) Firstly, the initial weight is adjusted to take account of:
- non-contacts during the interviewing time (during peak periods an interviewer may not finish an interview before their next assigned contact has crossed the counting line);
- people refusing to be interviewed.

(b) Some further adjustment of the weights within country of residence and nationality is then made to allow for interviews in which only minimum information is obtained from the respondents. These "minimum" interviews are then discounted. This procedure makes the assumption that "minimum" respondents are similar to those of a similar residency and nationality status who provide fuller information.

(c) Adjustments are then made for passengers arriving or departing outside the eligible times for sampling, usually over the night-time period between 11.00 pm and 7.00 am (these adjustments are based upon information from the Civil Aviation Authority (CAA)).

(d) The resulting weights are next summed across respondents to give estimated total passenger flows from the IPS sample data. These total flows are then scaled to bring them into line with actual numbers of international passengers passing through the main airports which are provided to ONS by the CAA. The passenger flow figures for Heathrow and Gatwick are adjusted before scaling to exclude "airside interliners" (i.e. passengers in transit to another flight) who do not pass through passport control and so technically do not enter the country.

(e) The weights are finally adjusted to allow for any imbalance in the sample. This involves comparing total arrivals and departures for each major country and port group over a period of a rolling year and, if the two totals are further apart than can be explained by statistical error, the weights of the relevant contacts are adjusted to reflect this.

This series of procedures leads to a final weight being assigned to each respondent. These final weights are then applied to the individual responses to produce the national estimates.

- Residual air, sea ports and the Channel Tunnel

For all other types of port, sample figures are directly scaled to known international passenger flows. For the residual airports these flows are derived from statistics provided by the CAA, whilst for the seaports, information was provided by the Department of Transport, Local Government and the Regions. Data on Channel Tunnel flows are supplied by both Eurotunnel (vehicle shuttles) and Eurostar (passenger trains). In the case of the vehicle shuttles, only vehicle flows are available; these are converted to passenger flows using information collected from a separate survey of vehicle occupancies conducted on behalf of ONS at the Eurotunnel terminals in the UK and France.

For residual airports, international passenger movement figures are assigned to groups of airports, subdivided between arrivals and departures. For long and short haul sea ports, the passenger movement figures are similarly assigned to groups of routes, subdivided between arrivals and departures. The sample for these grouped routes is then scaled to the passenger flows by dividing the number of contacts into the actual number of passengers.

In the calculation of these scaling weights, no allowance is made for non-response. However, by grouping airports or sea routes, allowances are made for unsampled ports and routes. Finally, the sample within each group is re-weighted for "minimum" interviews and sample imbalance (in the same way as for the main airports, see above) to arrive at a final weight for each respondent.

Additional sources of data

The method above explains how the national estimates are produced using the sample data from the IPS and control totals of passenger flows. Unfortunately, the IPS does not cover all possible passenger flows, so additional figures have to be obtained from other sources and added to the totals derived from the IPS. These additions are:

- UK residents on cruises departing from or arriving to UK shores (from the Department of the Environment, Transport and the Regions);

- Channel Islands expenditure and receipts from tourism (from the Economic Advisor's office in Jersey);

- rail fares purchased by overseas visitors to the UK and UK visitors abroad before the start of their visit (from British Rail International and Eurostar).

For years before 1999, additional information regarding travel to and from the Irish Republic, including American resident visitors leaving the UK via the Irish Republic, were provided to the ONS by the Central Statistics Office of the Irish Republic. These routes to and from the Irish Republic were introduced into the IPS in 1999.

Imputation

Inevitably, some respondents only partially respond and do not give details of their expenditure, fares or length of stay. For these respondents, ONS imputes the missing information based on the spending, fares and stay of similar types of contacts who do give the details. Spending for overseas residents visiting UK towns is also imputed.

Seasonal adjustment

The number of travellers and their spending both have a clear seasonal pattern, with more visits and spending in the summer than in the winter. Statistical techniques are used by ONS with the package 'X11ARIMA' to produce seasonally adjusted figures. These figures show visits and spending with an estimate for the seasonal component removed. They allow more meaningful comparisons to be made between months and quarters of the year and help to identify underlying trends. More details on seasonal adjustment procedures can be obtained from the IPS branch of ONS.

Constant prices

Usually, spending by overseas residents in the UK and UK residents abroad grows each year as the price of goods and services rise. Constant price figures are calculated by ONS to show real spending across years with the effects of price inflation removed.

For overseas residents in the UK, an index is created by splitting spending into its component parts (accommodation, meals etc.) using past IPS data and uprating these components by their related retail price indices. The resulting index is then used to rebase the overseas figures back to 1995 prices.

For UK residents abroad, spending is split by country of visit. Consumer price indices for particular countries are used with currency conversion rates to produce an index of price rises. The index is then used to rebase UK residents' spending to 1995 prices.

Appendix C

Definitions

1. The figures relate to the number of **visits**, not the number of visitors. Those entering or leaving the United Kingdom more than once in the same period are counted on each visit. The count of visits relates to UK residents returning to this country and to overseas residents leaving it.

2. **Day trips** (i.e. visits that do not involve an overnight stay) abroad by UK residents as well as day trips to the UK by overseas residents are included in the figures for visits and spending. Note 14 refers to overseas residents in transit through the UK.

3. An **overseas visitor** is a person who, being permanently resident in a country outside the UK, visits the UK for a period of less than 12 months. UK citizens resident overseas for 12 months or more coming home on leave are included in this category. **Visits abroad** are visits for a period of less than 12 months by people permanently resident in the UK (who may be of foreign nationality).

4. When a resident of the UK has visited more than one country, spending and stay for the entire visit are allocated to the country stayed in for the longest time.

5. Visits for **miscellaneous** purposes include those for study, to attend sporting events, for shopping, health, religious or other purposes, together with visits for more than one purpose when none predominates (e.g. visits both on business and on holiday). Overseas visitors staying overnight in the UK en route to other destinations are also included in the miscellaneous purposes category.

6. Estimates relating to tourist flows across the **land boundary** between the Irish Republic and Northern Ireland are, for convenience, included in the figures for sea. Where not shown separately, flows through the Channel Tunnel are also included under the figures for sea.

   Also excluded from the **regional analysis** tables (except the 'Total' section) are all visits that did not include an overnight stay in the UK. Visits by overseas residents to Northern Ireland, although included in the 'total' column, are not separately analysed. More than one region can be visited by an individual whilst in the UK so the total of the visits to all the regions will be greater than the total number of visits to the UK as a whole.

7. Adjustments are made to the reported cost of an **inclusive tour** so that only the amount earned by the country of visit (e.g. accommodation costs, car hire, etc.) is included. This estimate is then added to an individual's spending to give the total spending in the country of visit (see also note 9).

8. **Length of stay** for UK residents covers the time spent, including the journey, outside the UK, whilst for overseas residents it refers to the time spent within the UK.

9. **Spending** figures cover the same categories of traveller as the number of visits figures except that the figures for overseas residents additionally include the spending of same day transit passengers.

   Spending also includes foreign exchange earnings and expenditure due to travel relating to the Channel Islands. Spending excludes payments for air and sea travel to and from the UK. For any traveller on an inclusive tour, an estimate of the return fare is deducted from the total tour price.

10. Spending does not include the personal export of **cars** that have been purchased in the UK by overseas residents. Similarly spending excludes the personal import of cars by UK residents.

11. An estimate for purchases by overseas visitors at airport **duty-free** shops is included in the figures for spending. Such purchases on British carriers are excluded.

Exclusions

The following groups are excluded from the tables in this publication.

12. Trippers who cross the Channel or North Sea but do not alight from the boat.

13. Migrants and persons travelling to take up prearranged employment, together with military or diplomatic personnel, merchant seamen and airline personnel on duty.

14. Overseas residents passing through the UK on route to other destinations, but who do not stay overnight (often known as transit passengers). However any spending whilst in the UK is included in the spending figures.

Geographical areas

The geographical areas used in this report are unchanged from the previous publication.

15. **North America**: Canada (including Greenland and St. Pierre et Miquelon) and the USA (including Puerto Rico and US Virgin Islands).

16. **EU Europe**: Austria, Belgium, Denmark, France (including Monaco), Finland, Germany, Greece, Irish Republic, Italy (including San Marino and Vatican City), Luxembourg, Netherlands, Portugal (including Azores and Madeira), Spain (including Canary Islands, Spanish North Africa, Balearic Islands and Andorra) and Sweden.

17. **Non EU Europe**: Central & Eastern Europe, Cyprus, Faroe Islands, Gibraltar, Iceland, Malta, Norway, Switzerland (including Liechtenstein), Turkey, the former USSR and the states of former Yugoslavia.

18. **Central & Eastern Europe**: Albania, Bulgaria, Czech Republic, Slovakia, Hungary, Poland and Romania.

19. **North Africa**: Algeria, Egypt, Libya, Morocco, Sudan and Tunisia.

20. **Other Middle East**: Bahrain, Iran, Iraq, Jordan, Kuwait, Lebanon, Oman, Qatar, Saudi Arabia, Syria, United Arab Emirates and the Yemen.

21. **Central and South America**: Argentina, Belize, Bolivia, British Antarctica, Brazil, Chile, Colombia, Costa Rica, Ecuador, El Salvador, the Falkland Islands, French Guiana, Guatemala, Guyana, Honduras, Mexico, Nicaragua, Panama (including Canal Zone), Paraguay, Peru, Surinam, Uruguay and Venezuela.

22. **Caribbean**: Antigua, Bahamas, Barbados, Bermuda, British Virgin Islands, Cayman Islands, Cuba, Dominica, the Dominican Republic, Grenada, Haiti, Jamaica, Martinique, Montserrat, St. Kitts-Nevis-Anguilla, St. Lucia, St. Vincent and the Grenadines, Trinidad and Tobago, Turks and the Caicos Islands.

Although the information in this publication is by the country groups described above, almost 200 different countries of residence or visit can be identified by the IPS.

Appendix D

Response rates of the survey

Sample surveys such as the IPS depend on achieving high levels of response from the public. Non-respondents often have different characteristics of travel and expenditure compared with those who do respond and this can lead to biases being introduced into the results.

The response rates for the main airports, residual airports, sea routes and the Channel Tunnel are shown in **Table D1** below. A minimum response is one where the contact's nationality and country of residence are known but where the reason for visit, date visit began or country visited are not obtained. The overall response rate fell slightly in 2000, with full or partial responses being obtained from 81 per cent of the sample compared with 82 per cent in 1999. The overall response rates for sea and tunnel routes remained consistently higher than those at most of the main and residual airports.

IPS response rates 2000 and 1999 by type of response and UK port

	Complete or partial response (%)		Minimum response (%)		Total response (%)	
	2000	1999	2000	1999	2000	1999
Heathrow terminal 1	74	76	10	9	84	85
Heathrow terminal 2	69	73	13	12	82	85
Heathrow terminal 3	78	80	9	8	87	89
Heathrow terminal 4	85	85	7	7	92	92
Heathrow transits	81	83	6	6	87	89
Gatwick North	79	79	7	9	86	89
Gatwick South	81	80	6	8	87	88
Manchester terminal 1	87	83	6	6	92	89
Manchester terminal 2	84	84	5	5	89	89
Manchester terminal 3	88	87	6	5	94	91
Residual air	84	82	5	6	89	88
Sea	86	86	2	2	88	88
Channel Tunnel	89	90	4	5	93	94
Total	81	82	7	7	88	89

Appendix E

Accuracy of IPS estimates

The estimates of number of visits, nights and expenditure from the IPS are subject to sampling errors. Sampling errors result because every traveller to or from the UK is not interviewed on the survey. Sampling errors are determined both by the sample design and by the sample size - generally speaking, the larger the sample supporting a particular estimate, the (proportionately) smaller is its sampling error.

Table E.1 shows the sampling errors for the main 2000 estimates for both overseas residents visiting the UK and UK residents going abroad. 'Complex' sampling errors, which fully account for the clustered sample design of the survey, are shown in the table. Both standard errors and the 95% confidence intervals are quoted, the latter representing the interval into which there are 19 chances out of 20 that the true figure (had all travellers been surveyed) would fall. The 95% confidence intervals are given both in absolute and relative (percentage) terms - the estimate plus or minus the value, or percentage, gives the appropriate interval for each estimate.

Further details on the confidence intervals of data from the IPS and their interpretation can be obtained from the IPS Branch of ONS.

E.1 IPS sampling errors for 2000 estimates

	Estimate	Standard error	Absolute 95% confidence interval	Relative 95% confidence interval
Overseas visitors to the UK				
Number of visits (1000s)	25,004	379	743	3.0%
Number of visitor-nights (1000s)	203,186	3,919	7,680	3.8%
Total earnings (£ million)	12,603	184	360	2.9%
UK residents going abroad				
Number of visits (1000s)	56,089	441	864	1.5%
Number of visitor-nights (1000s)	563,208	6,034	11,827	2.1%
Total expenditure (£ million)	24,044	287	563	2.3%

Appendix F

Access to IPS data

Travel Trends is subject to Crown Copyright and as such proposals for reproduction of tables or contents should be addressed to:

The Copyright Section,
Office for National Statistics
B1/08 1 Drummond Gate
London SW1V 2QQ
Telephone: 020 7533 5652
Fax: 020 7533 5685

IPS monthly estimates
These are published in the '*ONS First Release*' series '*Overseas Travel and Tourism*' and are available by contacting Office for National Statistics on 020 7533 5725, or on the National Statistics website **www.statistics.gov.uk/press_release/TitleSearch.asp** by searching for 'Overseas Travel and Tourism'.

IPS quarterly results
These are published in electronic format in the '*Society MQ6*' titled '*Overseas Travel and Tourism*' and are available as downloadable PDFs on the National Statistics website **www.statistics.gov.uk/products/p1905.asp** free of charge. Users may, on request, still receive a printed copy of the publication through the new National Statistics print on demand service by contacting NS Direct on 01633 812078 or email ns.direct@statistics.gov.uk.

Other analyses:
General enquiries about the IPS should be directed to:
Office for National Statistics,
International Passenger Survey,
D1/19 Drummond Gate
London SW1V 2QQ.
Telephone 020 7533 5765
Fax 020 7533 5300
E-mail ips@ons.gov.uk

IPS Data sets
Travel*pac* is a compact version of the IPS database and is currently available on CD-ROM at a new price of £15 + VAT for the datasets from 1993 to 2000. Individual contact records from the full IPS database may be purchased and can be supplied on computer diskette or CD-ROM.

IPS data on the web

Some key data from the IPS are available from StatBase, the Government's on-line statistical service. In order to access StatBase you first need to link up with the National Statistics website **www.statistics.gov.uk**. Once you are connected to the website, click on the button marked StatBase. The StatBase 'family' of services consists of three main components:

StatSearch - a free service that contains a wealth of textual information that describes each of the National Statistic's information resources.

StatStore - another free service that contains a selection of data, including that published in Social Trends and Regional Trends.

TimeZone - a further free service providing access to a large portfolio of National Statistics time-series data

Please click on the button marked **StatStore** if you want to access the data contents of StatBase, including the IPS data.

Marketing agents

It is possible to commission more detailed analyses of the IPS data from marketing agents appointed by ONS. The marketing agents are:

Information Research Network

Incorporating SVP
Vigilant House
120 Wilton Road
London
SW1V 1JZ

Telephone: +44 (0) 20 7808 7107
Fax: +44 (0) 20 7808 7108
E-mail: info@irn-research.com
Web: www.irn-research.com

MDS Transmodal

6 Hunters Walk
Canal Street
Chester
CH1 4EB

Telephone: 01244-348301
Fax: 01244-348471
E-mail: queries@mdst.co.uk
Web: www.mdst.co.uk